THE SIMON AND SCHUSTER
STEP-BY-STEP ENCYCLOPEDIA
OF PRACTICAL GARDENING
Published in Cooperation with the Royal Horticultural Society

Fruit

by Harry Baker

Editor-in-chief Christopher Brickell
Technical editor Kenneth A. Beckett

Editor Jaqueline Baker
Art Editor Tony Spalding
Assistant Art Editor Janet Carrod
Assistant Editor John Moore
Designers Valerie Hill, Sean Keogh
   Winnie Malcolm, Michael Nawrocki
Editorial Assistant Helen Buttery
Executive Editor Chris Foulkes

ISBN 0 671 24834 0
Library of Congress Catalog Card Number 79 236 13

Fruit was edited and designed by
Mitchell Beazley Publishers Limited, Mill House,
87–89 Shaftesbury Avenue, London W1V 7AD

Typesetting by Tradespools Ltd, Frome, Somerset
Origination by Culver Graphics Ltd,
High Wycombe, Buckinghamshire
Printed in Spain by Printer industria gráfica sa.,
Sant Vicenç dels Horts, Barcelona
Depósito Legal B— 2107—1980

Contents

Introduction

Few gardeners will deny that one of the most rewarding aspects of gardening is growing and tasting freshly-picked sun-warmed fruits. They are far superior to store fruit because they are picked when they are at their best and their subtle flavors and textures have not been marred by handling and packing. Add to this the delight of a garden decked each spring with colorful blossoms, the perennial beauty of mature, shapely trees, and the pride in a well-stocked freezer or storeroom through the winter and you can really appreciate the joy of fruit growing.

Yet there are few books which give this fascinating and worthwhile pursuit the prominence it deserves. This book aims to correct that failure.

How to use this book
Fruit is divided into four major sections. The first deals with the practical aspects of fruit growing, from tools and equipment to planning the fruit garden. The second section concerns all soft fruits from strawberries to melons, which are the quickest to bear fruit and which are suitable for even a small garden. In the third section of the book tree fruits, which are slow to bear fruit but have a longer fruiting season, are discussed in detail and information is given about renovation of neglected trees, growing fruit in containers, and fruit storage. There is also a useful pollination guide. The fourth section covers diverse other kinds of fruit that usually grow in warm temperate regions.

The importance of the illustrations
Throughout the book the main text describes each fruit from planting to harvesting, explaining in detail the techniques and reasons behind the brief instructions in the step-by-step captions and pictures. All the illustrations have been carefully researched and the reader will find that they are amplified by the accompanying captions. In certain instances, special procedures or alternative operations have been "boxed" for greater clarity. Many fruit operations have never been illustrated or described in such detail before.

Climate and local conditions
Climate is important whether the gardener wishes to grow and ripen exotic fruits such as figs or temperate fruits such as apples and pears. Using a climate zone map of the United States (devised by the United States Department of Agriculture), each fruit is keyed in to its ideal growing area.

Fruit has been written mainly for gardeners in the temperate regions, with timings based on the comparatively mild areas encompassed by zones 6 and 7. For gardeners in more northern areas, timings may be two or three weeks later. For those in the South, timings are several weeks earlier. There is a general section on details of cultivation of fruits under glass or in the greenhouse, which can extend the fruiting season.

Because fruit is susceptible to frost damage, the fruit gardener must also take note of local climate conditions, the microclimate. The dangers of frost pockets and wind turbulence are discussed in terms of the choice of site, with suggestions on how to overcome them.

Once the site has been chosen the gardener needs to know how to get maximum benefit from it. The planning pages outline the possible yields and spacings of most fruits and fruit forms.

Fruits are usually long-term projects; some trees can bear fruit for a lifetime if given good care, and so it is particularly important to prepare the ground thoroughly before planting. A two-page section gives the essentials of soil content, soil depth, drainage, soil acidity (or alkalinity), fertilizers and digging.

Pests and diseases
To spray or not to spray is a question most gardeners are divided about. In *Fruit* the emphasis has been placed upon correct cultivation procedures and the selection of certified disease-free plants whenever possible. If the cultural instructions are followed, pests and diseases should be kept in check. If, despite this, the garden is seriously invaded by pests and diseases, or they are inherited in a new garden, advice on spraying has been included in a month-by-month gardening job reminder guide. A list of the most common pests and diseases and their treatments is in the front section of the book and each fruit page outlines those to which it is prone. A companion volume in this series, *Garden Pests and Diseases*, gives more comprehensive information on this subject.

The month-by-month guide also reminds the gardener of the tasks in the garden and their timings during the year.

Chemical control of weeds is another area of controversy. The policy of this book is to give full information on the various chemicals and their correct use for those who wish to use them. For those who do not, hand weeding and hoeing are suggested as alternatives. **Remember: keep all chemicals out of the reach of children; label the containers carefully; and always follow the manufacturer's instructions.**

Unusual fruits
For those gardeners already converted to the benefits of fruit growing who wish to try fruits not usually grown nowadays, full cultivation details are given for mulberries, elderberries, heathland fruits, quinces and nuts. A special section on warm temperate fruits will interest gardeners in warmer regions or those with a greenhouse who would like to try more "exotic" fruits.

Varieties
One of the most rewarding aspects of growing fruit is the choice of varieties available to the amateur. In number and quality they far outstrip fruits sold in stores; for example there are several hundreds of different apple and pear varieties but comparatively few are grown commercially. The commercial grower's requirements are understandably different from the amateur's; they are limited to those varieties that are highly productive, consistent and pack and travel well—unfortunately these are not necessarily those with the best flavor. There need be no such restrictions on the home grower, and to this end a list of currently available varieties personally selected by the authors has been included for each fruit where possible. They are not complete lists—such lists would fill a book in themselves—but they are a guide to the best varieties available.

The Royal Horticultural Society
Gardening is not an exact science and, as most gardeners know, part of its enjoyment is the degree of originality it is possible to achieve. For this reason, gardeners should be aware that local conditions, the ages of plants, and the varieties grown may cause the final results to differ slightly from those shown in the illustrations. Nevertheless, the gardener may rest assured that *Fruit* has been written with the experience and authoritative backing of the Royal Horticultural Society, which is renowned throughout the world as a leading body of horticultural practice. The cultural details and techniques in this book are those used and approved by the RHS after many years of testing and experience. These details and techniques have been verified by the American editors, or, if necessary, altered to comply with American horticultural conditions.

Glossary

Adventitious buds Normally growth buds develop between leaf and stem in a definite order. Adventitious buds are growth buds that arise without any relation to the leaves, usually in response to a wound.

Annual A plant that completes its life-cycle within one growing season.

Apex The tip of a stem, hence apical bud, the uppermost bud on the stem, and apical shoot, the uppermost stem on a system of branches.

Axil The angle between leaf and stem; hence axillary bud and axillary shoot, the bud or shoot arising between leaf and stem.

Biennial A plant with a life-cycle spread over two growing seasons.

Biennial bearer A tree bearing a good crop of blossom or fruit only in alternate years.

Branched head A branch system on a tree in which there is no central-leader shoot.

Break The development of lateral shoots as a result of pruning a shoot to an axillary bud.

Breastwood Shoots growing forward from plants trained against support structures.

Bush tree A tree pruned to give a dwarf form with about 2–2½ ft of clear stem.

Central leader The central vertical, dominant stem of a tree.

Chelated compound An organic compound containing a metal such as manganese or iron which is slowly released in the soil.

Clone A plant propagated asexually, with characteristics identical to its parent.

Cordon A tree pruned to form a main stem bearing spurs. It may be planted obliquely, at an acute angle to the ground or vertically.

Current year's growth/wood Shoots that have grown from buds in the present growing season.

Deblossoming The removal of individual flowers or flower trusses.

Defoliation The removal of leaves.

Dehorning The severe cutting back of main branches.

Disbudding The removal of surplus buds or shoots that are just beginning to grow.

Dormant buds Buds which, although formed normally, do not become active unless there is some injury to the shoot or branch system.

Dormant period The time in the life-cycle of a plant when no new growth is produced, usually in the winter.

Double working A way of overcoming the incompatibility between certain varieties of fruit and the desired rootstocks by grafting the former on to a compatible variety which is in turn grafted on to the rootstock.

Drywell A hole into which water drains.

Dwarf pyramid A tree pruned to form a pyramid-shaped central-leader tree about 7 ft high.

Espalier A tree trained with a vertical main stem and tiers of horizontal branches.

Extension growth Shoots that develop from the apical or terminal bud of a stem.

Eye A growth bud, especially of vines.

Fan A tree or shrub with the main branches trained like the ribs of a fan against a wall, fence or other support system.

Feathers The lateral shoots on a one-year-old (maiden) tree.

Flushes Irregular successive crops of flowers and fruit, as on ever-bearing strawberries.

Framework The "skeleton" of main branches.

Friable Describes a fine and crumbly soil with no hard or wet lumps.

Fruit buds Large, round prominent buds which produce flowers and fruit.

Germination The development of a seed into a seedling.

Girdling (bark-ringing) The removal of a ring of bark from the trunk of an unfruitful tree to check shoot growth and encourage fruiting.

Grafting Propagation by uniting a shoot or single bud of one plant—the scion—with the root system and stem of another—the stock or rootstock.

Growth or wood bud A small narrow bud that gives rise to a shoot.

Half-hardy A plant that cannot survive the winter without protection.

Harden off To acclimatize plants raised in warm conditions to colder conditions.

Hardy A plant that can survive winter conditions in the open.

Heading back The first tipping of the central-leader stem of a maiden tree.

Heel in To store stems, cuttings or plants in an upright or inclined position in a trench, which is then filled with earth and firmed.

Humus Fertile, decomposed organic matter.

Hybrid A plant produced by cross-pollinating two or more species or forms of a species.

Lateral A side growth that develops at an angle from the main stem of the tree.

Leader The terminal shoot of a tree or branch that determines the main direction of growth.

Maiden A one-year-old tree or shrub.

Maiden lateral A one-year-old lateral shoot.

Microclimate The climatic conditions in a particular small area.

Mulch A layer of material, such as straw or plastic sheeting, put on the soil surface primarily to conserve moisture and to suppress weeds.

Offset A young plant that develops close to or at the base of the parent plant.

Pan A hard layer of soil beneath the surface.

Perennial A plant that lives for more than three seasons.

pH The scale used to measure the acidity or alkalinity of the soil: 7.0 is neutral, above 7.0 is alkaline and below 7.0 is acid.

Pinching back or stopping To cut or nip out with fingers the growing tip of a shoot.

Plunge outside To bury container-grown plants up to their rims in an ash, peat or sand bed to protect the roots from frost in winter.

Prick out To transfer seedlings from a seed tray to another container or the open ground.

Primary branches The branches that are formed first, arising from the main stem.

Propagation The production of a new plant from an existing one, either sexually by seeds or asexually, for example by grafting.

Regulatory pruning Pruning to remove crossing, crowded and weak shoots and branches.

Renewal pruning Pruning to maintain a constant supply of young shoots.

Rod The main, woody stem of a vine.

Root cutting A piece of the root of a plant used for propagation.

Root-pruning Severing some or all of the main roots of a tree to reduce vigor.

Rooted tips The shoot tips of plants such as blackberries that have been buried in the soil and taken root to form a new plant.

Rootstock See **Grafting**.

Runner A rooting stem that grows along the surface of the soil, as in strawberries.

Scion See **Grafting**.

Secondary branches The branches that develop later from the primary branches.

Self-compatible, self-fertile or self-fruitful A plant that can produce seed after fertilization with pollen from the same flower or from other flowers on that plant or on a plant of the same clone.

Semi-dwarf A tree or shrub grown with about 3½–4½ ft of clear stem.

Snag A short stump of a branch left after incorrect pruning.

Spit depth The depth of a blade on a normal digging spade; about 10 in.

Sport or mutant A plant that differs genetically from the typical growth of the plant that produced it.

Spur A slow-growing short branch system that usually carries clusters of flower buds.

Spur-bearer A fruit tree that bears most of its fruit on spurs.

Standard A tree or shrub grown with 5–7 ft of clear stem.

Stock See **Grafting**.

Stopping See **Pinching back**.

Stub-back To cut back a lateral after it has fruited, leaving a 1 in stub.

Sub-lateral A side-shoot growing from a maiden lateral.

Sucker A shoot growing from a stem or root at or below ground level.

Systemic compound A pesticide or fungicide that totally or partially permeates the plant including the internal tissue.

Terminal bud A growth or fruit bud at the end of an unpruned one-year-old shoot.

Thin To reduce the number of seedlings, buds, flowers, fruitlets or branches.

Tip-bearer A tree that bears most of its fruits at the tips of one-year-old shoots.

Tipping The removal of the apical part of a shoot by pruning.

Trace elements Substances necessary for plant growth which are usually present in the soil in minute quantities.

True leaves Leaves typical of the mature plant as opposed to simpler seed leaves.

Truss A cluster of flowers or fruit.

Union The junction between rootstock and scion or between two scions grafted together.

Variety A named, cultivated form of a plant.

Vegetative growth Leaf and stem growth as opposed to flowers or fruit.

Water shoot A vigorous, sappy shoot growing from an adventitious or dormant bud on the trunk or older branches of a tree.

Wind-rock The loosening of the roots of plants by the force of the wind.

Climate 1

The most important aspects of climate the fruit gardener must consider when planning a fruit garden are temperature, rainfall and wind. Of these, temperature is the most crucial. Fruit plants can survive drought conditions and gales but they may fail to produce crops or even be killed by untimely low or high temperatures.

Broad climatic divisions are a useful basis for judging the general viability of a specific crop but local conditions must also be carefully considered (see pages 6–7).

Zones of hardiness

The map of hardiness in North America (right) was devised by the United States Department of Agriculture. It defines zones of consistent average, annual, minimum temperatures.

Throughout this book, the information on individual fruits includes the zones in which they are hardy or half-hardy.

The climate of zones 9 and 10 seems ideal for fruit growing, with mild winters and little frost to damage blossom or setting fruitlets: the growing season is long and there are many hours of sunshine for ripening. Although it is ideal for the typical zones 9 and 10 fruits (such as avocados, figs and citrus fruits), which are adapted to this climate and need long warm summers and fairly mild winters, it is not suitable for all fruits. Deciduous trees such as apples, pears, plums and cherries require a dormant period in each year and this is brought about by colder weather. In the southernmost zones, not all varieties are able to become truly dormant in the winter, because the temperature is too high. The trees usually become spindly with sparse, poor crops. These fruits, as well as gooseberries, currants and cane fruit (raspberries, for example), are adapted to more temperate conditions and are happiest in zones 6–8.

It is not difficult to grow fruits in zones in which they are half-hardy. Peaches, nectarines and apricots, for example, grow well in zone 5 provided they are planted in a sunny position and protected against low temperatures and frost. Alternatively, fruits can be planted in containers and moved under cover when conditions become unfavorable. Also, the conditions of a warmer

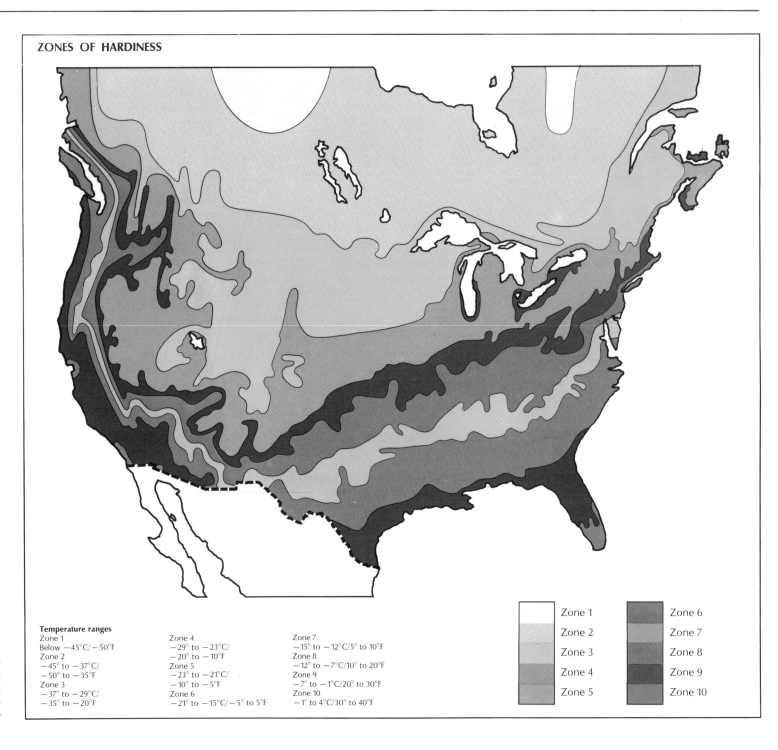

ZONES OF HARDINESS

Temperature ranges

Zone 1
Below −45°C/−50°F
Zone 2
−45° to −37°C/
−50° to −35°F
Zone 3
−37° to −29°C/
−35° to −20°F

Zone 4
−29° to −23°C/
−20° to −10°F
Zone 5
−23° to −21°C/
−10° to −5°F
Zone 6
−21° to −15°C/−5° to 5°F

Zone 7
−15° to −12°C/5° to 10°F
Zone 8
−12° to −7°C/10° to 20°F
Zone 9
−7° to −1°C/20° to 30°F
Zone 10
−1° to 4°C/30° to 40°F

Zone 1
Zone 2
Zone 3
Zone 4
Zone 5
Zone 6
Zone 7
Zone 8
Zone 9
Zone 10

zone can be artificially reproduced in a greenhouse, although this is expensive.

Coastal and lakeside fruit gardens

A large body of water, whether a freshwater lake or the sea, exerts a strong, modifying influence on a region's climate. Water takes longer to heat up and to cool down than land, so winter temperatures are usually higher and there is less risk of frost. As a result, it is possible to grow earlier flowering varieties of plants that are hardy to the zone and to grow half-hardy plants more easily.

Conversely, areas away from the sea's modifying influence are exposed to extremes.

Ocean currents also affect temperature. For example, the warm Gulf Stream affects the climates of Britain and western Norway to the extent that these coastal regions fall into a higher zone than that of other areas in the same northerly latitudes.

A large body of water can also have unfavorable effects on coastal areas. Winds tend to be strong because the uninterrupted expanse of water offers no resistance to slow them down. This can cause considerable damage to blossom, leaves, branches and fruit. In addition, winds blowing in from the sea are salt-laden and can burn leaves, young shoots and fruits. It is essential to provide shelter with wind-breaks in the form of fences or hedges (see pages 6–7). However, windy conditions do decrease the risk of radiation frosts.

Rainfall

The right amount of moisture is essential to the healthy growth of fruit crops, and both drought and excessive rainfall can be serious problems. Drought can be overcome to a considerable extent by regular watering and mulching, but excessive rain is difficult to combat.

Frequent rain and high humidity cause leaves to remain wet for prolonged periods, rendering them more prone to fungal infections. Fruits may fail to ripen and excessive rain may cause them to rot. If the soil becomes waterlogged, the roots may also rot. For example, it is difficult to obtain a good crop of disease-free apples in an area with an average rainfall of more than 35 in because of scab and canker, unless there is a very rigorous spraying program. Certain varieties of fruit withstand these conditions better than others; for example, cooking apples, in which appearance and flavor are not so important, tolerate heavy rainfall better than do dessert varieties of apples.

Temperature

The temperature at which grass usually begins to grow is about 6°C/43°F and this is regarded as the beginning of the growing season. The number of days per year at or above this temperature and, therefore, the length of the growing season, increases zone by zone, the shortest season being in zone 1 and the longest in zone 10.

The length of the growing season should be taken into consideration when deciding what fruits to grow. Some fruits, such as grapes, require a long season to ripen, whereas others, such as strawberries, require a short period. For practical purposes, the growing season can be thought of as the number of frost-free days from spring to fall. Grapes, for example, require about 180 frost-free days.

Although, as mentioned above, the minimum temperature for the growing season is about 6°C/43°F, some plants require consistently higher temperatures. For example, for melons, the ideal is a minimum night-time temperature of 24°C/75°F and a minimum daytime temperature of 30°C/86°F throughout their growing season, although an average of 24°C/75°F is satisfactory. Citrus fruits are also very sensitive to temperature. Seville oranges and mandarins, for example, require a minimum daytime temperature of 16°C/60°F throughout their growing season and do not reach their full flavor if temperatures are below 18°C/65°F while the fruit is ripening.

Frost

Frost in the spring can be more damaging to fruit plants than consistent low winter temperatures. Plants may survive low temperatures when they are dormant, but a sudden spring frost can kill new buds, shoots and sometimes flowers.

The degree of vulnerability depends upon the stage of bud development; the more advanced the fruit buds are, the greater the danger. Taking the apple as an example, frost damage can occur at green cluster stage at −3.5°C/26°F; at pink bud stage at −3°C/27°F; at full bloom stage at −2°C/28°F; at petal fall stage at −1.5°C/29°F; and at fruitlet stage at −1°C/30°F.

In areas susceptible to frost, choose, where possible, late-flowering varieties, those with long flowering seasons or those with a reputation for blossom hardiness. Suitable varieties of apples, for example, would be the medium-late to late-flowering 'Cortland', 'Dudley', 'Macoun', 'McIntosh' and 'Northern Spy'. Raspberries, blackberries and loganberries flower fairly late and are not likely to be much damaged by frost. Black currants are very susceptible to frost damage and red currants and gooseberries are also at risk. Strawberries can be damaged by ground frost but have such a long flowering season that it is rare to lose an entire year's crop. Frost pockets can occur in places where cold air collects, often producing local frost damage. See Choice of site, page 7.

Altitude

Altitude is also an important factor in that the higher it is, the cooler the climate and the shorter the growing season. There is also an increased risk of frost, and rainfall tends to be higher. Dessert fruits are usually grown commercially at altitudes of less than 400 ft, although this is a counsel of perfection and fruit can be grown at much higher altitudes. There are warmer microclimates in certain positions at higher levels, such as on south-facing slopes or between the folds of hills. In hotter climates, fruits that grow best at cooler temperatures can be planted on mountain slopes at comparatively high altitudes. Temperature drops by 0.5°C/1°F for every 250 ft of altitude.

The slope of the land is also a consideration. A steep slope is a handicap to essential cultivation and picking operations, and it usually means soil erosion and poor soil conditions are present. A gentle slope is preferable because it can help soil drainage as well as being easier to cultivate.

FROST DAMAGE

Strawberry flowers damaged by frost have developed black "eyes" (a). The ovaries have been killed and cannot develop into fruit. Apples scarred by frost develop russet patches and cracking (b). Fruits with this scarring may continue to grow if the ovaries have been only slightly damaged. Although frost-damaged pears can become distorted (c) as they grow, they are still edible.

Choice of site 1

If there is any choice within the garden, choose the sunniest site possible for fruit (see pages 8–9). Light and warmth are necessary to ripen the fruits and the wood and to promote the development of fruit buds for the next year's crop. Most fruits tolerate some shade but crop yields may be affected, particularly with warm temperate fruits such as apricots, peaches, nectarines, figs and grapes that must be in full sun. Other fruits grow reasonably well as long as they receive sunlight for at least half the day throughout the growing season. Dessert fruits, in which color and flavor are important, require more light than do cooking fruits. Bush and cane fruits, such as blackberries, will tolerate some shade provided the soil is not dry and the plants do not suffer from rain dripping from overhanging branches.

Wind protection
The fruit plot should be sheltered from strong winds which inhibit the movement of pollinating insects, damage growth and cause fruits to fall prematurely. In an exposed site, the gardener should provide a wind-break.

Wind turbulence

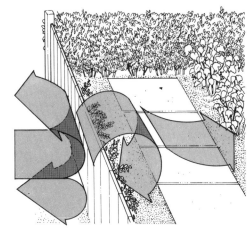

Avoid evergreen hedges and solid fences which may block the wind and cause severe turbulence among the plants next to them.

The type of wind-break depends upon the scale of planting; for example, a large orchard is best protected by a living wind-break such as a row of trees. For this, plant deciduous, fast growing, upright trees which leaf early in the spring, in preference to the more solid evergreens which block rather than filter the wind, creating turbulence among, and possibly damage to, the fruit they are supposed to protect. The most widely used are the alder, willow and poplar.

On a smaller scale there are many hedge plants that make a good screen if the smaller fruit tree forms are to be planted. Hedges such as beech and hornbeam can form attractive features in their own right. Nevertheless, the living wind-breaks compete with the fruit trees for light, water and nutrients and can be hosts to pests, diseases and birds. Also, where every bit of land is valuable, it is best to erect an artificial one.

The usual surround for a small suburban garden is a wall or fence against which fruit plants can be trained. These reduce the wind immediately behind the structure but may cause turbulence farther away.

The height of the wind-break also affects the area sheltered because the sheltered zone to leeward of a moderately solid wind-break may extend to about 30 times the height of the structure, although the effect beyond 20 times its height is slight.

Wind-breaks made of coconut matting or dense plastic netting erected on poles and wires are suitable for use in both large orchards and gardens because they can be placed where they are most needed to protect maturing crops or newly planted trees. They are preferable to a solid wall because they filter the air and prevent local turbulence.

To protect newly planted trees, drive $7\frac{1}{2}$ ft long supporting posts, about 3–4 in in diameter, 2 ft into the ground, spaced at 9–12 ft intervals. Place struts at an angle to the posts to ensure that they are strong enough to withstand the force of the wind. Stretch two strands of 8 gauge galvanized wire between the posts, one about 1 in above soil level and one 5 in below the tops. Fasten 5 ft deep plastic netting between the wires by folding the edges over and interlacing them with jute or other strong string.

An open wind-break

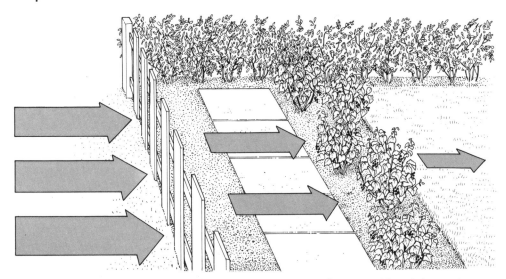

A more open fence or hedge filters the wind, reducing the wind's force by letting it flow through. Locate wind-breaks on the western and eastern sides of the garden where the wind is usually strongest and coldest and most damaging.

Erecting a wind-break

Drive $7\frac{1}{2}$ ft long supporting posts, about 3–4 in in dia., 2 ft into the ground, at about 9–12 ft intervals. Place struts on the lee side

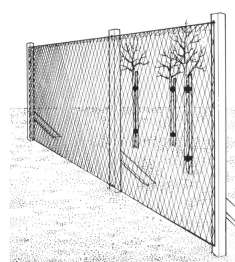

of the windbreak. Stretch 8 gauge wire between the posts. Tie plastic netting to the wires with string.

Choice of site 2

Frost protection

Avoid planting in a frost pocket if possible because all fruits are sensitive to cold during the growing season, particularly at blossom time, when a few degrees of frost can ruin the potential crop (see pages 4–5). Frost pockets are formed because cold air is denser than warm air and naturally flows downwards on sloping ground. The areas where this cold air collects, or is impeded, are most prone to severe radiation frosts and so are called frost pockets.

When planting a wind-break be careful not to create a frost hazard and, where such an obstruction already exists, it should be examined to see whether it can be removed or modified so that air drainage is improved. With a hedge, for example, it is possible to create a gap or remove some of the lower growth to allow the cold air to flow away down the slope. If there is no alternative to planting in a frost pocket, plant the larger fruit trees at the bottom and the smaller ones on the higher ground. Also consider planting late flowering varieties or those that are the most frost tolerant (see page 5).

It is impractical to try to protect large fruit trees in the garden but it is certainly worth while providing protection for the smaller fruit trees. The simplest way is to provide some kind of cover over the plants whenever frosts are anticipated. The cover should be removed once the danger of frost is over to allow access for pollinating insects and to let in light and air. Rows of cordons or espaliers can be draped with burlap or with two or three layers of the type of netting used for bird protection. Insert canes around the plants to prevent the cover rubbing against the blossoms. Wall-trained fruit trees can be protected in a similar way. Branches of black and red currants and cane fruits can be tied together in loose bundles for protection. Untie them once the buds break to avoid etiolation of the young growth. Strawberries in the open and the smaller fruit bushes can be covered with burlap, netting, straw or even two or three sheets of newspaper. Plants under cloches or frames are safe against mild frosts but the glass should be covered with straw or sacks in the event of severe cold. Remove the covering during the day.

The provision of artificial heat by oil burners is perhaps best reserved for crops under glass because of the cost. Burners in the open are ineffective unless used on a large scale, or in the Florida citrus groves. It may sometimes be worth while to cover bushes or wall-trained trees with a polyethylene tent and then put the burner inside. Make sure that the burner is working efficiently, and that there is no danger of the plastic catching fire.

Water as a means of frost protection is used commercially and this could be adapted to the garden. As water freezes latent heat is liberated and this protects the buds and flowers. It is important to keep them sprinkled more or less continuously throughout the period of frost with droplets of water about the size of raindrops. In long periods the branches become covered in ice and it is advisable, therefore, to prop up weak branches beforehand. Soil drainage must be efficient or the soil may become waterlogged which could seriously harm the roots (see pages 10–11). This is especially the case with heavy clay or other sticky soils that stop water from naturally seeping away.

Frost protection for large trees

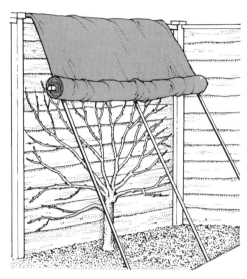

Wall-trained fruits such as the fig can be protected from frost by draping them with burlap or packing them with straw.

Frost pockets

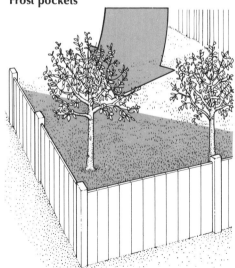

Avoid planting fruit trees and bushes in a frost pocket but if there is no alternative, improve the air drainage by creating a gap

to allow the cold air to flow away. Plant larger fruit trees and later flowering varieties of bush fruit.

FROST PROTECTION FOR SMALL PLANTS

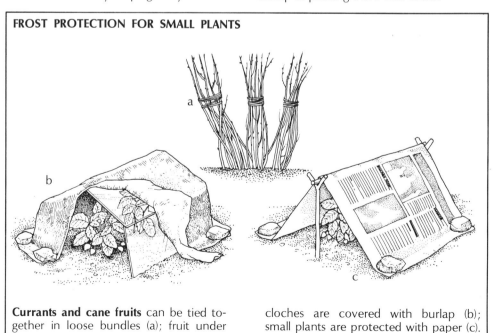

Currants and cane fruits can be tied together in loose bundles (a); fruit under cloches are covered with burlap (b); small plants are protected with paper (c).

Planning 1

The planting of tree, bush and cane fruits represents a long-term investment. Once planted there should be no need to move them until their cropping life is over. This could range from 20 to 50 years and more for tree fruits, and about 10–15 years for soft fruits. It is worthwhile, therefore, before planting to draw up a scale plan so that the plants are correctly sited.

The planner needs to take into account the approximate yield from each fruit to meet the family's requirements in relation to the amount of land available, the correct spacing and the right aspect.

Yield
The yield depends upon many factors, such as the fertility of the soil, the climate, and the variety and the size of the plant. As a guide, the table below lists approximate yields from reasonably mature plants of the fruits commonly grown outside.

Spacing
The eventual size and yield of a mature fruit plant are influenced by the environment, the variety and, with many tree fruits, the rootstock on which it is grafted. Trees grafted on vigorous rootstocks in time grow larger than trees grafted on dwarfing stocks, even though they may be the same variety. Nowadays, most trees are cultivated for small gardens and are usually grafted on non-vigorous stocks, except for the semi-dwarf or standard forms. Soft fruits are grown on their own roots.

The spacings given in the table below are intended only as a guide for the planner. For more detail, refer to the relevant fruit pages. Allow a wider spacing on very fertile soils.

Fruit against walls and fences
While in many gardens the bulk of the fruit crop comes from a plot of land specially set aside for this purpose, the use of walls, fences and trellises should not be neglected, particularly where space is limited. Their structure provides support for the plants and also for netting as protection against birds or frosts. Walls and solid fences have the added advantages of giving shelter and, where the aspect is sunny, extra warmth and light are reflected from the masonry or wood. The added warmth improves the quality of the fruits, promotes fruit bud development and makes it possible to grow the more exotic fruits where otherwise it might not be worthwhile.

Because wall and fence space is usually limited, use the restricted plant forms that are kept in shape and contained by summer pruning.

Apples and pears can be grown as cordons, espaliers or fans but stone fruits, such as apricots, peaches and cherries, do not respond to the cordon and espalier methods of training and are therefore grown only in fan-trained form. The climbing fruits, such as blackberries, hybrid berries and grapes, grow well against walls and fences. The grape vine in particular is perhaps the most versatile of all the trained fruits, being amenable to many forms of training against walls, fences or on pergolas but, of course, the aspect must be sunny.

The height of the supporting structure decides the shape or form in which the fruit is best trained.

Walls and fences up to 6 ft high are suitable for the low-trained tree forms such as the espalier, and for cordon and fan-trained gooseberries, red and white currants as well as blackberry and raspberry canes.

With walls and fences 6–8 ft high, it is possible to grow apples and pears (on dwarfing or semi-dwarfing stock) as cordons, fans or multiple-tiered espaliers, the number of tiers depending upon the height of the structure.

TREE FORMS

Oblique cordon

Espalier

Fan

Standard   Half-standard   Bush

There is no really dwarfing stock as yet developed for stone fruits, although it is anticipated there will be in the next five years, so the minimum height required for fan-trained apricots, peaches, nectarines, plums, and Morello cherries is 7 ft. There are successful peaches on semi-vigorous stocks grown on lower structures than this but they need regular pruning and tying down. The sweet cherry is a vigorous plant and needs a wall or fence of at least 8 ft. Trellis-work fencing gives structures extra height.

Aspect
The aspect of the wall, fence or trellis decides the kind of fruit that can be grown. In the northern hemisphere the warmest and sunniest aspect is the south-facing and the coldest and shadiest is the north, with the west and east somewhere between the two.

YIELDS AND SPACING

APPLES AND PEARS	Yield		Spacing	
Tree form	Apples	Pears	In rows	Rows apart
Bush	60–120 lb	40–100 lb	12–18 ft	12–18 ft
Dwarf bush	30–50 lb	20–40 lb	8–15 ft	8–15 ft
Dwarf pyramid	10–15 lb	8–12 lb	5–6 ft	6 ft
Espalier (2-tier)	20–25 lb	15–20 lb	10–18 ft	6 ft
Fan	12–30 lb	12–30 lb	12–18 ft	—
Single cordon	5–8 lb	4–6 lb	2½–3 ft	6 ft
Standard	100–400 lb	80–240 lb	18–30 ft	18–30 ft

OTHER TREE FRUITS				
Tree form			In rows	Rows apart
Bush (Morello cherry)		30–40 lb	12–18 ft	12–18 ft
Bush (plum and peach)		30–60 lb	12–18 ft	12–20 ft
Bush, semi-dwarf and standard (sweet cherry)		30–120 lb	15–40 ft	15–40 ft
Bush or small tree (fig)		15–20 lb	18–20 ft	18–20 ft
Fan (all stone fruits)		12–30 lb	12–18 ft	—
Fan (fig)		15–20 lb	12–15 ft	—
Fan (sweet cherry)		12–30 lb	18–25 ft	—
Pyramid (plum)		30–50 lb	10–12 ft	10–12 ft
Standard (plum, peach and apricot)		30–120 lb	18–25 ft	18–25 ft

SOFT FRUIT				
			In rows	Rows apart
Bush (black currant)		10–12 lb	5–6 ft	6 ft
Bush (gooseberry)		6–8 lb	4–5 ft	5 ft
Bush (red and white currant)		8–10 lb	5 ft	5 ft
Cordon (gooseberry, red and white currant)		1–3 lb	12–15 in	5 ft
Blackberry or hybrid berry		10–30 lb	8–15 ft	6–7 ft
Raspberry		1½ lb per ft of row	15–18 in	6 ft
Strawberry		8–10 oz per plant	12–15 in	2½–3 ft

Planning 2

South The southern, south-eastern and south-western aspects are best reserved for the sun-loving fruits, although most fruits would thrive in this situation. The soil at the base of a south-facing wall can become very dry, so ensure there is adequate moisture during the growing season by mulching and watering. This aspect is suitable for figs, peaches, nectarines, apricots, grapes, pears, plums, cherries and apples.

West The western aspect receives the hot afternoon sun. It is suitable for peaches, nectarines, apricots, sweet and sour cherries, grapes, pears, plums, apples, raspberries, blackberries, gooseberries, red and white currants.

East The eastern aspect is a dry situation receiving the fairly cool morning sun but shaded in the afternoon. Suitable fruits include the early pears, apples, plums, sweet and sour cherries, currants, gooseberries, blackberries and raspberries.

North The northern aspect is restricted to those fruits that are able to grow and ripen in cold situations with little sun. Suitable fruits are fan-trained sour cherries, early apples, cordon currants and gooseberries and blackberries. They will ripen later than those in full sun.

Wiring walls and fences

Horizontal wires firmly attached to the wall or fence are necessary to support the framework branches and for tying in the new growth. Use 14 gauge galvanized fencing wire for espaliers and cordons, and 16 gauge for fan-trained trees.

For espaliers, fix the wires so that they coincide with the height of the arms (tiers). Generally the tiers are 15–18 in apart but plant the espaliers first to see where the wires should be placed. The wires for oblique cordons are usually fixed every 2 ft, the highest wire being 6 in below the top of the wall or fence.

Fan-trained trees require horizontal wires every 6 in or two brick courses apart, starting at 15 in from the ground and continuing to the top of the wall or fence. Bolts to take the strain of the wires are not necessary on wires for fan-trained trees because the wires are placed closer together, so galvanized staples will suffice on wooden fences and lead anchors on walls.

Buying fruit plants

To ensure healthy new plants, it is best to buy fruit stock from a specialist fruit grower. Apart from having a better selection, the specialist is likely to stock varieties of a guaranteed high standard of purity, health and vigor.

Most state authorities inspect plants which are shipped in or out of the state to ensure that they are free of disease. Plants shipped within a state are, as a practical matter, usually inspected along with material going out of state, although they generally need not be inspected. Certified stock is usually healthy stock.

Also, before choosing any fruit plant check its pollination requirements. Some fruits such as sweet cherries, apples, pears and certain plums must be grown in compatible pairs or they will not produce fruit. Select the best varieties from the lists of recommended varieties and descriptions which head each fruit page. The varieties lists are given in abbreviated form for quick reference, and more detailed reading may be necessary.

WIRING WALLS AND FENCES

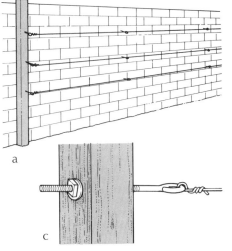
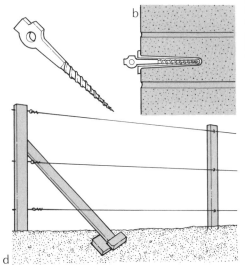

Wires must be held 1½–4 in away from walls by fixing 2 in square wooden battens (or 1½ in × 1½ in angle irons) to the masonry to hold the straining bolts and the ends of the wires (a). Screw or drive in 4 in galvanized or lead wall nails with anchors (b) every 5 ft to hold the wires between the battens. With the screw type, drill and plug the wall first. Wires should be kept taut by attaching straining bolts (c) to one end post. Use galvanized staples (d) to hold the wires on the intermediate and other end posts. Tighten the wires with the straining bolts before driving the staples home. A diagonal post is needed to brace the main post.

Planning a small fruit garden

North ⟹

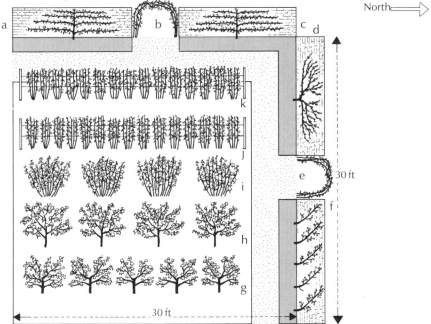

30 ft

30 ft

The above plot is a guide for planning a small intensively cultivated fruit garden. It can be modified to suit individual requirements. It contains: espalier pear (a); loganberry arch (b); espalier pear (c); fan peach (d); grape arch (e); cordon apples (f); gooseberries (g); red currants (h); black currants (i); June-fruiting raspberries (j); fall-fruiting raspberries (k).

Soil and soil drainage 1

Soil depth

Most soils will grow fruit of some kind, provided the land is reasonably well drained. The larger the fruit plant the greater the depth of workable, fertile, well-drained soil required. Strawberries need a minimum depth of 12 in, cane fruits, currants and gooseberries need 18 in, and tree fruits 24 in, with the exception of sweet cherries which require at least 30 in. Some fruits such as currants, gooseberries, blackberries, plums, damsons, pears and cooking apples will tolerate a little impeded drainage below 18 in, as will dessert apples, the plums that are sometimes called gages, and sour cherries, but to a lesser extent. For raspberries, peaches and sweet cherries good drainage is essential throughout. A thin soil over limestone is unsuitable for all but the smallest fruits such as strawberries. Raspberries do not thrive in soils over limestone unless plenty of organic matter is added.

Soil drainage

A basic idea of the natural drainage conditions of the garden can be discovered by a few simple observations. If the soil is heavy to dig and close textured, with pools of standing water after rainfall, the soil or sub-soil probably has a high clay content and water drains into and away from it very slowly. This type of soil can be improved by digging in bulky organics such as strawy compost, wood chips or bark, manure or peat and by improving the drainage.

Soils that are waterlogged for long periods must be drained, otherwise root death can occur, leading to extensive die-back or perhaps the total loss of the plant. For small plantings a trench leading to lower ground can be dug, but for larger plots a line of drains or even a herringbone system of plastic, concrete or tile drains may be necessary. Where it is impossible to drain the soil, the trees and bushes may be planted on mounds and the raspberries and strawberries on ridges.

If the soil is light and dries out fast, it probably has a low nutrient and high sand or gravel content, or it may be a shallow soil over limestone. Such soils can be improved by digging in plenty of bulky organics to help the soil retain moisture and nutrients. The ideal soil contains coarse sand, fine sand, clay and silt in roughly equal proportions. It is moist, not too sticky, but has a good crumbly texture, breaking up easily when squeezed by the fingers.

The pH level of the soil

The ideal soil for fruit should be slightly acid (about pH 6.5). The soil's acidity or alkalinity level, known as the pH, can be measured with a pH soil testing kit, which is available from garden stores or nurseries.

Lime is not needed for growing fruits unless the soil is very acid; for example, soils with a pH lower than 5.8 should be limed. Garden lime is usually carbonate of lime. Lime does exist in other forms but the carbonate (or ground limestone) is generally used. Rates of application vary from 2 oz to 1 lb per square yard according to the acidity of the soil. Do not apply lime directly to recently fertilized or manured soil, because the two substances react chemically together. Lime is best applied at least a month before or after other fertilizers. Preferably, apply the lime in the fall and the fertilizer in the spring.

Fruits grown in very alkaline or limestone soils may suffer from iron and manganese deficiencies resulting in chlorosis, which is a yellowing at the tips of shoots and between the veins on leaves, and in die-back of branches. To remedy these deficiencies apply iron and maganese in chelated (sequestered) form to the soil in late winter. In the long term the pH of alkaline soils should be reduced by using flowers of sulfur annually for several years. It is safe even among growing plants but is slow-acting, particularly in cold weather. The quantity of sulfur required varies according to texture, type of soil and, of course, by how much the pH is to be reduced. As a general guide, a sandy loam will need about half (4 oz) that for heavy loams, (8 oz per square yard). If it is not certain which type of soil predominates, apply a small quantity, say 2 oz per square yard, then after a few months test again and repeat the application until the required pH is reached. On natural limestone soils, the pH level will revert to its natural high pH and further treatments will be necessary.

Soil preparation

Bush, cane and tree fruits are relatively long lived so it is important to prepare the ground thoroughly. The first essential is to free the site from perennial weeds. Where there are a few only, fork them out and burn them, but if the ground is infested with them, apply weedkillers (see page 17).

If the gardener is reluctant to use these chemicals, or it is the wrong time of year, then double digging is necessary. Double digging is also essential where the sub-soil is hard or impervious and needs breaking up. For very large areas, if possible, borrow or hire a tractor equipped with a sub-soiler to break up compacted ground and a plow to turn the ground over. For widely spaced trees, provided the gardener is satisfied that there is no hard soil pan to be broken up, it is sufficient to prepare a 3 ft square at each planting site. For closely planted trees or a soft fruit plantation, single digging is all that is needed.

Single digging

Before digging mark out the plot. Stretch a line down the plot to divide it lengthwise into two. Using a spade, nick out a shallow furrow along the line. Remove the line.

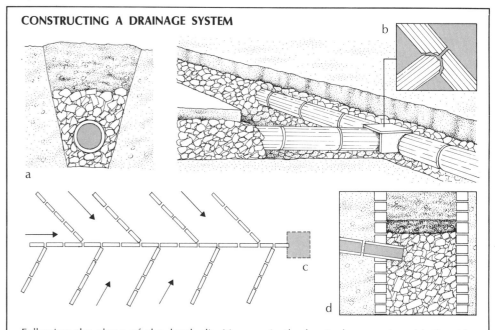

CONSTRUCTING A DRAINAGE SYSTEM

Following the slope of the land, dig V-shaped trenches (a) at the same level as the sub-soil, up to 3 ft deep and wide enough to take a 4 in dia. main pipe. At the same time dig side trenches for 3 in dia. drains. Cover the bottom with a 2 in layer of gravel. Lay the pipes on it.

The pipes (b) can be tile, but are today usually plastic. Use solid pipes rather than those that are perforated. Cover all the pipes with coarse rubble or stones, then finer rubble, finishing with a generous layer of top-soil.

In the herringbone system (c), the side drains meet the main drain at an angle of 60 degrees. The drains must run towards a ditch or drywell at a gradient of at least 1 in 40.

For the drywell (d), dig a hole 3–6 ft in dia. and at least 6 ft deep. The sides should be loosely bricked to allow water to seep through. Leave space for the main pipe to enter. The drywell can be filled with rocks, but this is not recommended as they reduce the water-holding capacity of the well by taking up space.

Dig out the first 12 in wide trench to a spade's depth (known as a spit deep) across half the plot. Pile the soil removed from this first trench at the same end but on the other side of the plot, just outside the marked-off area. Work backwards down the first half of the plot, filling in each trench with the broken-up earth from the trench being dug. If bulky organic matter is needed spread it over the soil at the recommended rate before beginning to dig, then dig it into the bottom of the trench before filling in. Use the soil from the beginning of the second half to fill in the last trench of the first. When the end of the second half is reached, use the heaped soil from the very first trench to fill in this last trench.

The key to successful deep digging is to work with a vertical spade. A slanting thrust achieves less depth and makes the work take longer. It is also good technique to drive the spade in at right angles across the trench to free the clod of earth to be lifted.

Double digging

Double digging is similar to single digging, except that the width of each trench dug is 24 in (instead of 12 in), or roughly three spade widths. It is advisable to mark each trench out with sticks and a garden line. This ensures that the surface of the dug soil remains even because a measured amount of soil is moved each time. Work from left to right across each trench width, starting with the spit farthest away from the preceding trench.

Break up the sub-soil at the bottom of the trench with a fork to a further spit depth. Break up the soil all around the bottom of the trench and not just the area in the middle.

Fork manure or compost into the broken up sub-soil at this stage. Fill in the trench with the soil from the next trench as for single digging, and so on.

Double digging grassland

Mark out the plot as described for double digging. Skim off the turf of the first trench to a depth of 2 in with a spade and place it at the same end but on the other side of the plot, just outside the marked-off area. Dig a 2 ft wide trench to a spade's depth and place the soil in a separate heap near the skimmed turf.

Break up the bottom of the trench with a fork to a 12 in depth.

Put the skimmed-off turf from the second trench grass downwards on to the loosened soil in the first trench and chop it up. Place the soil from the second trench on top and so on. The turf and soil from the first trench are used to fill in the last trench in the second half of the plot.

Soil nutrition

Digging is the opportune time to incorporate the bulky organics such as well-rotted manure or compost which are necessary for healthy growth and longevity of fruit. Bulky organics are also invaluable for improving the soil structure, making heavy clays more amenable to cultivation and light soils more moisture-retentive. The amount to apply depends upon the soil texture and fertility, and the manurial requirements of the crop. Fertile soils with a high humus content need very little, whereas light, "hungry" soils need heavy applications. A good average rate is one barrowload per 25 square feet.

The basic nutrients supplied by fertilizers are nitrogen, phosphates and potash, although some may contain small amounts of other nutrients. All three are important: potash for color, flavor and hardiness; phosphates for general health, and nitrogen for growth. A balanced compound fertilizer, such as 10-10-10, is recommended because it supplies equal amounts of nitrogen (N), phosphorus (P) and potash (K). Plums, pears and black currants require heavy dressings of nitrogen, but apples, raspberries and strawberries produce too much leaf and too little, poor quality fruit if given large amounts of nitrogen.

Do not use fertilizers containing chloride salts, such as muriate of potash, on soft fruits, particularly red currants, and use it with caution on tree fruits because chloride salts are toxic in large amounts.

Just before planting, apply the recommended rate of fertilizers for individual fruits, as specified on the following pages. Apply it as a top dressing and then fork it into the soil, working the soil down to a good crumbly tilth. For rapid absorption, apply liquid fertilizer to the roots of the plants.

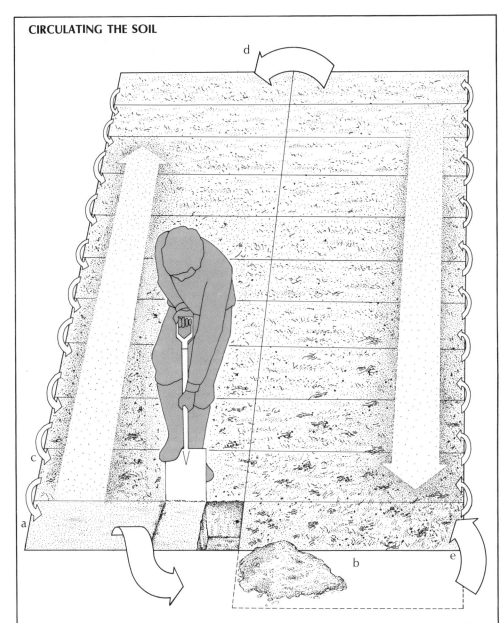

CIRCULATING THE SOIL

The plot is divided down the middle. Excavated soil from the first trench (a) is placed at the same end of the plot opposite the other half (b). The first trench is filled with soil from the second trench (c) and so on. The soil from the first trench in the second half fills in the last trench in the first half (d) and the last trench in the second half takes the soil removed from the first trench (e).

Tools and equipment 1

The fruit grower needs a few special tools in addition to the basic ones used in other gardening activities.

The illustrations show most of the tools and equipment needed for fruit growing.

Maintenance

Always clean garden tools and oil the metal parts as soon as possible after use. Store them in a dry place. Rusty tools mean harder work and they need replacement more quickly than tools that have been cared for.

Spade Choose good quality steel or stainless steel with a strong thin blade. Do not use a spade among established fruit plants because digging may damage the roots.

Fork Choose good quality steel or stainless steel with four well-spaced, rounded or square prongs for breaking up soil. Do not use around established fruit plants.

Dutch hoe (a) The easiest to use is a 4 in flat blade. It is ideal for shallow hoeing among established bush and cane fruits and strawberry rows.

Trowel and hand fork A trowel (b) is useful for making holes when planting strawberries, and a hand fork (c) is excellent for lifting rooted runners.

Garden line (d) A line of polypropylene string on a strong metal reel is used for marking out a plot and for spacing.

Irrigation equipment The equipment required depends upon the scale of planting. A one- or two-gallon watering can is sufficient for a small plot, but larger areas need a hose (e). Do not wet fruit or foliage (which encourages fungal diseases) but keep the spray from the hose low around the plants. Low-level sprinklers are also available or, better still, soil soakers that can be laid between the plants.

Labels Most fruit plants are long-lived, and so a permanent label is necessary. These can be made of wood, metal or plastic.

Gloves (f) A pair of leather or PVC gloves is essential for protecting the hands when pruning, particularly with thorny plants.

Shears Pruning established fruit trees needs a pair of heavy-duty shears with cutting blades about $2-2\frac{1}{2}$ in long. The two main types of shears are the anvil (g) and the parrot bill (h). The anvil type has a single cutting blade

which moves against a fixed soft anvil made of brass or plastic. The blade must be kept sharp and level with the anvil or it fails to cut cleanly and bruises the wood. Parrot bill shears have two blades; the lower blade supports the wood while the upper blade does the cutting. It has a scissor action and makes a clean cut without bruising the wood.

Points to note when buying shears are: a comfortable grip; a hardened steel blade; all parts replaceable; an easily sharpened and durable blade; a helper spring strong enough to return the blade to an open position after cutting; a safety-catch to lock the shears in the closed position.

Long-arm pruners (i) These are useful for people who do not want to climb ladders. One type has a 6–10 ft long metal pole with a blade attached by wire to a lever. This blade cuts with a slicing action, moving upwards against a fixed hook-shaped blade. Another type is basically a pair of shears on the end of a long rod.

Loppers (j) These are long-handled heavy-duty pruners, particularly useful for pruning well-established black currant bushes and for thinning out neglected trees. They are about 18 in long, with good leverage, able to cut branches up to $1\frac{1}{2}$ in in diameter.

Pruning saws These must be capable of cutting live green wood without the teeth clogging with wet sawdust. For this reason the teeth are widely spaced in the crosscut or fleam tooth pattern. There are three basic types: the one- or two-sided straight blade (k); the Grecian curved blade (l) and the bow saw (m). The straight-bladed saw is good for light pruning, fast cutting and neat cuts. The Grecian curved saw grips the wood well, which makes it better for cutting awkwardly placed branches. It cuts on the pull rather than the normal push stroke. The bow saw is used for heavy work, but sometimes the frame can get in the way.

The pole saw (n) is a pruning saw, usually the Grecian curved type, with a hollow handle into which a long metal pole can be inserted. It is useful for pruning branches that cannot be reached with an ordinary saw.

Knives (o) A $3\frac{1}{2}$ in straight-bladed knife with a strong handle is useful for grafting work, cutting off unwanted shoots and suckers, and

paring the edges of saw cuts before painting them. For propagation, a budding knife (p) is needed.

Ladders A ladder is useful for both pruning and fruit-picking. A tripod-style aluminum ladder (q) is a good choice for trees up to 15 ft high. It is stable, does not damage the tree by resting against it, and some have a knee-leaning rail which gives support and increases the height that can be reached. Some also have a platform on which to put a fruit container. Owners of larger trees need an ordinary extension ladder. There are also long cherry-picking ladders, used mainly by professional growers. Always ensure that the branch is strong enough to bear the weight of both gardener and ladder.

Fruit-picking devices (r) These can be used by people who do not own a ladder or are unable to use one. They usually consist of a long metal pole with an attachment at the end which cuts off or gathers the fruit and catches it in a bag or hopper. These bags are also available as an attachment to long-arm pruners.

Tree ties There are three basic types of manufactured tree ties: the adjustable buckle type (s), the nail-on type (t), and the chain-lock type (u). The first two have a collar or spacer between the tree and the stake to prevent chafing. The chain-lock type, suitable for young trees, is tied in a figure-of-eight; the cross-over acts as a cushion. Manufactured ties are made of weather-resistant materials such as plastic or rubber.

Alternatively, the gardener can make ties from, for example, bicycle tires, canvas, or strong cord. To use cord, tie a knot (preferably a clove hitch) near the top of the stake. Wind the cord three or four times round both the tree and the stake above this knot. Then make a collar by winding the cord as tightly as possible around the loose strands between them.

All ties should be checked regularly and removed and re-tied each year in April to allow the tree to expand.

Stakes Oak and preservative-treated softwood are all suitable materials for tree stakes. Oak stakes are comparable in price and durability to treated softwood. Pressure-treated softwood is more expensive but has

a much longer life because it is kiln-dried and then impregnated under pressure with a preservative. Stakes should be long enough to reach just below the lowest branches of a mature tree, allowing 18–24 in in the ground.

Sprayers These are used for applying pesticides, fungicides and sometimes weedkillers. There are various kinds: the double action sprayer, in which the liquid is held in an open container; the pneumatic type (v), in which the container is pressurized; and a container with an external pump, which may be operated by hand or by motor.

Sprayers should be strong, light and able to take different nozzles. It is important to choose the size and type most suited to the job. For applying weedkillers use a low-pressure sprayer; preferably with a nozzle giving a fan-shaped spray. For trees, a high pressure sprayer is needed for fungicides and insecticides, using a hollow cone nozzle. A small hand sprayer (w) of about $1\frac{1}{2}-2$ pints capacity is useful for short rows of strawberries, one or two bushes, or trees in pots. For a small garden of up to 30 ft × 30 ft, a free-standing sprayer with a flexible hose and metal spray tube and a capacity of $\frac{1}{2}-1$ gal is adequate. Many of these have a shoulder strap to make them portable. A knapsack sprayer with a capacity up to 4 gal is ideal for a larger garden of up to 100 × 60 ft. Extendable metal spray tubes are necessary for tree fruit gardens. In plots larger than one acre, a motorized sprayer may be a worthwhile investment.

Remember to wash out the sprayer thoroughly after use, especially after using weedkillers. Ideally, use a separate sprayer for weedkillers.

Tree guards In areas where animal pests such as rabbits are troublesome, tree guards are necessary. These can be either the manufactured plastic type or home-made ones of 1 in mesh galvanized wire netting.

Wire brush A stiff wire brush (x) is useful for cleaning up canker.

A can of bituminous paint (y) **and brush** (z) These are essential for sealing large pruning cuts. The brush should have stiff bristles. When using this corrosive paint, wear gardening gloves, cover adjacent foliage, such as grass, and do not allow the paint to spill.

Tools and equipment 2

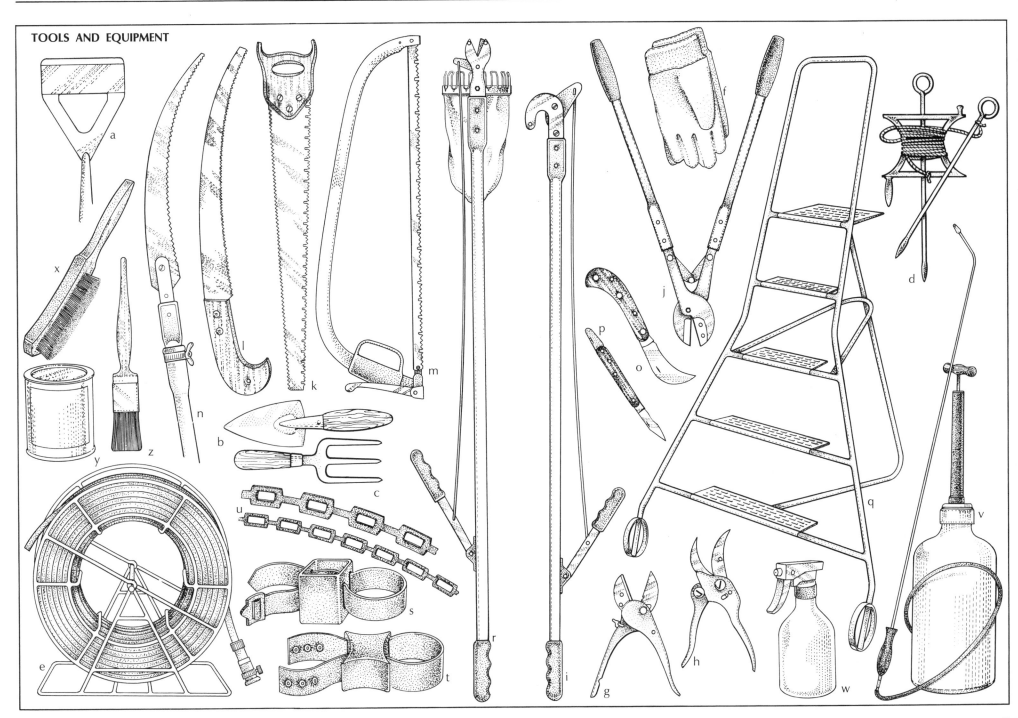

Pests and diseases 1

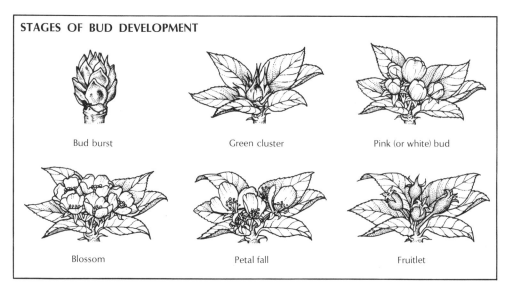

STAGES OF BUD DEVELOPMENT

Bud burst Green cluster Pink (or white) bud

Blossom Petal fall Fruitlet

Correct cultivation and weed control help to prevent trouble with pests and diseases, although chemical control may be necessary.

Types of chemical control
Fungicides and pesticides prevent or help to control infection and infestation.

The various pesticides act in different ways. A contact spray such as derris affects the insect itself. Ovicides such as DNOC kill the eggs. These take effect on contact, so it is important to cover all plant surfaces. A third group, systemic insecticides such as formothion, dimethoate and menazon, are taken up through the roots and leaves of the plant into the sap. They are thus very effective against sap-sucking insects. Complete coverage is preferable but not essential because systemics can be applied as a root drench.

Most fungicides only check or prevent attacks so they should be applied before the disease appears. The new partly systemic fungicides such as benomyl are slightly absorbed into the plant's tissues only but are effective for a short period even after symptoms are visible. However, resistant strains of the fungus may develop if systemic fungicides are used too frequently.

Precautions
Always follow the manufacturer's instructions when mixing and applying chemicals. Wash hands and equipment after using chemicals. Do not use the fungicide and pesticide sprayer for weedkillers. Some chemicals must be treated with extra caution. Malathion, captan and thiram should not be used on fruit that is to be preserved. Captan, dinocap, thiram and zineb may irritate the eyes, nose and mouth; wear a mask and goggles if susceptible to allergic reactions. Do not use sulfur on sulfur-sensitive varieties. Do not use pesticides when the flowers are open because they kill bees and other pollinating insects.

DISEASES
American gooseberry mildew Affecting gooseberries and currants, it forms a white, powdery coating on young leaves, shoots and fruits, later turning brown and felted. The shoots may be distorted at the tips.
Treatment: Cut out and burn diseased shoots in late August or September. Spray with dinocap before flowering, repeating as necessary. Or spray with benomyl as the first flowers open, repeating two, four and six weeks later. Keep the bushes open by regular pruning and avoid excessive nitrogen feeding.
Apple canker It affects apples and pears. Sunken discolored patches appear on the bark, becoming extended ellipses surrounded by concentric rings of shrunken bark. White fungus spores are visible on the sunken bark in summer. The branch becomes swollen above the canker and it may die.
Treatment: Cut out and burn diseased branches and spurs. On branches without die-back, cut out and burn diseased tissue. Paint the wounds with canker paint. Spray with bordeaux mixture or liquid copper after harvest but before leaf-fall. Repeat when half the leaves have fallen and at bud burst.
Bacterial canker Round brown spots appear on the leaves of apricots, cherries, peaches, and plums, later developing into holes. There are elongated, flattened, oozing cankers on the branches. The buds do not develop the following spring or they produce small, yellow leaves which curl, wither and die. The branches also die back.
Treatment: Remove badly cankered branches and dead wood. Spray with bordeaux mixture in mid-August, and one and two months later.
Bitter pit It causes sunken pits on apple skins, brown flesh spots and bitter taste.
Treatment: Prevent by watering and mulching during dry weather. Spray with calcium nitrate at 1oz per 2 gal of water in mid-June. Repeat ten days later. Ten days after that spray with 2 oz calcium nitrate per 2 gal and repeat at least three times at ten-day intervals.
Black knot Twigs of cherries, apricots and plums develop knotty, black excrescences.
Treatment: Remove twigs 4 in below knots. Spray with lime-sulfur at bud burst.
Boron deficiency The pear fruits on most branches are distorted and have brown spots in the flesh. The leaves are small and misshapen. There is some die-back of shoots and the bark is roughened and pimply.
Treatment: Apply 1oz of borax mixed with sand per 20 sq yds.
Brown rot Affects apricots, cherries, peaches, plums, nectarines and to some extent other fruits. The fruits are brown with soft, decaying flesh, later becoming covered with concentric rings of grayish spores.
Treatment: The disease usually occurs in warm, humid weather. If humidity is high, spray with captan every three days during period of bloom and prior to harvest.
Cane blight It affects only raspberries. A dark area can be seen on the canes just above ground level. The canes become very brittle and the leaves wither.
Treatment: Cut back diseased canes to below soil level and burn. Disinfect tools. Spray new canes with bordeaux mixture.
Cane spot It affects raspberries, loganberries, hybrid berries and, rarely, blackberries. Small purple spots appear on the canes in May to June, later enlarging and turning white with a purple border and then splitting to form pits or small cankers. The tips of shoots may die back, leaves may be spotted and fruit distorted.
Treatment: Cut out and burn badly spotted canes in fall. Spray raspberries with liquid copper or thiram (but not on fruit for preserving) at bud burst and just before flowering. Or spray with benomyl at bud burst and repeat every two weeks until the end of flowering. Spray loganberries with bordeaux mixture, liquid copper or thiram (but not on fruit for preserving) just before flowering and when the fruit sets.
Cedar-apple rust This disease occurs only in areas with red cedars. Leaves of apples, crab-apples, pears and quinces look rusty and distorted.
Treatment: Spray apples, and other similar fruit, in mid-spring with ferbam.
Chlorosis All trees may be affected if unable to take up sufficient iron from soil. Leaves turn yellow between the veins.
Treatment: Apply iron chelates to the soil.
Coral spot Red currants are very susceptible, but other currants and figs are also affected. The branches die back and coral red pustules appear on the dead shoots.
Treatment: Cut out affected branches several inches below the diseased tissues. Paint the wounds. Burn infected shoots and any other woody debris in the garden.
Crown gall A walnut-size gall can be seen at ground level on cane fruits or there is a chain of small galls higher up.
Treatment: Destroy diseased canes.
Die-back The shoots and branches die back. It is usually caused by fungi but occasionally by adverse cultural conditions.
Treatment: Cut back all dead wood to healthy tissue and paint the wounds. Check that feeding, watering and mulching are adequate.
Fireblight Affects pears and occasionally

Pests and diseases 2

apples. The shoots die back and the leaves become brown and withered. Cankers at the base of the diseased tissue ooze in spring.
Treatment: Do not over-fertilize trees, because this encourages strong growth which, in turn, encourages disease. Spraying several times during bloom with bordeaux mixture or copper may help. Cut out and burn diseased wood 6 in or more below blighted area.

Gray mold (*Botrytis cinerea*) Strawberries, cane fruits, currants and grapes are among the many fruits affected. The berries rot and are covered with gray-brown fluff.
Treatment: Remove and destroy infected fruits if possible. Spray with benomyl as soon as the flowers open, repeating two, four and six weeks later. Do not use on strawberries under glass or polyethylene.

Greasy spot It causes small oily brown spots on leaves of citrus trees.
Treatment: Spray with copper fungicides in the summer.

Gummosis Bark near the graft on citrus trees decays and gum flows from the infected areas on the trunk.
Treatment: This fungus disease is best controlled by proper planting and care of citrus. If trouble starts, check whether decayed bark extends more than half way around the trunk. If it does, destroy the tree. If it does not extend more than half way around the trunk, remove the decayed bark and a little of the adjacent live bark and disinfect the wound with 1 teaspoon of potassium permanganate in 1 pint of water. Cover the wound with tree paint when it heals.

Honey fungus It affects all fruit crops. White, fan-shaped patches of fungus appear beneath the bark on roots and on the trunk just above ground level. There are blackish growths on the roots and honey-colored toadstools grow at the base of the tree in the fall. Sudden death of the plant may occur.
Treatment: Dig out affected plants with as many roots as possible and burn them. Sterilize the soil with a two per cent solution of formaldehyde at 5 gal per square yard, or use a phenolic compound.

Leaf blotch Strawberries are affected by several diseases that cause browning of the leaves or dark spots that may be surrounded by various colors on leaves and stems. The

leaves die and the fruit often rots.
Treatment: Remove and burn affected leaves. Spray or dust with copper in the early fall and after bloom in the spring. Make several spring treatments if weather is wet.

Leaf spot of currants and gooseberries Dark brown spots can be seen on the leaves, later coalescing and turning the leaves brown. Premature leaf-fall results.
Treatment: Collect and burn all diseased leaves. Spray with zineb or thiram after flowering, repeating every 10–14 days, as necessary. Or spray with thiophanate-methyl as the flowers open, repeating two, four and six weeks later. Feed the bushes well to help overcome the disease.

Magnesium deficiency Orange, red or brown bands develop between the leaf veins, especially of apples, citrus fruits, grapes and raspberries.
Treatment: Spray at petal fall, or when the trouble shows, with magnesium sulfate at 8 oz per $2\frac{1}{2}$ gal of water. Repeat twice at 14-day intervals.

Melanose Leaves, fruits and shoots on citrus trees develop rough, irregular spots.
Treatment: Remove and burn infected parts. About a week after fruit set, spray trees with a neutral copper fungicide and wettable sulfur.

Peach leaf curl Reddish blisters appear on the leaves. Later, the leaves swell and have a powdery white covering of spores. Premature leaf-fall results.
Treatment: Spray with bordeaux mixture or liquid copper in January or February. Repeat 10–14 days later and just before leaf-fall.

Powdery mildew Apple, grape, melon, peach and quince are affected. A white powdery coating of fungus spores appears on emerging shoots and young leaves. Apple and pear shoots are stunted, the fruits fail to set or develop brown patches, and the leaves fall. The skins of grapes become discolored and shrivel and split.
Treatment: Remove silvered shoots at pruning. Cut off infected shoots of apples, peaches and quinces in spring and summer. Spray apples and quinces with dinocap at the pink bud stage. Repeat every 7–14 days until mid-July. Spray grapes with dinocap at first symptoms, repeating two, four and six weeks

later. For melons, spray with benomyl or dinocap at first symptoms. Repeat every two weeks, as necessary. On peaches use a sulfur fungicide at first symptoms, repeating every two weeks as necessary.

Quince leaf blight Dark red irregular spots appear on leaves, later becoming blackish. The leaves may turn brown or yellow and fall prematurely and the fruit may be spotted and deformed. Shoot tips die back.
Treatment: Rake up and burn fallen leaves. Cut out dead shoots in winter. Spray with bordeaux mixture when leaves are fully developed, and in summer, if necessary.

Raspberry virus diseases These are very troublesome; loganberries, blackberries susceptible to viruses and related organisms, and other cane fruits may also be affected. Yellow blotching or mottling is visible on the leaves. Growth is poor and the crop reduced.
Treatment: Remove and burn all affected plants at the same time. Plant new canes certified as healthy in a new site 50 ft away or change the soil on the old site to a depth of $1\frac{1}{2}$ ft.

Reversion This affects only black currants and is spread by the big bud mite. Mature leaves on the basal shoots are narrow with fewer than five pairs of veins on each main lobe. The flowers are bright magenta-colored and there is a reduced fruit yield.
Treatment: Control big bud mite (see page 16). Destroy all diseased bushes at the same time. Plant new certified bushes on a fresh site.

Scab Affects apples, pears, peaches, pecans and citrus fruits. Brown or black scabs are visible on the fruits which are sometimes mis-shapen and cracked. Olive-green blotches develop on the leaves and they fall prematurely. There is a general loss of vigor and a reduced crop. Pimples on the young shoots later burst the bark as cracks or scabs.
Treatment: Rake up and burn all leaves in fall. Cut out cracked and scabby shoots.

Shothole Affects cherries, peaches and nectarines, and plums causing brown spots on leaves which later become holes. Only weak trees are affected.
Treatment: Proper feeding should prevent a recurrence but, if not, spray with copper fungicide at half strength in summer and at full strength just before leaf-fall.

Silver leaf It can affect most tree fruits, currants and gooseberries, but it is most troublesome on plums, appearing as silvering leaves which may turn brown. There is progressive die-back of branches and a purplish fungus grows on the dead wood, later turning white or brown. Inner tissues are stained brown or purple.
Treatment: If there is fungus on the trunk, destroy the tree. Otherwise, cut back dead branches to 6 in behind the staining of inner tissues. Paint the wounds. Sterilize all tools after use on diseased trees.

Split stone Affects peaches and nectarines. Fruits crack at the stalk end producing a hole through which earwigs can enter. The stone is split and the kernel (if formed) rots.
Treatment: Hand pollinate the flowers. Lime the soil if necessary. Water when required.

Spur blight This affects raspberries and sometimes loganberries. Dark purple blotches appear around the nodes on canes. They later enlarge, turn silver and become covered with minute black dots. Buds wither and die or produce shoots which die back in spring.
Treatment: Cut out and burn diseased canes. Spray with benomyl, dichlofluanid, thiram or captan when the new canes are a few inches high. Repeat two, four and six weeks later. Or spray with bordeaux mixture or liquid copper at bud burst, repeating when the flower tips are just showing white.

Strawberry mildew Purple patches are visible on leaves, which curl upwards. Grayish fungal spores develop on the undersides and spread to flowers and berries.
Treatment: Dust with sulfur or spray with dinocap just before flowering. Repeat every 10–14 days until two weeks before harvest. Or spray with benomyl just after flowering, repeating two and four weeks later. After harvest, cut off old leaves and spray with fungicide.

Strawberry virus diseases Various diseases cause stunting or death. The symptoms are most obvious from April to September. The leaves become dwarfed and puckered with yellow edges and yellow or purple mottling. A virus-related organism causes old leaves to turn red and young leaves yellow. The flowers have green petals and the fruits fail to ripen. Eventually the plant dies.

Pests and diseases 3

Treatment: Destroy all affected plants at the same time. Do not take runners. Plant disease-resistant strawberries in a fresh site or change the soil on the old site to a depth of 1ft × 1½ ft wide.

Wilt Several wilts affect melons. Lower leaves turn yellow and wilt and then the whole plant wilts and collapses.

Treatment: Destroy diseased plants and sterilize the soil. Replant with disease-resistant varieties.

PESTS

Aphids (Greenfly) Aphids suck sap from the leaves and shoots of most tree, bush, cane and other soft fruits, causing leaf curling and distortion, reddish discoloration, stunted growth and black sooty mold. They spread virus diseases.

Treatment: Spray with miscible oil in late winter (but not strawberries) to kill over-wintering eggs. Use a systemic insecticide, such as formothion, in the spring if aphids are present, repeating as necessary.

Apple curculio A brown beetle with humped back that makes puncture holes in apples, cherries, pears and quinces. The mis-shapen fruit falls.

Treatment: Apply a general-purpose fruit spray at two-week intervals throughout the growing season.

Apple maggot White larvae tunnel into apples, cherries, blueberries.

Treatment: Spray on a regular schedule with a general-purpose fruit spray.

Apple sawfly Caterpillars tunnel into the fruitlets, causing them to fall in June. A ribbon-like scar forms on the remaining fruits.

Treatment: Spray with lindare, dimethoate or fenitrothion one week after petal fall. Pick up and burn infested fruitlets.

Big bud mite A pest of black currants. It lives inside buds, making them swollen and rounded (instead of narrow and pointed) and they fail to develop in spring. The mites spread reversion disease (see page 15).

Treatment: Pick off and burn big buds during the winter. Spray with benomyl at the first open flower and again two and four weeks later. Destroy badly infested bushes and re-plant with virus-free stock on a fresh site.

Cankerworms These inchworms, or measur-ing worms, are seen looping and hanging from long threads on many kinds of tree fruits. If present in numbers, they can defoliate the trees rapidly.

Treatment: Apply a general-purpose fruit spray on a regular schedule.

Caspid bugs Affect currants, gooseberries and apples. Capsids suck sap from shoot tips, leaves and fruits. Leaves at the shoot tips develop with tattered holes. Mature apple fruits have corky scabs or bumps on the skin.

Treatment: Spray with a systemic insecticide such as formothion shortly after flowering has finished.

Caterpillars Caterpillars of various kinds feed in the spring, causing damaged and ragged buds, leaves and blossoms. Tent caterpillars are particularly troublesome on cherries and apples in spring and also in the fall.

Treatment: Spray with fenitrothion or tri-chlorphon as the young leaves appear. Place a sticky greaseband around the trunk to trap emerging wingless female winter moths. Keep bands sticky and in position until late March. Do not burn nests, as this damages the tree.

Codling moth Caterpillars of small gray-brown moths tunnel into the mature fruit of apples and English walnuts.

Treatment: Spray with fenitrothion in mid-June, repeating three weeks later. A regular spray schedule with a general-purpose fruit spray is also effective.

Gooseberry sawfly These caterpillars are up to 1in long, creamy-green with black dots. They can completely defoliate gooseberry and red currant plants.

Treatment: Spray with derris or malathion as soon as caterpillars are seen, repeating as necessary from late April onwards.

Japanese beetles Handsome, metallic-green beetles with coppery wings that feast on grape leaves and may attack other fruits.

Treatment: Many of the beetles can be picked off by hand into a can of kerosene. But, for general control, spray with carbaryl.

Mealy bugs Sap-feeding pests of apples, citrus fruits, grapes and other fruits. The small white-pink insects can be seen in the leaf axils covered with a white fluffy wax.

Treatment: Control by spraying with mala-thion 2 or 3 times at 2 week intervals.

Nematodes A microscopic soil insect that attacks citrus tree roots, causing a general malaise of the trees.

Treatment: Fumigate the soil with SMDC or other fumigant.

Oriental fruit moth A gray and brown moth with pink larvae that attacks leaves and twig tips on peaches and bores into the fruit through the stems. They also attack quinces and other deciduous fruits.

Treatment: Spray regularly with a general-purpose fruit spray.

Peach tree borer This yellow caterpillar bores into the trunks of peaches and related stone fruits, leaving masses of gum oozing from the holes they make.

Treatment: Fumigate the soil around the trees with para-dichlorobenzene in the fall. Spray endosulfan on the trunks and branches when the buds start to open in the spring.

Plum curculio Similar to apple curculio and treated in the same way.

Plum sawfly Its grubs tunnel into the young fruits and cause them to fall early.

Treatment: Spray with fenitrothion or di-methoate at 7–10 days after petal fall.

Raspberry beetle The maggot-like larvae damage the ripening fruits of raspberry, blackberry, loganberry and similar fruits.

Treatment: Prevent damage by spraying at dusk with derris or malathion on the raspberry when first pink fruit is seen; on the logan-berry when flowering is almost over; and on the blackberry when flowering starts.

Red spider mite A tiny, sap-feeding pest of apples, plums and many other fruits. It causes a yellowish mottling of the leaves which can dry up and fall early.

Treatment: Apply a winter wash in February to control over-wintering eggs. Check the mite with a dinocap spray or use a systemic insec-ticide such as dimethoate or formothion in summer if it persists. Give two or three applications at 7–10 day intervals.

Scale insects These are sap-feeding pests with shell-like coverings which are attached to the bark. The various kinds attack fruits such as apples, peaches and pears.

Treatment: Control with a dormant oil spray in late winter. Apply malathion in late May and late June.

Slugs These damage fruits on strawberries.

Treatment: Scatter metaldehyde baits among the plants. Keep the garden clear and tidy in winter to reduce numbers.

Vine weevil Grubs feed on the roots of grapes and strawberries, sometimes destroy-ing the plants. The adult beetles eat irregular-shaped notches from the leaf margins at night, but this is less serious.

Treatment: Drench the root area with lindare.

Wasps These feed on the ripe fruit of apples, pears, plums and grapes.

Treatment: Enclose fruit trusses in bags made from muslin or old nylon stockings. Destroy wasp nests by placing carbaryl dust in the entrance at dusk.

Woolly aphid This aphid sucks sap from cracks in the bark and young shoots of apples. The colonies can be recognized by their white fluffy waxy coating.

Treatment: Spray or paint the colonies with a systemic insecticide such as formothion or dimethoate when the aphid appears in late May to June.

ANIMAL PESTS

Birds There are a number of methods of protecting food crops from damage or des-truction by birds. Such methods include bags and sleeving, collars, cotton as a deterrent, fruit cages and netting. See page 17.

Mice Mice eat the bark on trunks and roots of fruit trees, and if they succeed in girdling a trunk, the tree dies.

Treatment: Keep grass cut around trunks and pull mulches away from them. Surround trunks with $\frac{1}{4}$ in wire mesh that extends about 4 in below ground and 20 in above.

Rabbits Like mice, they eat tree bark and may kill trees by girdling.

Treatment: Use traps to catch rabbits. En-close trunks in wire mesh.

Squirrels If other food is scarce, squirrels eat the fruits of peaches, pears and apples, even while these are still green.

Treatment: Trapping.

Deer These animals can be pests when they strip apples off trees in the fall. In winter, they injure many different trees by nibbling on tender shoots and by rubbing their antlers on the trunks.

Treatment: Repellents sprayed on trees in winter are reasonably effective, but they can-not be used during summer and fall.

Weed control/Fruit cages

Weed control

Weeds are basically any plants growing where they are not wanted. They compete with the cultivated plants for nutrients and moisture and may harbor pests and diseases.

Many gardeners find that digging before planting, removing all perennial roots at the same time, and regular hoeing help to control weeds. For those gardeners who prefer not to use weedkillers, these methods are sufficient. If there is a large garden, limited time or weeds are well-established, herbicides may be more effective.

Herbicides

Herbicides are chemicals that destroy plants by scorching or by internal poisoning after they have been absorbed into the water-conducting tissues. If the correct chemical is used and the instructions are followed to the letter, one annual application is usually sufficient, except on neglected land where there is a lot of dormant seed.

The chemicals used can be very dangerous to humans, pets and fruit plants and so should always be handled with extreme care. Use separate sprayers for weedkillers and pesticides. Avoid spray drift, taking care not to contaminate any water course or pond.

Four chemicals, paraquat, simazine, dalapon and glyphosate, are sufficient for the amateur fruit grower. They are available under a variety of brand names but look for the active chemical constituents on the label.

Paraquat This kills all green tissue on contact by scorching and burning, so avoid spray drift. It is suitable for annual weeds and perennial weeds with no underground food reserves. On clay soils it is quickly inactivated on reaching the ground and there is no danger of fruit plants absorbing it through their roots. The risk is greater on sandy soils so wet the soil as little as possible. It is most effective in cool weather. In winter, the dose can normally be halved.

Take care not to wet the foliage of any fruit plants. Avoid spraying the trunks of apple, pear, plum and cherry trees less than three years old.

Simazine Taken up by germinating weed seeds before their emergence, simazine will not kill established weeds or weed seedlings.

Incorrect dosage can render the soil sterile for some months, so the manufacturer's instructions should be followed precisely. Simazine persists in the soil so allow seven months to elapse after spraying before attempting to grow crops from seed. It can be used to keep clean land weed-free among newly planted and established crops of apples, pears, black currants, gooseberries and cane fruits. Do not use near stone fruits or near strawberries grown in a sandy soil.

Dalapon This kills grasses and some related plants by absorption through the leaves and distribution through the system. It is suitable for use against annual and perennial grasses around apple and pear trees that have been established at least four years. Check the manufacturer's instructions because some varieties are adversely affected. Do not use it among stone fruits. It is readily taken up by the roots of trees and bushes so use only enough to spray the grass foliage without excessive run-off. It remains effective in the soil for between six and eight weeks.

Glyphosate Applied to the foliage of weeds, this is most effective when they are in active growth. It destroys annual and perennial weeds, especially grasses, creeping thistle and docks. It is inactivated on contact with the soil and crops can be sown or planted three or four weeks after treatment, or as soon as all the weeds are dead.

Protection against birds

Ripening fruit grown in the open needs protection against such birds as blackbirds, thrushes and starlings, which can inflict considerable damage on the crop. Winter protection may be necessary against birds which can destroy over-wintering buds, particularly on plums, cherries and bush fruit.

Commercial bird scarers are available but birds quickly become used to them. Bird repellents have a low success rate. In wet winters, the material washes off and in hard weather the birds eat the buds no matter what chemical is used.

Fruit cages Soft fruits, with the possible exception of strawberries, are usually grown in a group together and so can be surrounded by a single enclosure. Use $\frac{1}{2}-\frac{3}{4}$ in wire, polyethylene, nylon or plastic netting, 6–7 ft high, supported by wires stretched between the tops of posts, spaced 6 ft apart. Cover the top of the cage with $\frac{3}{4}$ in mesh netting. For very large cages, it may be necessary to drape the "roof" over battens nailed to the tops of the supporting posts. The roof netting can be polyethylene, nylon or plastic. Wire mesh is not suitable because zinc toxicity may be caused by condensation drops from the galvanizing. The netting should be left on in winter, except in heavy snowfall areas. Open the cage during the flowering period to allow access to pollinating insects because, even when the mesh is large, insects tend to avoid fruit bushes in an enclosed cage.

Ready-made cages are convenient and time-saving but more expensive.

Netting Fruit trees and bushes can be protected by draping them with lightweight nylon or plastic netting. To protect strawberries, drape netting over the plants, supported on posts at least 18 in high (see pages 21–3).

Cotton Black cotton thread wound between branches will deter birds but it is a time-consuming task if the trees are large or numerous. Do not use nylon thread because it can strangle birds or trap their feet.

Bags and sleeving Individual fruits can be protected by securing paper, muslin or perforated polyethylene bags or sleeves around them provided the tree or crop is small.

Collars Cardboard collars fitted around the stalks of tree fruits prevent birds perching close enough to peck the fruit. Again, this is practicable only on small trees or crops.

HERBICIDES		
Time of application	Weeds affected	Herbicide
APPLES AND PEARS		
Before weeds appear	Germinating seeds	Simazine
After weeds appear	Annuals, perennials without underground food reserves	Paraquat
Early spring or fall	Actively growing grass	Dalapon
End winter to late bud burst	Annuals, grasses, other perennials	Glyphosate
GOOSEBERRIES AND CURRANTS		
Before weeds appear	Germinating seeds	Simazine
After weeds appear	Annuals, perennials without underground food reserves	Paraquat
After leaf-fall	Grasses	Dalapon
CANE FRUITS		
Before weeds appear	Germinating seeds	Simazine
After weeds appear	Annuals, perennials without underground food reserves	Paraquat
STONE FRUITS		
March onwards, repeating as required	Annuals, perennials without underground food reserves	Paraquat
End winter to late bud burst	Annuals, grasses, other perennials	Glyphosate
STRAWBERRIES		
December	Germinating seeds	Simazine
July/August, after harvest	Germinating weeds	Simazine
Between harvest and flowering	Annuals, unwanted suckers	Paraquat

Month-by-month guide

This guide is intended as a reminder of the jobs to be done each month in the fruit garden. For full details of cultivation, see under the specific fruits. The timing of the tasks is based on the climate of zone 6. In colder zones, the same tasks are done somewhat later in the spring and earlier in the fall; in warmer zones, they are done earlier in the spring and later in the fall.

JANUARY
Order new plants from nursery catalogs. Delivery to be made in the spring.

Check whether snow and ice are injuring tree limbs. Prop up weak limbs. Remove damaged wood.

Check whether mice, rabbits or deer are feeding on tree bark and take appropriate steps to protect it.

FEBRUARY
Check for damage to trees by mice, rabbits, deer, ice storms, or heavy snowfalls.

MARCH
Prune all plants as required.

Apply dormant oil spray to apples, pears, peaches or other similar fruits.

Prepare beds for new strawberries, raspberries, other small fruits.

Tighten up and repair trellises for grapes, blackberries, raspberries and similar fruits.

APRIL
Fertilize plants. For most, this is the only feeding required.

Mulch tree and bush fruits with organic matter to keep down weeds, hold in moisture, nourish the soil.

As buds break on apples, pears, peaches and other similar fruits start regular spray schedule.

Plant new fruits delivered from nursery.

Sow melon seeds indoors for an early crop. Prepare planting bed outdoors.

Remove hay from strawberry bed.

MAY
Start training grapes, blackberries, raspberries and other trellis-grown fruit.

Make initial thinning of tree fruits.

Mulch newly planted strawberries. Protect established strawberries against birds with nets.

Continue regular spray program. Destroy tent caterpillar nests.

Set out melon plants. Protect with cloches or polyethylene tents if there is any likelihood of another frost.

JUNE
Make second application of fertilizer to plants that require it (For example, blueberries).

Thin fruits.

Train grapes and other similar fruits on trellises.

Cut back laterals on red and white currants and gooseberries.

Pinch out growing points on espaliers and cordons.

Continue regular spray program.

Harvest strawberries. Remove blossoms on new strawberry plants until end of month.

JULY
Last date for fertilizing all woody plants (if they require it). After this, fertilizer forces plants into soft growth that may be damaged by winter cold.

Water in dry spells.

Continue regular spray program. Spray peaches and related plants for brown rot if weather is humid.

Continue training grapes, ever-bearing raspberries.

Prune cordons and espaliers (until September).

Place supports under heavily laden branches of apples, pears and similar fruits.

Protect plants, such as blueberries and raspberries, from birds.

Cut back strawberries that have finished fruiting and apply fertilizer.

Pick raspberries, gooseberries, blackberries, blueberries, currants, cherries, early peaches, apricots, nectarines.

AUGUST
Water in dry spells.

Continue regular spray program. Spray for brown rot on peaches and similar fruits, if weather is humid. Watch out for Japanese beetles on grapes and spray as necessary with carbaryl.

Continue training grapes.

Cut out old raspberry canes, tie in new ones, and remove unwanted suckers.

Harvest peaches, nectarines, apricots, blueberries, blackberries, plums, crabapples, early apples and pears, grapes, melons.

SEPTEMBER
Spray late peaches, plums for brown rot if weather is humid. Cut out old canes of blackberries and related hybrids after harvest and thin others if too crowded.

Water grapes heavily after final harvest to help protect against winter injury.

Harvest all tree fruits, melons, ever-bearing strawberries and raspberries, blackberries, grapes.

OCTOBER
Cut out old canes from blackberries and related hybrids. Clean up strawberry bed.

Lime soil as necessary.

Fumigate soil with paradischlorobenzene if peach tree borers are present.

Harvest late apples, pears, peaches, quinces, grapes, ever-bearing raspberries.

NOVEMBER
Apply winter mulch of hay or straw to strawberry bed after ground is frozen.

Pull back organic mulches from around trunks of apples and other trees that may be attacked by mice.

Place supports under tree branches that may be damaged by ice or snow.

DECEMBER
Take a rest. The garden should be in order.

Fruit in the greenhouse

There is much satisfaction and no great difficulty in growing out-of-season fruits if a greenhouse is available. Most tree fruits and soft fruits may be grown under glass. The warmth and protection of a greenhouse not only hastens maturity of the fruits, but also protects them from weather hazards such as gales, frosts and torrential rain, and pests such as birds. There are, however, several factors to consider before attempting to grow fruit under glass.

If a greenhouse has first to be purchased, its cost and its possible heating bills through the years must be set against the value of the fruit crops likely to be obtained. There is also the size factor. Unless a few potted trees are all that is to be grown, a greenhouse of not less than 10 ft × 8 ft is the smallest to be considered. One peach, nectarine, grape or fig tree grown in the greenhouse border needs wall or roof space at least equal to this size, and more if possible. A further relevant factor is that, in general, the larger the greenhouse, the cheaper is each square yard of growing space. If fruits crop regularly and as well as they should, then in a comparatively few years the greenhouse should pay for itself.

The situation is rather different for hardy fruits such as apples, pears, cherries and plums, which are grown in pots and brought into the greenhouse to advance their time of fruiting, then taken outside for the rest of the year. Plants in containers are "plunged" outside by burying the pot up to the rim in a bed of ashes or sand or in well-drained ground, after fruiting and until early April. It is worth while growing these fruits in a greenhouse only if they are alternated with such fruits as melons. Of course, if fruit growing under glass is looked upon as a hobby, these "commercial" considerations do not apply.

Site

Whether or not the greenhouse is to be heated, it should be sited in a sheltered place where the low winter sun is not obstructed. Frequent strong winds can soon dissipate both artificial and sun heat and lower the temperature accordingly. Ideally, a lean-to greenhouse is best, built against a south- or west-facing wall. If no artificial heat is used, the lean-to is especially valuable, because the back wall absorbs the sun's heat and releases it slowly over a period. The wall is also ideal for training such fruits as peaches and figs.

Heating the greenhouse

Although heating is not necessary to advance the maturity of fruits grown under glass, it is essential for really early crops. Heating a greenhouse can be expensive and sorting the best buy from the various methods available is difficult. The main fuel-types are: solid fuel such as coal, coke and wood; oil; gas and electricity. All fuels can be burned to heat water which circulates in pipes, or to heat the surrounding air by convection or using fans or ducts. Solar heating, a method that uses the sun's power to heat water or air which is stored in specially insulated containers for immediate or future use, has recently been developed to heat greenhouses, and is used particularly in the USA. This method will probably become more popular.

Methods of heating Solid fuel systems are cheaper to run but equipment and installation charges are high. Where natural gas is available, there are very cheap and efficient heating units. Oil can be used in various ways, either burned to heat air directly or to work a boiler system, but the high cost of oil makes heating by this method more expensive than the previous methods. Most expensive of all is electricity, but the equipment is not unduly costly and there is much to be said for a system that provides instant, clean heat at the touch of a switch. Provided that a minimum temperature of 7°C/45°F is maintained (all that is necessary for fruit growing) and an efficient thermostat control is used, electricity need not cost as much as might be supposed. Also, when used to power a fan heater, it has the added advantage of maintaining a buoyant, moving atmosphere which is beneficial to the plants and helps to minimize such diseases as gray mold.

Heating is not usually required until late in the fall and can often cease in April, so fuel bills need not be high if tender plants are not grown all the year.

Maintenance and hygiene

During late spring to early fall, the glass needs shading during warm, sunny spells. Roller blinds are the best method, ideally coupled to an automatic opener. This method is, however, expensive to install. A favorite alternative is to apply a liquid shading compound either sprayed or painted on to the glass. It is best to select a formulation that can easily be rubbed or washed off when not required.

In the sheltered, equable conditions within a greenhouse, certain pests and diseases can flourish and become troublesome. For this reason hygiene is important. Apart from spraying or dusting infected plants with the appropriate pesticide or fungicide, the greenhouse interior should be washed down with an approved disinfectant, either when the plants are dormant or once potted plants have been taken outside. Ideally all the metal, wood and brickwork should be scrubbed annually, paying attention to crevices where the female red spider mite over-winters. Forcible spraying is a less efficient alternative.

Benching should be similarly treated and all debris (including unused canes, boxes and pots) should be removed. Trees plunged outside should be sprayed with a winter wash before moving them back into the greenhouse. Permanently housed plants should be similarly treated while dormant.

Soil

Unlike plants in the open, plants in the greenhouse border are totally dependent on how good the border soil is because their roots are restricted. Ordinary top-soil from the garden is not always suitable.

A good border soil should consist of a mixture of seven parts fibrous loam (if possible made from sods stacked for six months before use), three parts peat and two parts coarse grit. Add base fertilizer at the rate of 8 oz per 2 gal bucketful of soil.

If re-soiling an existing border, it is an opportune time to check on the drainage. If the sub-soil is a layer of impermeable clay or if the ground seems waterlogged, construct a drainage system or a drywell (see pages 10–11).

Cultivation

The following notes describe the general routine for all fruit when grown under glass. For cultivation of fruit in tubs and pots, see pages 80–1.

All the hardy fruits in this book are best planted or potted in the fall, ideally just as the leaves fall or soon afterwards. From then on they must be kept cool. Trees under glass need plenty of fresh air, so leave the ventilators (and the door on warm days) of the greenhouse wide open unless gales or frosts are forecast.

During the dormant season from November to February, trees in the greenhouse border should be mulched with well-rotted manure or compost, or with peat and a balanced fertilizer such as 10-10-10 at 2 oz per square yard.

In early January, move in plants in containers that were plunged outside after fruiting last year and shut the ventilators to build up warmth. On mild days, the trees are sprayed, ideally with rainwater. After a few weeks, artificial heat may be turned on if required. As the weather warms up some ventilation is needed and floors and benching should be damped down daily.

A regular watch must be kept for pests and remedial action taken as soon as possible. In particular look out for red spider mite and aphids (see pages 14–16).

When the flowers begin to open, stop the overhead spraying with water and damp down on sunny days only.

In some cases, hand pollination is needed (see page 43). Once flowering has ceased and fruitlets are visible, resume regular routine program of damping and spraying. Plants in pots should be given a liquid feed at this stage, and the feed should be repeated at ten day intervals.

At all times make sure that the plants do not lack water. Potted trees need watering daily, and often twice a day during hot spells. Border-grown plants need water at least once a week and two or three times a week in warm weather.

When fruits begin to ripen, cease overhead spraying but resume after picking and continue until just before leaf-fall. Potted trees should be plunged outside once all the fruit has been picked. They must be re-potted annually just after leaf-fall (see pages 80–1 for details of re-potting).

Soft fruits

Introduction
Soft fruit is an umbrella term for several low-growing shrubs and perennials that bear soft, juicy fruit. They are not all closely related and they have a variety of growth habits. Botanically the best-known fruits can be placed into two groups: those belonging to the rose family (Rosaceae), including the raspberry, blackberry, loganberry and allied hybrids, and the strawberry; and those classified in the gooseberry family (Grossulariaceae) including the black, red and white currant, and the gooseberry. Three fruits not included in these two families are grapes (Vitidaceae), the melon (Cucurbitaceae) and the blueberry (Ericaceae). However, all the fruits in the soft fruit category have the common advantage of bearing fruit soon after planting—in some cases (such as the melon) within the same year. Also, soft fruits are particularly suitable for the small garden because they need far less room than do tree fruits such as apples, pears and plums.

Site
With good basic culture, all the soft fruits are easily grown and, once established, provide annual crops without fail. Although best grown in an open, sunny position, they do reasonably well in partial shade or in a site that gets afternoon sun only. Low-lying areas that are susceptible to late spring frosts should be avoided if possible.

If space in the garden is restricted, use walls and fences for grapes and climbing cane fruits, as well as for gooseberries and red and white currants as cordons or fans (see pages 8–9). Soft fruits such as strawberries, grapes and currants can also be grown in containers, in window boxes or in tubs on a patio, and climbing fruits can be trained over pergolas and arches (see pages 88–9).

In a small garden the fruits to be grown must be chosen carefully. If there is room, for example, for only six bushes it is tempting to grow one of each of all the main soft fruits. But it is more sensible and profitable to grow a minimum of three bushes of two favorite sorts only. In this way enough fruit can be picked for the family's needs, with some left over for jam-making perhaps, or for freezing.

Personal preference will, of course, dictate the choice of fruits. If only a few sorts can be grown, black or red currants, raspberries and strawberries are a good choice because, apart from their excellent taste, all are good croppers relative to their size and those in stores are seldom as fresh as those picked straight from the garden.

With the use of cloches, cold frames or polyethylene tunnels the season of some soft fruits (strawberries in particular) can be extended both in the early summer and in the fall.

Protection against birds
Another advantage of growing soft fruits is the comparative ease of providing protection against pests. Very few gardens escape bird damage to ripe fruit in summer and fall, or to fruit buds in winter and spring. This means some sort of year-round protection is needed. A permanent fruit cage is highly recommended because it provides both efficient bird protection and allows easy access to the plants for picking, spraying, pruning and top-dressing (see page 17).

Clearing the site
Although most soft fruits grow well enough in any moderately fertile soil, it is always worth while doing some initial preparation. See pages 10–11 for details of soil preparation and drainage. A first essential is to make sure that all perennial weeds are removed. Nowadays there are selective herbicides for this purpose (see page 17), although some gardeners may prefer to double dig before planting which buries the weeds. Clean, cultivated ground needs single digging before planting (see pages 10–11), and hand picking occasional weeds during this operation is all that is needed.

Planting
Strawberry plants are set out with a trowel in much the same way as any bedding plant or young perennial. Raspberry canes and blackberry layers (plants) can usually be dealt with in the same way, depending upon how much root they have. At the most a small spade is all that is necessary.

Bush fruits generally have a more extensive root system and, because they are a fairly long-term crop, their planting ritual should be more elaborate. Plant bushes from November to March, depending on the region and weather and horticultural conditions.

Dig a hole which is deeper and wider than the roots when they are spread out. The bottom of the hole should be loosened with a fork and if little or no organic matter was dug into the area initially, a spadeful or two can now be worked in. Use well-rotted manure or garden compost, or peat and bonemeal.

Set the plant in the hole and spread out the roots. Fill in the hole with the soil, occasionally giving the bush a gentle shake up and down so that the soil filters among the roots and makes close contact with them. Firm the soil gently throughout with the feet. When all the plants are in position, rake the site over so that it is level and apply a light dressing of a balanced fertilizer.

Strawberries 1

JUNE-BEARING STRAWBERRIES

EARLY
'Dixieland' Large, firm berries. Especially good in South, but adapted to other areas.
'Earlibelle' Very early. Does best in deep South. Bright red berries turning dark red. Medium-large.

'Earlidawn' Very early. Big, tart berries and lots of them. Susceptible to verticillium wilt and should be avoided if this is a problem in the area.
'Holiday' Very early. Very productive. Solid red.
'Premier' Standard commercial variety, but good in home garden. Widely grown. Medium-size berries.

'Puget Beauty' Fine variety for the Northwest. Long, medium-large berries. Aromatic and sweet.
'Redglow' Especially flavorful, medium-big berries, but not in large quantities.
'Spring Beauty' High-yielding and puts out a great many runners. Berries orange-red, large and sweet.

MID-SEASON
'Catskill' Unusually large berries are bright crimson and extra sweet. Productive. High resistance to verticillium wilt.
'Dunlap' Also called 'Senator Dunlap'. Highly weather-resistant and adaptable. Fairly small, red berries with outstanding flavor.

The strawberry cultivated today has resulted from the interbreeding of a number of *Fragaria* species, principally the North American *F. virginiana* as well as the South American *F. chiloensis*. This intermingling of genetic characteristics has resulted in a fruit of great variety in taste and color, with a cropping ability and season of such versatility that it can be grown from the Tropics to the cool temperate regions of the world. It is no wonder the strawberry is the most popular soft fruit.

For the purposes of cultivation the strawberry is divided into three categories: the ordinary June-fruiting strawberry; the so-called ever-bearing strawberry that produces one crop in the spring and a second crop in the fall; and the alpine strawberry (*Fragaria vesca*, subspecies *alpina*), a mountain form of wild strawberry (see page 23).

Standard strawberries

The ordinary, or June-bearing strawberry, crops once only in the early summer. A few do crop again in fall and these are called "two crop" varieties, but they are cultivated in the same way as the others. The expected yield per strawberry plant is about 8–10 oz.

Cultivation

Some gardeners prefer to grow strawberries as an annual crop, planting new runners each year. This method produces high quality fruits but a lower yield than that of larger two- or three-year-old plants.

Soil and situation Most soils are suitable for strawberries, but they should be well drained. On waterlogged land, if a drainage system is not practicable, grow strawberries on ridges 2–3 in high. They prefer a slightly acid (pH 6.0–6.5) light loam in a frost-free, sunny situation. They will, however, tolerate some shade and because many varieties flower over a long period, the later flowers should escape spring frosts. Strawberries are readily attacked by soil-borne pests and diseases and a system of soil rotation should be practiced. Do not grow them for more than three or four years in any one site. For this reason, strawberries are best grown with the vegetables rather than with the more permanent fruit plants.

Soil preparation A strawberry bed will be down for three or four years, and the initial preparations should be thorough so that the land is made fertile and free from perennial weeds. In July dig in well-rotted manure or compost at about the rate of 14 lb to the square yard. Rake off any surplus because bulky organics on the surface encourage slugs, snails and millipedes. Once applied, no more organics should be needed for the life of the bed. Just before planting, lightly fork in a balanced fertilizer such as 10-10-10 at 3 oz per square yard.

Planting and spacing The earlier the planting, the better the maiden crop in the following year. Plant in early spring after the ground has started to warm up. It is not necessary to wait until frost danger has passed. In the warmest American climates, however, it is better to plant in October. Plant the runners in moist soil with the crown of the strawberry just level with the soil surface; planting too deep may result in the rotting of the buds and planting too shallow may cause drying out. Plant with a trowel or hand fork, spreading out the roots well. Replace the soil and firm it. Space the plants 18 in apart in rows 3 ft apart. On a light soil they can be 15 in apart with $2\frac{1}{2}$ ft between the rows. Plants to be grown for two years need only 12 in spacing.

Pollination The flowers are pollinated by bees and such crawling insects as pollen beetles. Imperfect pollination results in malformed fruits. All modern varieties are self-fertile.

Watering and feeding Water regularly for the first few weeks after planting and whenever dry conditions occur during the growing season, but try to keep water away from the ripening berries because this encourages gray mold (*Botrytis cinerea*). The risk is less with trickle or drip irrigation because only the soil is wetted. Damp conditions overnight also encourage botrytis; water in the morning so that the plants are dry by nightfall. In mid-August each year, apply a balanced fertilizer at $\frac{1}{2}$ oz per square yard along each side of the row. No other feeding is necessary unless growth has been poor. In this case apply sulfate of ammonia at $\frac{1}{2}$ oz per square yard in April, taking care to prevent fertilizer touching the foliage because it will scorch it.

Weed control Weeds compete for nutrients and water. Keep the rows clean by shallow hoeing and tuck any runners into the row to fill gaps. Pay particular attention to cleaning up between the rows before mulching. Weedkillers may be used (see page 17).

In general, shallow cultivation of strawberries keeps weed growth in check. But care should be taken to weed strawberry beds each fall, and particular attention should be paid to the removal of all weeds.

1 In late winter or the preceding fall, dig in well-rotted manure or compost at a rate of 14 lb per square yard. Rake off any surplus manure.

2 About April, plant the strawberries 18 in apart in rows 3 ft apart. Spread out the roots, keeping the crowns level with the soil surface. Firm the soil.

3 For the first few weeks after planting and during all succeeding dry spells in the growing season, water regularly. Keep water away from ripening berries.

4 Up to July 15 in the first year, pick off all blossoms to force strength into the plants for a big crop next year.

5 When the fruits begin to swell, scatter slug pellets along the rows. Cover the ground beneath the berries and between rows with barley or wheat straw.

6 Protect the fruit from birds. Support nets with posts at least 18 in tall. Cover posts with jars or pots first.

Strawberries 2

'Fairfax' Large berries turning deep red when fully ripe. Excellent quality and flavor. Moderately productive.
'Guardian' Large berries, bright red throughout and very sweet. Vigorous plants with enormous yield.
'Midway' Large, tart berries. Heavy producer. Very susceptible to verticillium wilt.

'New Empire' Ripens mid-season to late, over a long season. Huge berries.
'Raritan' Medium-size berries produced in great supply for a long time.
'Surecrop' Extremely reliable producer of big, deep red berries.
'Tennessee Beauty' Popular in the middle South. Medium-size berries.

LATE
'Deep Red' Huge, dark red berries. Ornamental dark green plants putting out many runners.
'Fletcher' Performs best in cool areas. Medium-size berries.
'Sparkle' Starts producing toward end of mid-season. Medium-size berries, sparkling red and of excellent flavor and

quality. Very productive and popular.
'New Marlate' Extra large berries of delicious flavor. Vigorous.
'Sparkle' Starts producing toward end of mid-season. Medium-size berries, sparkling red and of excellent flavor.
'Spring Giant' Berries up to 2½ in in diameter, bright red, highly flavored. Plants are unusually tall.

Disbudding During the first season, remove all flowers until mid-July. If the plants are allowed to set fruit in the first few months, vegetative growth will be retarded and the next year's crop will be small. In succeeding years, of course, disbudding is unnecessary.

Mulching When the fruits of two-year-old plants begin to swell and weigh down the trusses, scatter slug pellets along the rows. Then put straw down around the plants. This is to keep the fruits clean, so tuck the straw right under the berries and also cover the ground between the rows to help to keep down weeds. Do not straw down earlier than this because the straw prevents the heat from the earth reaching the flowers, which may then be damaged by frost at night. Preferably use barley straw which is soft or, as a second choice, wheat straw.

Protection from birds The best method of protection is to cover the strawberry bed with a large cage, using ¾ in or 1 in plastic netting, supported by posts and wire or string. The height should be at least 18 in; about 4 ft is the ideal height for picking in comfort. Put glass jars or plastic plant pots over the posts to prevent them from tearing the netting. A simpler method is to spread

Alternatives to mulching

If straw is not available. strawberries can also be grown through black polyethylene. First, prepare the bed by raising a 3 in high ridge of soil. Water it well. Lay plastic over the ridge, tucking in the edges under the soil. Plant the strawberries

lightweight plastic directly over the plants. It can be folded back when picking is to be done.

Harvesting

The best time to pick strawberries is in the morning when the berries are still cool. Pick them complete with stalks; try not to handle the flesh because it bruises easily.

At the end of the season

Immediately after cropping, remove the straw and cut off the old plant leaves (about 3 in above the crown) and unwanted runners using shears or a sickle. Alternatively, a rotary lawn mower can be run directly over the entire bed. Tuck in runners needed to fill in any gaps in the row. In the second year, a matted row can be grown by allowing runners to root in the row and reducing the space available, so that the quantity of fruit is greater but the quality suffers. The space between the rows is kept clear. Defoliation is good horticultural practice because it rejuvenates the plant and removes leaves and stems, which may be a source of pests and diseases. But it must be done as soon as cropping is over to avoid damaging fresh growth and reducing the crop the next year.

through slits in the plastic at 15–18 in intervals. Leave a 6 in bare strip between plastic strips to enable rain to permeate to the roots. Black polyethylene sheeting does slow down evaporation, but the soil under it will eventually become dry.

Winter protection

In zones 3–7, as soon as the fall temperature drops to 20°C/68°F, spread straw or salt or marsh hay over the entire bed. The covering should be at least 3 in deep between rows; and enough to conceal the plants themselves. The purpose of the covering is to protect the plants against frost and other winter injuries. If the temperature does not drop to 20°C/68°F before the end of November, the plants should be covered at that time in any case.

The covering is removed in the spring after growth is well started. If it is left on too long, the foliage will yellow.

Propagation

Strawberries are easily propagated from runners which the parent plant begins to produce as the crop is coming to an end. The aim is to obtain well-rooted runners for early planting and it is achieved by pegging down the strongest runners so that they make good contact with the soil. In June or July choose healthy parent plants which have cropped well. From each select four or five strong runners. Peg them down either into moist open ground or into 3 in pots buried level with the soil. Pot-grown runners are best because they are easier to transplant. Fill the pots with a seed-starting mixture or a 50–50 mixture of loam and peat. Peg close to the embryo plant but do not sever it from the parent at this stage. For the pegs, use 4 in pieces of thin galvanized wire bent to a U-shape. Straightened out paper clips are ideal.

In four to six weeks there should be a good root system. Sever from the parent, lift and plant out into the new bed. Keep them well watered.

Planting under mist or in a closed propagating case are other useful ways of obtaining very early runners. With these, sever the embryo plants from the parents at the first sign of roots—root initials—and peg them into 1½–2 in peat pots.

Varieties

Strawberries soon become infected with virus diseases, so it is important to plant only virus-free stock. It is best to obtain plants from a specialist propagator who guarantees healthy stock.

PROPAGATION

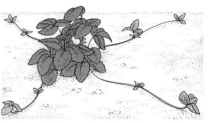

1 In June to August, select four or five runners from healthy, cropping plants.

2 With U-shaped wires, peg runners into open ground or into 3 in pots buried level and filled with a potting compost.

3 In four to six weeks they should have rooted. Sever from parents close to plants.

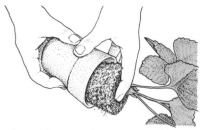

4 Lift out the potted runners and knock out from the pot. Plant out into the new bed and water well.

Strawberries 3

EVER-BEARING STRAWBERRIES
'Geneva' Excellent large, sweet berries, but have a tendency to rot in damp weather. Produces fairly late in the spring.
'Luscious Red' From Minnesota, therefore quite hardy. Long, pointed, medium-size berries.
'Ogallala' Drought-resistant plants doing best in cool climates. Berries are large, dark red and have a faint wild strawberry flavor.
'Ozark Beauty' Unusually productive. Big, sweet, wedge-shaped berries. Extremely popular.
'Superfection' Tart, rounded, light red berries. Among the most widely planted ever-bearing varieties.

'Chief Bemidji' Very hardy. Big, solid red berries. Good for southern gardens as well as those elsewhere. Excellent producer over a long period. Huge, sweet, orange-red berries.
ALPINES June to October.
'Baron Solemacher' Superb flavor. Masses of tiny dark red fruits. Widely grown. Prefers slight shade.

'Alexandria' Sweet and juicy. Very bright red. Fruits long (over ½ in) and large for an alpine. Good cropper.
'Fraise des Bois' Good flavor. Fruits very small. Bright red. Prolific continuous cropper.
'Alpine Yellow' Strongly flavored, very small golden-yellow fruits. Not as heavy a cropper as the red varieties.

Ever-bearing strawberries

Ever-bearing strawberries have the characteristic of producing fruit in the spring and again in the fall. It is useful to cover the fall crop with cloches to extend the season, possibly in late October. It is best to grow ever-bearers for one year only because the size and weight of the crop deteriorate in the second year. Replant with new runners each year.

Cultivation

The basic requirements of soil, spacing, mulching and feeding are the same as for June-bearing strawberries. The soil should be highly fertile and moisture-retentive. Be sure to water well in late summer and fall.

Plant in the early spring and remove the first flush of flowers to ensure a good crop later in the season.

In the fall, when cropping is finished, clean up the rows, remove the old straw, surplus runners and one or two of the older leaves, and burn the debris. Cover with straw or hay in the late fall to protect against winter damage.

Do not fertilize the plants in the spring of the following year, but apply a balanced fertilizer immediately after all the spring berries have been picked to encourage a second, smaller, crop in the fall. Then remove plants entirely.

Alpine strawberries

Several varieties have been selected for garden and commercial cultivation. They make an attractive edging plant, having masses of small white flowers. They bear dark red fruits continuously or in flushes from June until November.

Cultivation

Alpine strawberries are usually grown from seed and kept for no more than two years before re-sowing. There are a few varieties that produce runners, but most do not. Maintaining virus-free stock is difficult.

Sowing Sow the seeds in March under glass. Sow into seed boxes containing a moist seed-starting mixture. Maintain them at a temperature of 18°–20°C/64°–68°F. Cover the boxes with glass and shade until the seeds germinate. When two true leaves appear, prick out the seedlings 1 in apart into flats or peat pots.

Soil preparation, planting and feeding The soil should be rich, well drained and slightly acid (pH 6.0–6.5). Just before planting apply sulfate of potash at ½ oz per square yard. Once the danger of frosts is over, but by the end of May, plant out the seedlings in the prepared, moist soil. Plant in the open or in light shade. Space the seedlings 1 ft apart with 2½ ft between the rows. Water them in dry weather (about 3–4 gal per square yard every 7–10 days). For better cropping, when the flowers appear, feed every two weeks with a liquid fertilizer.

Harvesting

Pick carefully. Slight crushing, sugaring, and overnight soaking brings out the flavor.

PROPAGATION

Some ever-bearing strawberries produce runners and are propagated in the same way as are June-bearing strawberries, but a few varieties do not and these are propagated by division.

From late August to early September, dig up a mature plant and break off the new crowns or buds with as many roots as possible. Transfer them to the new strawberry bed and plant them immediately in the usual way. Do not plant the crowns too deep or they will rot.

1 In March, sow into seed boxes of moist seed compost.

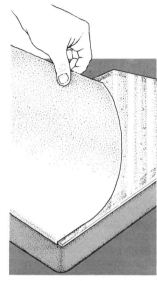

2 Cover with glass and shade until germination. Maintain a temperature of 18°–20°C/64°–68°F.

3 When the seedlings have two true leaves, prick out 1 in apart into flats or individual peat pots.

4 Just before planting, apply sulfate of potash at ½ oz per square yard to moist well-dug soil, forking it in lightly.

5 Once the danger of frosts is over, plant out the seedlings in the prepared bed, 1 ft apart in rows 2½ ft apart.

6 In dry periods, water the plants thoroughly every 7–10 days. For better crops, feed every two weeks with liquid manure.

Raspberries 1

STANDARD RASPBERRY VARIETIES
'Amber' Amber-yellow berries superior in quality to other yellows and comparable to most reds (which are generally better than the yellows). Fruits rather late. Not hardy in zone 3.
'Boyne' Red berries of good quality. Vigorous, very hardy plants grown in North Dakota and Manitoba.

'Canby' Canes nearly thornless. Large, sweet red berries ripening before
'Chief' Profuse small red berries, but of only fair quality.
'Early Red' Red berries of better-than-average flavor. Hardy and very early.
'Latham' Probably the most popular standard red raspberry. Very large, mildly sweet, firm fruits of moderate quality.

Hardy and tolerant of virus diseases.
'Sumner' Dependable variety well adapted to heavier soils. Big, red berries ripening over a long period.
'Taylor' Excellent large, conical, light red berries in profusion. Delicious flavor. Vigorous, hardy, erect plants.
'Willamette' Enormous, conical, dark red berries in abundance.

Like the strawberry, the raspberry is one of the quickest fruits to crop, bearing a reasonable amount in the second year and full cropping thereafter. A good average yield is 1½–2 lb per foot run of row.

Cultivation

Most red raspberries (there are also a few with yellow fruit) flower in late spring and the fruits ripen in early to midsummer, depending upon the variety and the weather: such varieties are called standard or summer-bearing raspberries.

The stems, or canes, are biennial in that they grow vegetatively in their first year, flower and fruit in their second year and then die back to ground level. The root system is perennial and of suckering habit, producing each growing season new replacement canes from adventitious buds on the roots and new buds from old stem bases.

Some raspberry varieties have the characteristic of flowering on the first year's growth on the topmost part. These are called ever-bearing raspberries as they produce a small crop of fruit in early summer and a larger crop in early fall. All grow in zones 3–7. Because their cultural requirements differ in some respects, they are described separately (see page 26).

Soil and situation Red raspberries grow best on a slightly acid soil of pH 6.0–6.7 that is moisture-retentive but well drained. They can be grown in dry, sandy and limy soils of low fertility, provided plenty of water is given during dry weather and bulky organic manures are liberally applied. Raspberries will not tolerate poor drainage, and even temporary waterlogging can lead to the death of the root system and subsequent death of the canes. In alkaline soils above pH 7.0, iron and manganese deficiencies may occur. See pages 10–11 for reduction of soil alkalinity and correction of iron and/or manganese deficiencies.

The site must be sheltered because strong winds damage the canes and inhibit the movement of pollinating insects. Preferably, they should be planted in full sun, although they grow quite well in partial shade with a minimum of half a day's sun, provided they are not directly under trees and the soil is not too dry.

Soil preparation Prepare the ground in late fall or late winter by forking out all weeds, particularly perennials. Then dig a trench along the intended row three spades wide by one spade deep. Cover the bottom of the trench with well-rotted manure or compost to a depth of 3–4 in and fork it into the base so that it is thoroughly mixed with the soil. With double-dug grassland there is no need for this operation because the buried turf takes the place of the organic manure. Finally fill in the trench and fork in a balanced fertilizer such as 10-10-10 at the rate of 3 oz per square yard.

Planting and spacing If possible the rows should run north-south so that one row does not shade another too much.

In early spring, plant the canes 18 in apart in the rows. If more than one row is planted, space the rows 6 ft apart, or 5 ft apart if using the single fence system. Spread the roots out well and plant them about 3 in deep; deep planting inhibits new canes (suckers).

After planting, cut down the canes to a bud about 9–12 in above the ground. Later, when the new canes appear, cut down the old stump to ground level before it fruits. This means foregoing a crop in the first summer but it ensures good establishment and the production of strong new canes in subsequent years.

Supporting the canes

To prevent the canes from bowing over when heavy with fruit and to keep the fruits clean it is generally advisable to support the canes. The usual method is a post and wire fence for which there are various alternative systems. It is easier to erect the fence before planting, although it may be left until the end of the first summer.

Single fence: vertically trained canes This is the most popular method and consists of single wires stretched horizontally at heights of 2½, 3½ and 5½ ft. It requires the least space of the various fencing systems and is ideal for the small garden. The fruiting canes are tied individually to the wires and thus are secure

1 In early fall, take out a trench in prepared ground three spades wide by one spade deep. Cover the bottom of the trench with a 3–4 in layer of well-rotted manure or compost and fork in thoroughly.

2 Then, fill in the trench and fork in 3 oz per square yard of a balanced fertilizer such as 10-10-10.

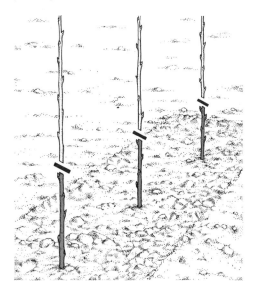

3 From March to April, plant the canes at 18 in intervals. Spread the roots out well and plant about 3 in deep. Cut down the canes to a bud about 9–12 in above the ground.

4 In late March, apply sulfate of ammonia at ½ oz per square yard. Mulch with a 2 in layer of garden compost, keeping it well clear of the canes.

Raspberries 2

EVER-BEARING RASPBERRY VARIETIES
'Fall Red' From New Hampshire and very hardy. Large, bright red berries of fine flavor and aroma. Ripens very early.
'Heritage' Flavor fair. Berries firm, small to medium, round, conical, light red. Cropping heavy. Requires a warm situation.
'Indian Summer' Soft, crumbly red

berries of good flavor. Brilliant red. Abundant producer.
'September' Flavor fair. Berries crumbly, small to medium, conical, dark red. Cropping and vigor moderate.
Yellow autumn-fruiting raspberry
'Fallgold' Sweet, mild flavor. Berries medium to large, golden-yellow, conical. Canes vigorous, prolific.

against winter winds. They are exposed to the sun, which enhances the quality of the fruits and reduces the incidence of fungal disease. The system has the disadvantages that the new canes are at risk of being trampled on during picking and of being damaged by strong winds in July unless temporarily supported by string tied to the lower wires.

Drive in preserved 7½ ft posts 18 in into the ground 12–15 ft apart. Use 14 gauge galvanized fence wire.

Erect the end posts first and strut them and then drive in the intermediate posts. Finally fix the wires to the posts using straining bolts at one end and staples on the intermediates and at the opposite end.

Double fence: parallel wires The double fence is erected in a similar way to the single fence but because the top wires are not as high, the posts are only 6½ ft tall. Cross bars 2½ ft long by 2 in across to carry the parallel wires are fixed to the end posts and to the intermediate posts. In exposed situations, double posts should be used instead of cross bars. Parallel wires are spaced 2 ft apart at 3 ft and 5 ft from the ground. Stretch wire as cross ties every 2 ft along the wires to prevent the canes falling down in the row.

This method has the advantage of enabling a larger number of canes to be trained in and a greater yield to be obtained from much the same area. Picking the fruits from the center is difficult, however, and there is a higher risk of fungal diseases because of the more crowded conditions.

In an exposed garden the untied canes may be damaged on the wires, so the canes should be tied to the wires.

Scandinavian system (training in a low "V")

This is a double fence system with only one set of parallel wires spaced 3 ft apart at 3 ft from the ground.

Drive two sets of posts 4½ ft long 18 in into the ground, 3 ft apart every 12–15 ft in the row.

The fruiting canes are not tied but woven around the wires to form a "V" when viewed from the end of the row. The replacement canes are allowed to grow up the center unsupported.

With this method the fruit is presented at a low picking height and the replacement

canes are safe within the row. However, there is the risk of fungal troubles because of the crowded conditions of the canes on the wires and in the row. If more than one row is planted, space the rows 6 ft apart.

Single post system This is a method particularly suited to a very small garden. It consists of a single post to which each plant is tied. The posts are 7½ ft long by 2½ in top diameter, driven 18 in into the ground.

Initial pruning

In the first two seasons after planting, the number of canes may be few, but thereafter there should be more than enough.

In the second year thin out the weakest canes in the early spring so that the remainder grow more strongly, and pull out unwanted canes growing well away from the row. Allow about 8–10 canes to a plant.

Pruning and training established plants

As soon as fruiting is over, cut down to ground level the old canes which have fruited. Select the healthiest and strongest of the young canes, retaining about four to eight per stool.

If using the single fence system, tie the canes to the wires, 3–4 in apart. Either tie each one separately with a 6 in twist tie or secure them to the wires by continuous lacing using jute or strong string. Tie an occasional knot as a precaution against the string breaking later on.

With the Scandinavian system the canes are laced around a single wire, equally on each side. Gently bend them over at the point they reach the wire and then twist the canes around the wire. No tying is necessary. Do this in late August or early September when the canes are still supple. Depending upon the length of the canes, this could mean four or six canes being twisted around each other and the supporting wires like a rope. The average number of canes from each plant should be about four to six.

For the single post system the fruiting canes are tied to the posts and the replacement canes looped in as and when necessary.
Tipping the canes (This is not applicable to the Scandinavian system). In early spring, about March, cut the canes to a bud 6 in

above the top wire. This removes winter damage to the tips and encourages the lowest buds to break.

For very vigorous varieties grown on the single fence system, where tipping would remove a lot of the cane, loop and tie the canes back on to the top wire and then prune about 6 in off the tips. This method gives extra length of canes, hence more crop, but the top wire must be strong.

Feeding and watering

In early spring each year apply 1 oz of sulfate of potash per square yard. Every third year add 2 oz of superphosphate per square yard. In late March apply sulfate of ammonia at ½ oz per square yard. The fertilizers should be applied as a top dressing covering about 18 in each side of the row.

Also, in late March, mulch with a 2 in layer of garden compost, damp peat or manure, keeping the material just clear of the canes. The mulch helps to conserve moisture in the summer and inhibits weed seeds from germinating.

Throughout the growing season keep down weeds and unwanted suckers by shallow hoeing. Be careful not to damage or disturb the roots of the raspberries. If preferred, herbicides can be used (see page 17).

In dry weather water the raspberries regularly but, to minimize the risk of fungal troubles, keep the water off the canes.

Protect the fruit from birds with netting.

Propagation

Raspberries are easily propagated by forking up surplus canes with as many roots as possible in early spring. The canes must be healthy and strong. Virus-infected plants should be dug up and burned.

Harvesting

Pick the fruits without the stalk and core, unless the raspberries are required for showing, when they are harvested with the stalk attached, using scissors. Picking of standard varieties continues for about a month. In general, pick raspberries when they are fresh, if possible, for better flavor. Use shallow containers to prevent the fruits from crushing each other.

SUPPORT SYSTEMS

Single post system

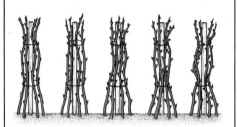

Drive 7½ ft long 2½ in dia. posts 18 in into the ground at each planting station.

Single fence system

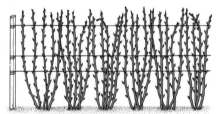

Drive 7½ ft posts 18 in into the ground at 12–15 ft intervals. Stretch 14 gauge galvanized wires between the posts at 2½, 3½ and 5½ ft.

Double fence system

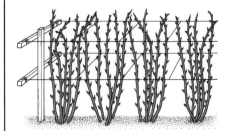

Drive 6½ ft posts 18 in into the ground 12–15 ft apart. Fix 2 in dia. cross bars 2½ ft long to the end posts and to each intermediate post. Then, stretch parallel wires 2 ft apart between the posts at 3 ft and 5 ft from the ground. Stretch wires as cross ties every 2 ft along the wires.

Raspberries 3

Pests and diseases

If aphids are present, spray with dimethoate, formothion or malathion in spring. An oil spray in winter gets rid of the over-wintering eggs. To prevent raspberry beetle grubs feeding on the fruits in summer, spray at dusk with malathion or derris when the first pink berry is seen.

The most serious diseases of raspberries are viruses, which cause the leaves to become mottled or blotched and the canes to be stunted. Seek expert advice before destroying canes because the symptoms are similar to those caused by raspberry leaf mite and bud mite. New canes should be planted elsewhere.

Canes affected by cane blight in summer will wilt, snap off easily and die. If fruiting spurs become blighted, cut out and burn affected canes. Spray new canes with bordeaux mixture.

Cut out and burn canes badly affected by cane spot and prevent it by spraying with liquid copper or thiram at bud burst and pre-blossom time, or with benomyl every two weeks from bud burst to petal fall.

Spur blight causes dark purple blotches around the buds and shoots wither in early spring. Cut out and burn affected canes. Spray new canes when they are a few inches high with benomyl, thiram or captan repeating two, four and six weeks later.

Prevent gray mold (*Botrytis*) on ripening fruit by spraying three times with benomyl at flowering and at two week intervals. Remove and destroy infected fruits.

Selecting healthy plants

It is important to buy only certified stock, wherever possible, to ensure the plants are virus-free and healthy. Healthy plants should last at least ten years before starting to degenerate from virus infection. When this occurs, remove the plants and start a new row in soil that has not grown raspberries or other *Rubus* species before. Alternatively, re-soil over an area 2 ft wide by 1 ft deep.

EVER-BEARING RASPBERRIES

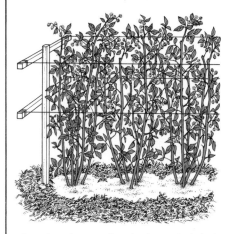

Ever-bearing raspberries bear their fruit on the top part of the current season's canes, extending back from the top over 12 in or more, depending upon the variety. The fruits ripen in early summer a little ahead of standard varieties and again from the beginning of September until stopped by the fall frosts. Ever-bearing raspberries should be picked as soon as ripe and, if necessary, every day. The fall crops can be quite heavy.

The cultural requirements (soil preparation, planting, spacing, initial pruning and feeding) are the same as for the summer-bearing kind. Use the parallel wire method of support described on page 25. The fruits are produced when the weather is becoming cooler, so they are best planted in the sunniest position possible, otherwise too few raspberries may ripen before the first frosts arrive.

Pruning established plants Such ever-bearers do not produce a large spring crop. It is better to grow them for fall use only and to put in standard varieties for summer use. Each February cut down all canes in the row to ground level. In the following spring, new canes are produced which crop in the fall. As the canes are not in the row for more than a year, it is not necessary to thin them unless they are particularly crowded. Pull out any which are growing away from the row.

The first year

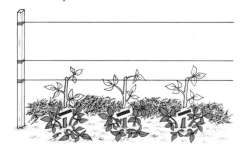

1 In spring, when the new canes appear, cut down the old stumps to ground level.

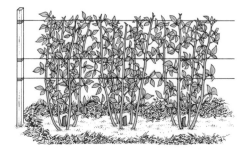

2 In June to September, as new canes develop, tie them 4 in apart on to the wires.

Second and subsequent years

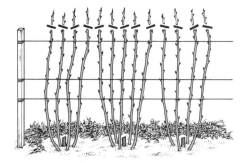

3 In March, cut the canes to a bud 6 in above the top wire. Mulch the plants.

4 In midsummer, fruit is carried on laterals from last year's canes. Thin out the weakest new growth to leave strong canes 4 in apart. Pull out new shoots growing away from the row.

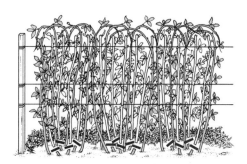

5 When fruiting is over, cut the fruited canes down to ground level. Tie in new canes 4 in apart. If growth is vigorous loop the new canes over to form a series of arches.

6 Each year in early spring, apply 1 oz of sulfate of potash per square yard as a top dressing 18 in each side of the row. Every third year apply 2 oz superphosphate per square yard.

Raspberries 4

BLACK RASPBERRY VARIETIES
'Allen' Large fruits of superior dessert quality. Very productive, hardy and vigorous. Early.
'Black Knight' Ever-bearing variety cropping in summer and fall, but primarily in summer. Large, sweet berries.
'Bristol' Very popular variety with high-quality, firm berries in mid-season. The

berries may be a bit difficult to pick. Extremely productive and vigorous.
'Dundee' Somewhat dull black fruits of good quality. Productive, hardy, vigorous plants are somewhat more tolerant of poorly drained soils than other varieties. Canes easily damaged by wind.
'Huron' Big, glossy black, high quality berries a bit later than most.

'Munger' Best variety for the Northwest, where black raspberries are very widely grown.

PURPLE RASPBERRY VARIETIES
'Clyde' Extra large, firm, glossy dark purple berries ripening in mid-season. Very vigorous, hardy, disease-resistant plants.

'Marion' Very large, dull purple berries ripening a little after 'Sodus'. Productive. May be injured by severe winter weather.
'Sodus' Most popular purple variety. Large, tart berries ripening later than most reds and purples. Vigorous plants suitable to all zones.

Black and purple raspberries are generally known under the name of black raspberry, just as red and yellow raspberries are usually known as red raspberries. They are also closely related to the reds, although they are larger and more productive and greatly tolerant of heat, although less resistant to cold.

Plants with black berries, which are also called blackcaps, ripen earlier than those with purple berries, but purple berries have bigger fruit with a more distinctive flavor. The berries are not as juicy as red raspberries and are used primarily to make appetizing jams and jellies.

Both the black and the purple raspberry grow in zones 4–8.

Culture

Black and purple raspberries are somewhat more susceptible to disease than red raspberries and a little more care should be taken in finding a site for them. Do not plant for several years in soil in which potatoes, tomatoes, peppers, eggplants or a previous crop of raspberries have been grown; and be sure to plant 300–400 ft away from all wild brambles and cultivated red and yellow raspberries.

The soil, moisture and fertilization requirements of black raspberries are essentially similar to those needed by the red raspberry.

Propagation

Black and purple raspberries are reproduced by inserting the tips of young canes into the soil to a depth of 4–6 in. Left to their own devices, plants tip-layer themselves but do not produce such good plants as can the gardener. The best time to do this is in mid-summer in loose soil with ample moisture.

The plants should be well rooted by late fall and ready for transplanting to the garden in early spring. Cut off the old stem at the ground as soon as new growth starts.

Training and pruning

The plants are best grown in a double-fence system similar to that used for red raspberries. If the soil holds moisture well, set the plants 3 ft apart and 1 in deeper than they previously grew. In drier soils, increase spacing between plants to as much as 6 ft.

No pruning is necessary in the first year. Thereafter, in late winter or early spring, cut off all weak canes at the ground, leaving 4–6 good canes per plant. Remove weak and dead laterals, and trim back the remaining laterals on black varieties to 6–8 in; on purple varieties to 10 in. Then in early summer, before berries start to ripen, nip about 3 in off the ends of the upright canes to force the growth of the laterals.

Finally, as soon as all fruit has been picked, prune out all the canes that bore fruit to give more light and room to the new canes. Burn all prunings promptly.

Harvesting

Black raspberries deteriorate more slowly than reds so it is not necessary to pick them so frequently.

Planting and spacing

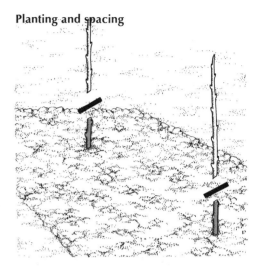

In spring, place medium-length canes 4 ft apart in rows 6 ft apart. Do not plant deeply. Cut the canes down to 6 in above the ground.

Training and pruning

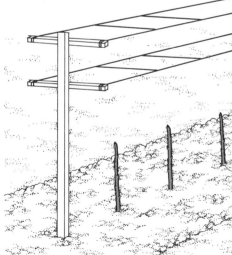

1 Fix two parallel wires between T-shaped supports 5 ft high. The wires should be 18 in apart. Place the canes between the wires.

2 After first year, in late winter or early spring, cut off all weak canes at the ground, leaving 4–6 good canes per plant. Remove weak and dead laterals and trim back the remaining laterals.

Propagation

1 In midsummer, dig a hole 4–6 in deep near the mature raspberries in loose soil with ample moisture. Insert the tip of a young cane into the bottom of the hole and fix with a staple.

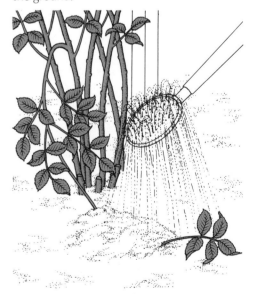

2 Fill in the hole, tamp down the soil, and water well. When the tip has rooted, sever from the parent plant with 10 in of stem and plant out.

Blackberries 1

The blackberry is a rambling cane fruit found growing wild in many milder parts of the United States. The canes are of arching habit, thick, strong and often aggressively thorned, although there are good thornless cultivated varieties. The plants are usually deciduous, but not always so in mild winters. They grow in zones 5–8.

A good average yield from a well-established blackberry plant is 10–30 lb of fruit, depending upon the size of the plant and the variety.

Cultivation

Cultivated blackberries are much larger and more luscious than wild varieties. They need little preventive spraying and can be planted in a spare corner of the garden to which their wide-spreading roots should be confined.

Soil and situation Blackberries grow in a wide range of soils and will tolerate slightly impeded drainage. If thin dry soils cannot be avoided, improve their moisture retentiveness and fertility with bulky organics.

Blackberries flower relatively late, from May onwards, and bloom over a long period, and so frost is seldom a problem. They are among the few fruits that can be successfully grown in a frost pocket, although this should be avoided if possible. They will also tolerate partial shade but fare better in full sun. Because of their rambling habit, they need some support.

Planting Prepare the ground in the fall. Fork out perennial weeds. Then, if the ground is poor, apply a 2–3 in deep layer of well-rotted manure, compost or peat over an area 2–2½ ft square at each planting site and dig it in thoroughly. Rake in 3 oz of a balanced fertilizer such as 10-10-10 over the same area.

Plant while dormant in early spring. Young plants, in the form of rooted tips or one-year-old bedded tips, can be obtained from a nursery. Using a hand trowel or fork, dig a hole wide and deep enough to take the roots spread out well. Plant the canes to the nursery depth. After planting, firm the soil and then cut down each cane to a bud at about 10 in above the ground.

Spacing Plant the canes 4 ft apart in rows 6 ft apart. One plant is often sufficient.

Support Support is generally necessary to keep the canes off the ground for easy picking and to keep the plants tidy. Individual plants can either be tied to sturdy stakes, or a wire fence trellis can be erected with wires every 12 in between 3 and 6 ft. Erect the wires before planting the canes.

Training The fruiting canes should be trained to keep them separate from the young replacement canes to facilitate picking and to reduce the risk of the spread of fungal diseases from the old to the new.

The three methods commonly used are the fan, weaving, and rope system trained one way. The fan is best reserved for less vigorous berries. The weaving system takes full advantage of the long canes of vigorous kinds but there is much handling at pruning time. The one-way system keeps handling to a minimum, but wastes space because young rods are trained along the wires only to one side of the plant. These fruit the following year. When new rods appear they are trained in the opposite direction.

Initial pruning In the first summer after planting, a number of young canes should spring up from the root system. Tie these securely to the lower wires in a weaving fashion. In the second summer these canes should flower and fruit. At the same time new growth springs from the base of the plant. This young growth should be secured and trained in the adopted method.

When fruiting is over, untie the old canes and cut them down to ground level. With the fan and weaving systems the young canes are then trained in to take their place. With the one-way system, the young canes are already tied in. The young growth will fruit in the next year, and so the cycle is repeated.

Subsequent pruning Pruning in the third and subsequent years consists of cutting out the canes that have fruited and replacing them with the new canes. If the replacement canes are few, the best of the old canes can be used again, but the older growth does not yield the best quality berries. Each April cut back any winter-damaged tips to a healthy bud.

Feeding and watering In early spring apply 2 oz of a balanced fertilizer such as 10-10-10 as a top dressing over one square yard around the base of each plant.

A little later, mulch with a 2 in layer of garden compost, peat or manure, keeping the material just clear of the canes. In dry weather water the plants but, to minimize the risk of fungal troubles, avoid the canes.

Pollination

All varieties are self-compatible and only one plant is needed.

Harvesting

Blackberries are ready for picking when they are black, plump and sweet. Some varieties turn black before they are fully ripe. Pick all fruit when it is ripe even if not required, because this helps the later fruit to achieve a good size.

Pests and diseases

Blackberries are prone to the same pests and diseases as raspberries (see pages 24–27).

OTHER BERRIES

Boysenberries, dewberries, loganberries and youngberries are all closely related to the blackberry and red raspberry, but generally grow much larger and are of trailing habit. They grow only in warm climates, usually to zone 8, but sometimes to zone 7. All are available in thorny and thornless varieties.

Boysenberries have very large reddish-black fruits with a dusty bloom. They are soft, tartly sweet and have a delicious aroma.

Loganberries have light reddish fruits covered with fine hairs. They are tarter than boysenberries.

Youngberries are very similar to boysenberries, but the fruits are shiny and a little sweeter.

Dewberries are somewhat hardier and have sweet black berries sometimes measuring 1½ in long. They ripen a week or so earlier than blackberries. 'Lucretia' is generally considered the best variety.

Culture

All of these plants have the same requirements as blackberries. Because the canes run to great length, they should be trained on a trellis. Cut out those that have fruited after harvest in August. Cut back new canes, growing on the trellis, to 6–8 ft and remove all but 12–16 of the canes. Early the following spring, cut the laterals to 1 ft.

In areas where the plants are marginally hardy, remove the canes from the trellis in the fall and cover with straw. This should be some protection from frost.

PROPAGATION

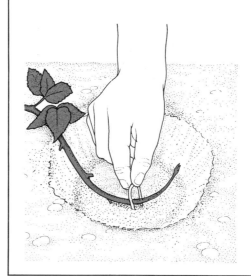

Blackberries (like black raspberries) are propagated by tip-rooting. The new canes are tip-rooted in August and September. A 6 in hole is dug with a trowel near the plant, and the tip of a young cane is bent down into it. The soil is then replaced and firmed. As new canes are produced, more tips can be buried. In the following spring, the rooted tips are severed from the parent plant with about 10 in of stem, and then dug up and planted out in a new position. A few varieties produce suckers, which should be lifted with as much root as possible and planted out in the new bed.

Another method is by leaf bud cuttings taken in July and August and rooted in a cold frame. This method is useful for rapid propagation when stock is limited, and when there are other growing restrictions.

Blackberries 2

Cultivation

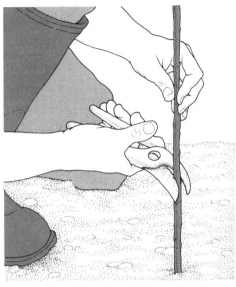

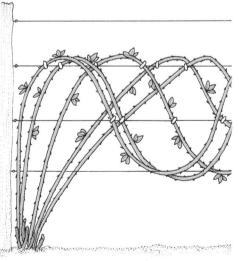

1 In fall, clear the ground of perennial weeds. If the ground is poor, dig in a 2–3 in layer of well-rotted manure over an area 2–2½ ft square. Fork in 2 oz of balanced fertilizer over the same area.

2 In early spring, dig a hole to take the plant with the roots spread out well. Plant to the same depth as it was at the nursery. Firm the soil and cut the cane to a bud 10 in above the ground.

3 Fork in 3 oz of a balanced fertilizer such as 10-10-10 per square yard around the base of each plant.

4 Later, apply a 2 in layer of garden compost keeping it just clear of the canes. During dry weather, water the plants but keep the water off the canes.

Weaving system

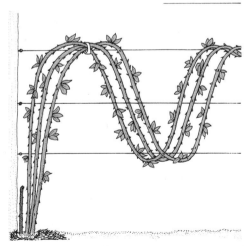

The second year

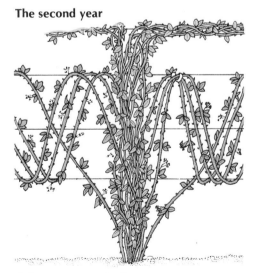

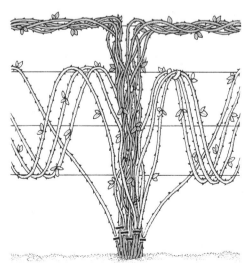

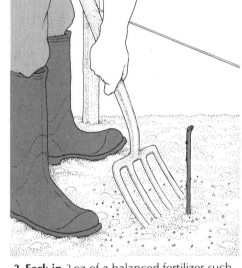

1 In summer, as the young canes appear, tie them to a strong wire support. Weave them in and out of the bottom three wires.

2 In summer, train the new canes up through the center of the bush and along the top wire. Fruit is carried on laterals of last year's canes.

3 After fruiting, cut out all fruited canes to base. If there are few new canes, retain the best of the old.

4 At the same time, untie the current season's canes and weave them round the lower three wires. In fall, remove the weak tips from the young canes.

Black currants 1

BLACK CURRANTS

EARLY
'Boskoop Giant' Juicy, moderately sweet, good flavor. A thin, rather tender skin. Berries very large. Cropping heavy. Bush very vigorous and slightly spreading. Susceptible to leaf spot.

'Blackdown' Sweet flavor. Berries firm, medium to large. Cropping good. Bush medium to large, rather spreading. Very resistant to American gooseberry mildew.

MID-SEASON
'Wellington XXX' Sweet, good flavor. Berries medium to large. A tough skin. A heavy cropper. Growth vigorous and spreading and needs careful pruning to keep upright. Sensitive to lime sulfur.
'Blacksmith' Good flavor. Skin rather thin and tender. Berries large. Cropping heavy. Bush vigorous, large and spreading. Not suitable for the small garden.
'Ben Lomond' Flavor good, acid. Berries large, cropping very heavy. Bush upright and compact, spreads a little under the weight of the crop. Flowers late and has some resistance to frost. Carries a good resistance to American gooseberry mildew.

The black currant (*Ribes nigrum*) is a native of central and eastern Europe from Scandinavia to Bulgaria, also northern and central Asia to the Himalayas. It can be found growing wild, generally in damp woody places.

Selection in cultivation has given rise to stronger-growing and highly productive varieties. Black currants are grown on a stool system—that is, many shoots spring from below the ground rather than from a single stem. A well-grown black currant bush may reach 5–6 ft in height and spread and should last 15 years or more before it needs to be replaced. A good average yield from an established black currant is about 10–12 lb.

Cultivation

The black currant is an alternate host for white pine blister rust, a serious pest that kills those trees. Many of the states in which white pine grows forbid the planting of black currants because of the adverse effect on white pine.

Therefore, any gardener considering planting such fruit should first check with the state agricultural extension service or forestry department before ordering. Some nurseries will be able to advise if restrictions exist.

The black currant is the worst of the several alternate host plants of white pine blister rust. Consequently, black currants are difficult to find in American nurseries and only one variety, 'Boskoop Giant', is commonly offered by those nurseries that sell black currants.

Soil and situation Black currants can be grown in a wide range of soils. Ideally it should be slightly acid (about pH 6.5), highly fertile, moisture-retentive and well-drained, although black currants will tolerate slightly impeded drainage. Light soils need plenty of bulky organics. Excessively acid soils should be limed to bring the pH up to 6.5.

The site should be frost-free and sheltered from strong winds so that pollinating insects such as bees are not inhibited. Most varieties bloom early in the spring and the flowers are extremely vulnerable to frost. In frost-prone areas, plant late-flowering or more frost-tolerant varieties and cover the plants on frosty nights. Black currants will tolerate partial shade but prefer a sunny position.

Preparing the soil Prepare the ground in early fall, clearing away all weeds. Apply a 3 in layer of manure or compost over the whole area. If manure and compost are not available, apply a 2 in layer of peat with bonemeal at 3 oz per square yard. If the ground is fairly clean single dig the materials in, but if rough and weedy double dig the area. Rake in a balanced fertilizer such as 10-10-10 at the rate of 3 oz per square yard.

Planting and spacing Buy two-year-old certified bushes. Select plants with not less than three strong shoots.

Plant during dormancy in early spring. Space bushes 5 ft apart in the row (6 ft apart for more vigorous varieties), with 6 ft between rows.

Dig out a hole wide enough to take the roots spread out well. To encourage a strong stool system plant bushes about 2 in deeper than they were in the nursery—the soil mark on the stems gives an indication. Fill in the hole and firm.

Initial pruning After planting, cut all shoots to within 2 in of soil level. This encourages the production of strong young shoots from the base, and creates a good stool system for heavy cropping in the future, although it means foregoing a crop in the first summer. If the plants are certified free of disease, the pruned shoots may be used as cuttings. They root easily, so buy only half the number of bushes required and fill the vacant positions with two to three cuttings to each station.

After the hard initial pruning the young bush should produce three or four strong shoots from the base, each shoot being 18 in or more in length. If growth is poor, they should be cut down again in the winter. Assuming a strong bush has been formed, no pruning is required at the end of the first year; the young shoots are left to fruit in the following summer.

Pruning an established bush Black currants bear the best fruit on the wood produced in the previous summer, although they also crop on the older wood. Prune in early fall or at any time in the dormant season until early April.

The objective with an established bush is to stimulate a constant succession of strong young shoots to carry fruit in the next season by fairly hard-pruning, cutting at or as near the base as possible, and by heavy feeding.

It is important to be able to distinguish the young wood from the old. This is fairly easy because the bark of the young shoots is much lighter in color than that of three years old or more.

There is no need to limit the number of main branches nor to have the center open. However, about a quarter to a third of the oldest wood should be removed annually. Cut back to a strong young shoot at or near the base or, if there is none, cut out the branch altogether.

Remove any thin mildewed shoots including those suffering from die-back in the center. Leave a working space between one bush and the next.

Feeding and watering Black currants thrive on heavy manuring and high summer moisture. Each March apply a balanced fertilizer such as 10-10-10 over the whole plantation at 3 oz per square yard. Additionally, in April apply sulfate of ammonia at 1 oz per square yard; on acid soils apply an artificial fertilizer containing calcium carbonate and ammonium nitrate. Follow this with a 3 in thick mulch of manure or compost around each bush.

In dry weather apply $4\frac{1}{2}$ gal of water per square yard every ten days, but keep the water off the stems as much as possible to lessen the risk of fungal trouble.

Weed control The bushes are shallow-rooted. Do not dig around the plant but keep the weeds down by shallow hoeing or by hand weeding or by using herbicides.

Pollination

Black currants are self-compatible and are pollinated mainly by bees.

Frost and bird protection

The flowers are extremely vulnerable to spring frosts which cause the fruitlets to drop. On nights when frosts are likely, drape the bushes with burlap or a few layers of bird netting (see pages 6–7); remove the cover in the mornings. Net the fruits against birds when the first fruits begin to color.

Harvesting

Pick selectively when the currants ripen but before they begin to fall or shrivel.

Pests and diseases

The most serious pests of black currants are aphids, the black currant gall mite, and red spider mite. Use a systemic insecticide against aphids, benomyl for gall mite, and malathion, dimethoate or derris to control red spider mite.

Of the diseases, the most troublesome are reversion disease, gooseberry mildew, leaf spot and botrytis. Bushes affected by reversion should be dug up and burned. Mildew can be controlled by regular spraying with benomyl; this will also control leaf spot. Alternative fungicides are zineb or thiram. For botrytis use benomyl at flowering time.

PROPAGATION

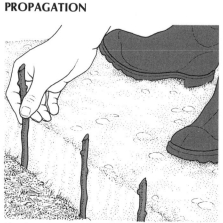

Black currants are propagated from cuttings 8–10 in long and about a pencil's width thick, from well-budded healthy wood of the current year's growth. Take the cuttings in October or November. Make a sloping cut just above a bud at the top and a straight cut just below a bud at the base. Insert the cuttings deeply with only two buds showing above the surface in well-drained light soil. Space the cuttings 6 in apart and firm them in the row.

At the end of the first growing season dig up and plant the rooted cuttings 12 in apart. Cut them down to within 1 in of the ground. This hard pruning should create a stooled bush.

Black currants 2

LATE
'Baldwin' (Hilltop strain). The most widely grown variety. Acid flavor, rich in vitamin C. Tough skin. Berries medium and hang well without splitting over a long period. Cropping moderate to good. Bush of medium vigor, fairly compact. Suitable for the small garden.
'Jet' Flavor good, acid. Berries firm, small to medium. Trusses extremely long, hang well, easy to pick. Cropping very heavy. Bush large and vigorous. Flowers very late. Carries some resistance to gooseberry mildew.

1 In early spring, clear the ground of weeds. Dig in a 3 in layer of manure or compost. Rake in a balanced fertilizer such as 10-10-10 at 3 oz per square yard.

2 Dig a hole wide and deep enough to take the roots spread out well. Plant the bush 2 in deeper than it was at the nursery. Fill in the hole and firm the soil.

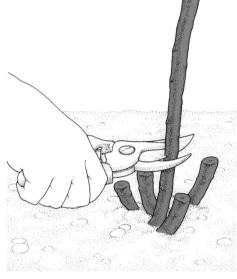

3 After planting, cut down all shoots to within 2 in of soil level.

The second year

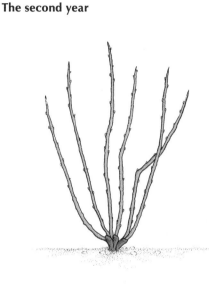

4 In the fall, the severe pruning has resulted in strong new shoots appearing from the base. These will fruit the following year. No pruning is required.

5 In March, apply a balanced fertilizer such as 10-10-10 at 3 oz per square yard. A month later, apply 1 oz sulfate of ammonia per square yard.

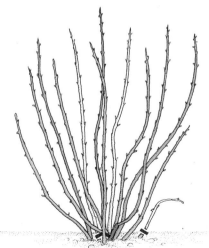

6 In July, the bush fruits best on last year's wood. New basal growths develop.

The third year

7 In winter, thin out weak shoots and any branches that are too low, broken or mildewed.

In subsequent years

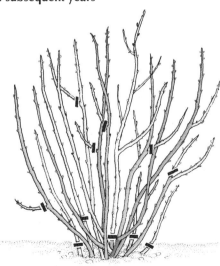

8 Every winter, remove about one-third of the bush. Cut out badly-placed, damaged wood. Cut back fruited branches to a strong shoot.

Red and white currants 1

RED AND WHITE CURRANT VARIETIES
'Cascade' Popular old variety with red, rather mild-flavored fruits in compact clusters. Early.
'Perfection' Reasonably productive, somewhat spreading plants with large bright crimson berries in mid-season.
'Red Lake' Vigorous, upright plant with big, light red berries in large clusters.

Fruits remain on the plant long after ripening.
'White Imperial' Choice white-fruited variety. Medium-size berries. Clusters are not always well filled.
'Wilder' Dependable, mid-season currant with big, dark red berries of good quality in mid-season. Vigorous, productive, upright plant.

'Viking' Late red fruits in sizeable quantities. May be immune to rust.

Red and white currants are basically derived from two European species, *Ribes rubrum* and *R. spicatum*. Red currants sometimes occur as garden escapes from bird-sown seed and *R. rubrum* is also found naturalized in many areas.

Cultivation

The fruit buds are produced in clusters at the base of the one-year-old shoots and on short spurs on the older wood. Because of this fruiting habit there is a permanent framework of branches, unlike the black currant for which a succession of young wood is needed.

The red currant is usually grown as an open-centered bush on a 4–6 in stem or leg, rather like a miniature apple tree, with a height and spread of about 5–6 ft. This method of growth makes cultivation around the plant easier and keeps the fruit clear of the ground. The red currant is also grown as a single or multiple cordon, and, more rarely, as a standard or fan. A well-grown bush should yield at least 8–10 lb of fruit and a single cordon about 2–3 lb. Plants should bear well for at least ten years.

The smooth-skinned, glistening red berries are attractive and ideal for jelly, pies, juice and for wine making.

Red and white currants are, like black currants, alternate hosts to white pine blister rust, and so have planting restrictions in many states. The state agricultural extension service or forestry department should be consulted before ordering.

The white currant is a mutation or sport of the red currant and for cultural purposes is treated in exactly the same way. The berries, of somewhat milder flavor than the red, are also useful for jelly and for wine making.

Soil and situation Ideally, the soil should be neutral to slightly acid (about pH 6.7). Red and white currants are less tolerant of poor drainage than the black currant but, provided the soil is reasonably well drained and not deficient in potash, they are tolerant of a wide range of conditions.

The flowers of the red and white currants are hardier than those of the black currant, so it is a useful plant for north-facing walls and fences and for shaded areas, provided the soil is not dry and over-hanging trees do not drip on the plants. They grow in zones 3–8. A sunny position is best if the berries are to acquire their full flavor. The site should be sheltered but not a frost pocket.

Soil preparation Prepare the soil in the fall or late winter by clearing away all weeds. Apply a light dressing of well-rotted manure or compost about 1½ in thick over the whole area. If farmyard manure or compost are not available, apply a 1 in layer of damp peat. If the ground is fairly clean, single dig the dressing in; but if weedy, double dig the area. Rake in a balanced fertilizer, such as 10-10-10, at the rate of 2 oz per square yard and sulfate of potash at ½ oz per yard.

Selection of plants Buy plants from a reliable source because certified stock is not available. One- or two-year-old bushes are usually supplied by the grower. Select a plant with a clear stem, or leg, of about 4–6 in with a head of about 3–6 evenly balanced shoots. The single (or multiple) cordon may be two or three years old and should consist of one (or more) straight stems with sideshoots.

Planting and spacing Plant during the dormant season in March or April, unless the plants are container-grown, when they can be planted at any time.

Space bushes 5 ft × 5 ft (5 ft × 6 ft on fertile land) and single cordons 15 in apart, or 12 in apart on light soils. Allow 12 in between each stem of a multiple cordon; for example, double cordons should be planted 24 in apart from the main stem at ground level. Cordons should be trained up a vertical cane for straight growth and support. If planting cordons in the open, before planting erect a wire fence with horizontal wires at 2 ft and 4 ft and tie canes to the wires at each planting station.

Next, take out a hole large enough to contain the roots well spread out, and plant the bush or cordon to the same depth as it was in the nursery. Fill in and firm the soil.

Feeding and watering Each March apply a balanced fertilizer, such as 10-10-10, over the whole planting at 2 oz per square yard and sulfate of potash at ½ oz per square yard. On light soils also apply a mulch of rotted manure, compost or peat 2 in thick around each bush. If manure, compost or peat are not available, apply sulfate of ammonia at 1 oz per square yard. Water copiously in dry weather.

1 In late winter, dig in a 1½ in layer of well-rotted manure. Then, rake in a balanced fertilizer, such as 10-10-10, at 2 oz per square yard and sulfate of potash at ½ oz per square yard.

2 In early spring, dig a hole large enough to take the roots well spread out and plant the bush to the same depth as it was at the nursery. Delay planting if the ground is very wet or frozen.

3 Each March, apply 10-10-10 at 2 oz per square yard and sulfate of potash at ½ oz per square yard. On light soils also apply a 2 in mulch of rotted manure, compost or peat around each bush.

4 During the winter, protect the fruit buds with netting against attack by birds and frost at blossom time. Remove it during the day at flowering time.

Red and white currants 2

Pruning bush currants
The objective is to create a goblet-shaped bush with about 8–10 main branches growing upwards and outwards on a 4–6 in clear stem with an open center. Prune in the same way as the gooseberry bush (see pages 36–7) except that the leaders are pruned to outward-facing buds, unless the branches are drooping, when they are pruned to upward-facing buds.

Pruning the single cordon: initial pruning
On planting a one-year-old rooted cutting, shorten the central leader by about one-half to an outward-facing bud. Cut back all other laterals to about 1 in at a bud, and remove any buds lower than 4 in to create a short clear stem. If planting an older pre-shaped cordon, shorten the leader by one-third and prune maiden laterals to one bud.

In late June to early July cut back the current season's side-shoots to 4–5 leaves. Tie the leader to the cane as and when necessary throughout the growing season, but do not prune it.

Second and subsequent years A cordon is pruned in much the same way as a bush. Each summer at the end of June or early in July prune the current season's side-shoots to 4–5 leaves. Do not carry out summer pruning earlier than this or secondary growth may be stimulated. The leader is trained and tied to the cane, but not pruned in the summer until it has reached the required height, usually about 5–6 ft. From then on it is summer-pruned to 4–5 leaves.

Each winter, cut all the previously summer-pruned laterals to about 1 in at a bud. Prune the leader to a bud leaving 6 in of new growth. Once the leader has reached the required height, it is also pruned to leave one bud of the previous summer's growth. This helps to maintain the cordon at approximately the same height for some years.

Multiple cordons, such as the double- and triple-stemmed cordon, are pruned in exactly the same way as the single, except that in the early formative years suitably low placed laterals are used to form the main stems of each goblet-shaped bush.

Weed control
Red and white currants are shallow rooted. Do not dig around the plants but keep the weeds down by shallow hoeing or by using herbicides.

Pollination
Red currants are self-fertile and insect pollinated, so pollination is not a problem.

Frost and bird protection
Red and white currant flowers are fairly hardy, although they will not tolerate hard frosts. Cover them with burlap or two or three layers of bird netting on frosty nights.

The berries are extremely attractive to birds in the summer, as are the fruit buds in the winter. Net the bushes in the winter and at fruit ripening time. Remove the netting at flowering time, because it inhibits insect pollination.

Harvesting
Red and white currants are ripe in July or August and should be picked as soon as they are clear in color. Pick whole clusters to avoid injury to the delicate fruit.

Propagation
Propagate new red and white currant plants in the fall from hardwood cuttings, which should be 12 in long or more. Before planting the cuttings, remove all the buds except the top three or four. Insert into the soil with the third bud within 2 in of the soil surface and label the cuttings. After they have rooted (in about a year's time) plant out the cuttings. This method produces rooted cuttings with four good branches and a short leg.

Pests and diseases
The most serious pests are aphids and, to a lesser extent, sawflies and currant fruit flies. Control aphids with a systemic insecticide rotenone.

Occasionally anthracnose and cane blight can be troublesome. Early season sprays of ferbam give satisfactory control of anthracnose. If the canes are blighted, cut back to healthy wood and burn the prunings.

The first year: Cordon

1 In winter, when planting a one-year-old shorten the central leader by about one-half to an outward-facing bud. Cut back all laterals to 1 in at a bud and remove any lower than 4 in.

2 From late June to early July, cut back the current season's side-shoots to 4–5 leaves. Tie the leader to the cane as it extends but do not prune it.

Second and subsequent years

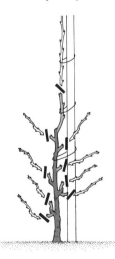

3 In winter, prune the leader to a bud leaving 6 in of new growth. Cut all previously summer-pruned laterals to 1 in at a bud. In later years, cut the leader back to one bud.

4 From late June to early July, prune the current season's side-shoots to 4–5 leaves. Tie the leader to the cane as it extends.

Gooseberries 1

GOOSEBERRIES
'**Chautauqua**' Large, greenish-yellow fruits. Rather early. Planted small, it is inclined to spread.
'**Downing**' Excellent medium-size green berries. Very productive and widely planted.
'**Fredonia**' Large, dark red berries. Late.
'**Glendale**' Dull red, medium fruits.

Large, vigorous plant. One of the best varieties for warmer regions since it withstands heat better than the average variety.
'**Pixwell**' Medium-large red berries. Produces heavily. Plant is less thorny than most gooseberries.

TYPES OF GOOSEBERRIES

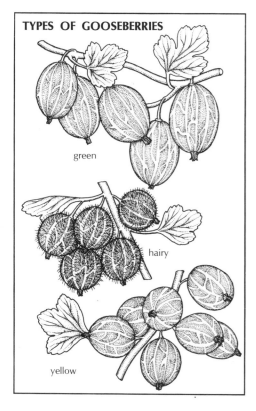

green

hairy

yellow

The gooseberry (*Ribes uva-crispa*) is a deciduous thorny shrub growing in zones 3–8.

Like the red currant, the gooseberry bears its fruit on spurs on the older wood and at the base of the previous summer's lateral growth. For this reason it is grown with a permanent framework of branches, usually in the form of an open-centered bush on a short stem, or led, of about 4–6 in. It is also widely grown as a cordon in single or multiple form and occasionally as a standard on a 3½ ft stem or as a fan.

The fruits may be smooth or hairy, yellow, white, green or red according to variety.

A well-grown bush should reach a height and spread of 5 ft and crop well for 12 years or more. A good average yield from a bush is 5–6 lb, and from a cordon 1–2 lb.

Like currants, gooseberries are alternate hosts of white pine blister rust and can be planted only in areas where this disease is not a problem. The local state agricultural extension service or forestry department should be contacted before ordering plants.

Cultivation

One-, two-, or three-year-old bushes can be bought from a grower. A one-year-old bush should have about 3–5 shoots evenly placed around the stem, a two-year-old about 5–7 and a three-year-old 6–8 primary and secondary branches. Gooseberries are self-fertile, so they can be planted singly.

Soil and situation The soil requirements of the gooseberry are similar to those of the red currant. The soil should not be allowed to become potash-deficient. The plant tolerates a little impeded drainage, provided it occurs below 18 in. The ideal soil, however, is a slightly acid (pH 6.7), well-drained medium loam.

The gooseberry is tolerant of cool, partial shade, but grows best in an open sunny site, which should be sheltered against strong winds, especially at flowering time in early April. Do not plant it in a frost pocket.

Soil preparation Prepare the soil in the fall or late winter. It is essential to eliminate perennial weeds because the gooseberry is thorny and not easy to weed around. On light soils, dig in a 1½–2 in layer of well-rotted manure or compost over the whole area. On rich soils there is less need for bulky organics because too much of them encourages soft growth, which is prone to snapping and to mildew. Rake in a balanced fertilizer such as 10-10-10 at 2 oz per square yard and sulfate of potash at ½ oz per square yard.

Planting and spacing Plant during the dormant season in March or April, preferably when the soil is warm.

Dig a hole wide and deep enough to contain the root system with the roots well spread out. Before planting, clean off any suckers at the base of the plants and any shoots too near the ground, then plant it to leave a clear stem of 4–6 in. Fill in the hole and firm the soil.

Space the bushes 5 ft apart, or on highly fertile ground 5 ft by 6 ft apart, and single cordons 1 ft apart. Allow 1 ft space for each stem of a multiple cordon. For straight growth and support, train a cordon up a cane. If growing cordons in the open, erect a wire fence with horizontal wires at 2 ft and 4 ft and tie the canes to it.

Feeding and watering Each March apply a balanced fertilizer such as 10-10-10 over the whole plot at 2 oz per square yard and sulfate of potash at ½ oz per square yard. Mulch around the base of the plant with a 2 in layer of well-rotted manure, compost or peat on light soils, but less on medium or fertile soils. In the absence of bulky organics apply sulfate of ammonia at 1 oz per square yard.

Water copiously in dry weather but do not water irregularly or heavily at the ripening stage because this causes the fruit to split.

The second year

1 Clear the soil of perennial weeds. Rake in a balanced fertilizer such as 10-10-10 at 2 oz per square yard and sulfate of potash at ½ oz per square yard.

2 In early spring, dig a hole wide and deep enough to take the roots spread out well. Plant the bush so that there is a clear stem of 4–6 in above ground.

3 At the same time, cut back each framework branch by one-half to an inward- and upward-pointing bud. Clean off the suckers at the base and any shoots too near the ground.

4 In winter, shorten the leaders by one-half to inward- and upward-facing buds. Select well-placed shoots to form further permanent branches and cut back by one-half. Remove suckers and low stems.

Gooseberries 2

Formative pruning: Bush

Most varieties have a tendency to form drooping growth and, in order to maintain an erect bush, counteract this habit by pruning the leaders to inward- or upward-facing buds or back to upright laterals. The center of the plant is kept open to make picking and spraying easier, to ripen the wood and fruits, and to improve air circulation (which lessens the risk of mildew).

When planting a one-year-old bush, cut back each framework branch by one-half to an outward-facing bud if the shoot is upright. Cut back to an inward-facing bud if the shoot is weeping.

The second year (or a two-year-old bush)

In late winter, shorten the leaders by one-half. Select well-placed shoots to form further permanent branches and cut back by one-half. Remove any suckers or low-growing shoots growing from the stem.

The third year (or a three-year-old bush)

The bush should have developed a main framework of about 6–8 branches with well-spaced leading shoots; it is at the start of its cropping life. In winter, shorten the leaders by one-half to a bud facing in the required growth direction. Cut out shoots crowding the center and shorten those not required

for the framework to about 2 in. Thereafter, prune the bush both in the summer and in the winter.

Pruning an established bush

Each summer, in late June to early July, prune all laterals (that is, the current season's growth) back to five leaves. This opens up the bush and removes any mildew and aphids at the tips of the shoots. Do not prune gooseberries earlier because this might induce secondary growth. Do not prune the leaders unless they are affected by aphids or mildew.

Each winter, cut back the leaders by one-half to a bud facing in the required direction. If the branch is weeping badly and there is a suitably placed upright lateral on it, then cut back to this.

Next deal with the laterals that were pruned the previous summer. Where smaller quantities of large high-quality dessert fruits are required, cut all of these laterals back to about two buds. Where a large amount of fruit is required, pruning should be moderated accordingly. Vigorous varieties should be pruned less severely because this could encourage excessive growth. Cut out dead and diseased wood, and any growth crowding the center of the bush.

As the bushes become older and branches less productive or too spreading, leave in some suitably placed strong, young shoots to replace the old which are then cut out.

The third year

Pruning a single cordon Prune in the same way as the red currant cordon (see page 33).

Weed control

As with most bush fruits, the gooseberry is shallow rooted. Keep the weeds down by light hoeing or with herbicides.

Protection against frost and birds

The gooseberry flowers early, during April, and spring frosts can substantially reduce the crop. On frosty nights protect the plants when they are in flower. Cover with burlap or two or three layers of bird netting, but remove it during the day to allow in light and give access for pollinating insects.

The fruit buds are attractive to bullfinches and sparrows in the winter and the ripening fruits to blackbirds and thrushes in the summer. Net the bushes in the winter and when the fruits begin to ripen. For further information on netting against birds, see under separate headings (page 17).

Thinning and harvesting the fruits

For large dessert fruits start thinning the fruits in June, removing every other one, and use the thinnings for cooking.

For small or medium dessert fruits, do not thin the fruits but leave them to ripen and develop their full flavor. Pick gooseberries for cooking when they are a good size, but still green, from late June.

Propagation

Propagate gooseberries using 12 in hardwood cuttings taken from healthy shoots in late September. First remove the weak tip and all but four buds from the upper part of the cutting. This produces a miniature, open-centered bush on a short leg. Dip the base of the cuttings in a hormone rooting powder. Insert the cuttings in the open ground with their lowest buds 2 in above the soil surface. Leave the cuttings in the nursery bed for the growing season. Lift and replant, exposing more of the stem.

Pests and diseases

The pests and diseases that plague the gooseberry are similar to those that attack the currants. For example, aphids and anthracnose (see page 33).

The third year

5 In winter, shorten the leaders by one-half to a bud facing in the required growth direction. Cut out shoots crowding the center. Shorten laterals not required for the framework to about 2 in.

6 When the fruits are large enough for cooking, thin the fruits by removing every other one. Cover the bush with burlap or bird netting to protect the fruits from birds.

The established bush

1 In late June to early July, prune all the laterals produced that season to five leaves. This opens up the bush and removes aphids at the tips of the shoots. Do not prune the leaders.

2 In winter, cut back the leaders by one-half. Cut back laterals pruned in the previous summer to about two buds. Cut out diseased and dead wood and growth that crowds the center.

Heathland fruits 1

BLUEBERRIES
The following varieties are derived from *Vaccinium corymbosum*. They will set fruit with their own pollen but for maximum crops at least two varieties should be planted together.
'Berkeley' Very large, light blue berries of good flavor. Medium vigor.
'Bluecrop' Fast-growing variety with big

clusters of large, light blue berries. A consistently heavy cropper of good quality. Bush upright, then spreading. Vigorous.
'Earliblue' Similar to 'Bluecrop' but the berries ripen earlier.

There are numerous closely related blueberry-like shrubs growing wild in the United States. They are known as bilberries, blueberries, deerberries, farkleberries, and huckleberries. Almost all belong to the genus *Vaccinium*, but huckleberries have the botanical name of *gaylussacia*. The most important of such berries are the low-bush blueberries, but even those are seldom cultivated in the accepted sense.

However, where they are the dominant plant (blueberry barrens), they are often managed commercially by burning over every two to three years in winter. This eliminates weed growth from the base. They are not cultivated because they provide less fruit and much smaller (but generally tastier) fruit than the taller high bush varieties.

They are, however, easy to cultivate, requiring almost the same conditions as the high bush blueberries. They tolerate drier soils and need full sun for good crops. Low-bush blueberries grow in zones 3–5.

They are best planted 12–15 in apart each way in beds 3 ft wide with access paths in between. Feeding is the same as for high bush blueberries.

Pruning as such is not necessary, but in the second or third year cut back hard half the plants to promote young, vigorous stems. One or two years later the other half is cut back. Thereafter the plants are treated regularly in this way. Harvesting and storing is as for high bush blueberries. Pests and diseases are not a problem.

High bush blueberries

The principal species of high bush blueberry is *Vaccinium corymbosum*. It forms bushes to about 12 ft in height with narrow oval leaves about 2 in long and white, sometimes pink-tinted flowers in dense clusters. The fruits are $\frac{1}{2}$ in wide. The blueberry is a decorative shrub, especially in the fall when the leaves turn red, and it can be grown as an ornamental with rhododendrons and other acid soil shrubs.

In the deep South, where *V. corymbosum* does not grow, cultivated blueberries have been developed from the native species, *V. virgatum*. These are known as rabbiteye blueberries and grow to 15 ft, but are otherwise similar to *V. corymbosum*.

Soil and situation Blueberries require moist but well-drained acid soil with a pH of 4.0–5.5 If the pH is much above the upper limit, chlorosis occurs and the plants may die. Suitably acid sandy or clay soils should be liberally enriched with peat moss or oak or pine leaf-mold at not less than one large bucketful per square yard.

As with most members of the heather and rhododendron family (Ericaceae), blueberries rely upon an association with a fungus for their existence. The fungus thrives where organic matter is abundant, so it is important to apply plenty of peat or acid leaf-mold to the soil. If the soil is thin and sandy, apply the organic material to the whole site. For most soils, it is usually sufficient to dig out 1 ft square holes at each planting station and till these with an equal mixture of peat and soil, or leaf-mold and soil.

Include some coarse sand if the surrounding soil is heavy. Dried blood at 2 oz per hole may also be added if the soil is poor. Alternatively, apply sulfate of ammonia to the soil surface at $\frac{1}{2}$ oz per hole after planting. It is also possible to grow bushes in large pots or tubs.

The site may be in sun or slight shade and should be sheltered from strong winds. Blueberries derived from *V. corymbosum* are hardy and grow in zones 5–7, but do not thrive if the temperature falls regularly below −28°C/−18°F. A frost-free growing season of at least five months is needed and ideally a warm summer with plenty of rain. Rabbiteye varieties grow in zones 7–9.

Planting Two- to three-year-old plants are usually available in containers. In fall or spring set out the plants 5 ft apart in rows 6 ft apart. If the plants are pot-grown, gently knock them out of their containers and carefully spread out the perimeter roots without breaking up the root ball, fill the planting holes with an equal mixture of peat and compost and firm fairly lightly. Then, using a trowel, make a small hole large enough to take the root ball, set the plant in the middle and firm the soil. Larger plants are planted as described in the Introduction to Soft Fruits (page 20).

Pruning Regular pruning is not essential. If young plants fail to branch naturally, in spring cut back the longest stems by about one-third. After the third year, bushes that are becoming dense should be thinned, removing the oldest, barest stems to ground level or to a low strong side-shoot.

Feeding and watering In spring, apply a dressing of dried blood at 2 oz per square

High bush blueberries

1 Before planting, dig out a 1 ft square hole at each planting station. Fill it with an equal mixture of peat, or leaf-mold, and soil.

2 In spring, plant the bushes 5 ft apart in rows 6 ft apart. With a trowel make a hole large enough to take the root ball. Set the plant in it. Firm the soil.

3 In spring each year, apply a dressing of sulfate of ammonia at 1 oz per square yard. At the same time, mulch with peat, oak leaf-mold, sawdust, or chopped bark.

The established bush

4 In late winter, cut back some of the fruited branches that have become twiggy to a vigorous shoot. Cut close to base any damaged or dead branches.

Heathland fruits 2

'Jersey' A vigorous variety of erect habit bearing large handsome foliage. The large, light blue berries are sweet and of good flavor. Excellent as a dual purpose bush for the shrub border.
'Rancocas' This variety produces a good crop of quality, small fruits over a long harvesting period. Good shapely habit. The following varieties are derived from

Vaccinium virgatum. Two different varieties must be planted.
'Tifblue' Large, bright blue berries of excellent quality. Ripens in mid-season (late May–June).
'Woodward' Very large, medium blue, tasty berries. Mid-season.

yard or sulfate of ammonia at 1 oz per square yard. On poorer soils, every other year in winter apply a general fertilizer, such as 10-10-10, at 2–3 oz per square yard. To maintain the humus content, mulch annually in spring with peat, oak-leaf mold or pine needles to a depth of 1–2 in. Other important sources of humus are composted sawdust and chopped bark.

Blueberries need plenty of moisture in the summer. In dry weather, water them copiously, preferably (although not necessarily) with collected rainwater.

Harvesting and storing
The berries should be picked when they are blue-black with a white waxy bloom and start to soften. They should be eaten fresh within a few days, but if spread thinly on trays and kept in a cool cellar or refrigerator they will last for at least a couple of weeks.

Pests and diseases
Blueberries have few problems that cannot be taken care of with a general-purpose fruit spray. The spray should be used if and when problems arise. Birds, however, are a prime nuisance and once the berries have formed, protection is essential (see page 17).

Cranberries
The common or small cranberry (*Vaccinium oxycoccus* or *Oxycoccus palustris*) has long wiry stems with tiny, narrow, pointed leaves. The small, pink flowers are carried in clusters. The fruits are about $\frac{1}{3}$ in wide, red or pink, sometimes with brown-red spots. Cranberries are sold in the market and are the fruits of *Vaccinium macrocarpum* (*Oxycoccus macrocarpus*). This is a slightly more robust species than the common cranberry with blunt-tipped leaves and much larger fruits. It grows from zone 6 northward.

Cultivation
In the United States, the cranberry crop is of rather minor importance and has developed into a highly specialized form of agriculture including the construction of artificial bogs which can be flooded and drained. It requires moister conditions than the blueberry to thrive and, ideally, a soil of greater acidity.

Despite this, cranberries are easy to grow if the right rooting medium can be provided.
Soil and situation Cranberries need a constantly moist soil of high organic content with a pH of 3.2–4.5. A naturally moist, acid soil is ideal, but if not naturally peaty, fork generous amounts of moss peat into the top 6–9 in. Or, prepare trenches as described in the box opposite. Cranberries should be cultivated in a sunny site.
Planting Plant one- or two-year-old divisions, rooted cuttings or seedlings 12 in apart each way in spring. Any long trailing stems should be partly buried, or held down by sand or small pegs to prevent them from being blown about. Rooting usually occurs along the pegged-down stems.
Pruning and feeding No pruning is required, but any semi-erect wispy stems can be sheared off annually in early spring. Feeding is not usually necessary, but if growth is poor, apply sulfate of ammonia at $\frac{1}{2}$ oz per square yard. Plants in peat-filled trenches benefit from a light dressing of general fertilizer every other year. An old matted bed can be rejuvenated by almost covering it with a layer of fine peat and sand.

Harvesting and storing
See high bush blueberries (see page 36).

Pests and diseases
A malathion spray when the flower buds are swelling and again as the flowers fade provides control of grubs that attack the fruit.

Varieties
Among the vigorous and free-fruiting varieties of *Vaccinium macrocarpum* are 'Early Black', 'Hawes', 'McFarlin', 'Searless Jumbo'. 'Stevens' is a particularly good new variety.
Highbush Cranberry The only similarity this shrub has to the cranberry is its small, acid, red fruit appearing in midsummer. The plant is actually *Viburnum trilobum*—a 10 ft ornamental deciduous shrub with large flower clusters in spring. It is not quite as hardy as the true cranberry.

Plant it in the spring in sun or partial shade and grow like any strictly ornamental viburnum. Fruit production starts when the plant is about three years old. Pick while firm.

PREPARING THE CRANBERRY BED

Where the soil is acid but not naturally moist, dig shallow trenches about 3 ft wide by 9 in deep and line them with heavy-duty polyethylene. Return the soil with peat to the waterproofed trench and lightly firm. Spread and rake in sulfate of ammonia at $\frac{1}{2}$ oz per square yard.

This trench method can be used on

alkaline soils, filling in this case with pure peat moss or a mixture with up to half by bulk of coarse washed sand. The same fertilizers should be used.

Before planting, unless the ground is already wet, soak the bed thoroughly. It is best to use rainwater as this is the most natural nourishment.

Cranberries

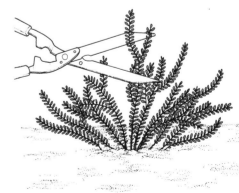

1 In spring, plant the divisions, cuttings or seedlings 12 in apart in the prepared ground. Bury any trailing stems.

2 In early spring, shear off any semi-erect wispy stems. If growth is poor, apply $\frac{1}{2}$ oz sulfate of ammonia per square yard.

Grapes 1

AMERICAN GRAPE VARIETIES

'Beta' Small, black berries. Early. Not good for eating but fine for juice and jelly. Very hardy.
'Brighton' Medium-sized red fruits in medium-size clusters. Mid-season. Self-unfruitful. Hardy.
'Catawba' Medium-size, purple-red fruits of fine flavor. Often made into wine. Late. Hardy.
'Concord' Best known of all large, black-fruited varieties. Delicious flavor. Mid-season. Hardy.
'Delaware' Superb small, red grape. Early. Vines are fairly weak but hardy.
'Extra' Large blue fruits with a flavor typical of the wild post oak grape. Grown in the Southeast.
'Fredonia' Large, black fruits of the 'Concord' type and among the best. Ripens ahead of 'Concord'. Hardy.
'Golden Muscat' Popular yellow-fruited variety ripening late. Large, full clusters. Distinctive muscat flavor.
'Nimrod' Greenish-white, seedless variety similar to the following. Hardy. Not a slipskin.
'Interlaken Seedless' Descended from famous 'Thompson Seedless' grape. Small, greenish-white fruits without slipskins. Mid-season. Hardy.
'Niagara' Delicious white variety with large fruit in large clusters. Strong foxy flavor. Mid-season. Hardy.
'Norton' Recommended for juice. Small blue fruits. Hardy.

The art of growing grapes, or viticulture, has a long and illustrious history. The vine grows wild in the temperate regions of North America, western Asia, southern Europe and parts of North Africa and it is thought to have originated in Asia Minor.

The vine is a perennial deciduous climber that clings to supports by tendrils. The leaves are hand- or heart-shaped and 4–8 in in size.

The grapes most commonly grown by home gardeners in the northern part of the United States are the so-called American, or bunch, grapes, descendants of wild grapes. The blue, black, green, red and yellow berries usually have slip-skins (separable from the pulp) and ripen from mid-summer on. They are largely self-fruitful. Although American bunch grapes can be grown from zones 3–10, they do best in zones 5–7.

Muscadine grapes are generally grown in the South (zones 7–9). These form much larger vines up to 90 ft long and produce fruits singly or in loose clusters. Several self-fruitful varieties are available but most varieties are self-unfruitful. Since the fruit of self-fruitful varieties is inferior to that of the self-unfruitful varieties, self-fruitful varieties are best used to pollinate the self-unfruitful varieties.

Vinifera, or wine, grapes are descended from European grapes and are best employed in wine-making. A number of varieties, all with skins inseparable from the pulp, are eaten at table and are considered among the best grapes for this purpose. Some varieties are also used for raisins. All vinifera grapes are self-fruitful, producing berries in extremely large clusters. They grow best in California, but there are numerous hardy varieties that can be grown as far north as zone 6. There are also many new hybrid varieties resulting from crosses of American and vinifera grapes. These combine characteristics of the parents and are therefore difficult to classify.

Cultivation

Grapes are sun-loving plants and must be grown where they will be exposed to the sun all day or at least for the greater part of the day. But the base of the plant need not be in full sun although it is essential that the upper part of the plant catches as much strong sunlight as possible. (Grapes growing wild in forests often take root at the foot of trees and soon clamber above the trees).

The location selected for the vines should have good air drainage. In colder areas, protection from winter winds is necessary.

Soil

The vines are fairly tolerant of a wide range of soils, although the soils must be deep and well drained, and not too sandy. The plants require a soil pH of 5.5–7.0. If there is any possibility that the soil may become badly waterlogged, a good drainage system should be installed.

Two or three weeks before actual planting, prepare the soil by double-digging to break up any hard layers and to clear away perennial weeds. Dig in leafmold or well-rotted manure at the rate of about one wheelbarrow load per 20 square feet. Also rake in a balanced fertilizer such as 10-10-10 at the rate of 3 oz per square yard.

Planting

Plant one-year-old vines in early spring before they start to leaf out. Dig large, deep holes; spread out the roots; firm them well; and water thoroughly. Then cut off all but one strong cane and trim this back to eight buds.

Maintenance

Except for pruning and training, grapes do not demand a great deal of attention.

In dry spells, they should be watered deeply, but, as the fruit begins to mature, the water supply should be reduced somewhat. This helps the maturation process and also inhibits succulent growth. In the fall, however, after the fruit has been picked, one heavy watering is necessary to help protect the vines from winter injury.

Unless the plants are doing poorly, they need little fertilizer. Give each plant 2–4 oz of ammonium nitrate or a somewhat more balanced fertilizer in early spring. This should carry them through the growing season.

Keep encroaching weeds pulled. An application of an organic mulch around the plants discourages weed growth in addition to supplying the necessary nutrients for healthy growth.

Training and pruning

The training and pruning of grapes are matters of critical importance. The main purposes of training are to keep the large, fast-growing vines under control, to facilitate care and harvesting, and to expose all parts of the plants to the sun. The purposes of pruning are to maintain vigorous growth, to provide new canes for the next year, and to limit the number of fruit-producing buds so that the vines do not produce too much small fruit of inferior quality.

Various training systems are used for all three types of grapes.

American bunch grapes
Four-Arm Kniffin system This is the most popular method of training American bunch grapes since it gives good production and requires little summer tying of the vines.

The trellis required consists of 4–6 in posts and galvanized steel wires. Space the posts 16 ft apart. Sink the end posts 3 ft into the ground and brace them with diagonal struts or guy wires. Sink the intermediate posts 2 ft. The posts normally extend 5 ft above ground,

Staking and planting

1 Bore or dig holes and drive 8 ft posts 3 ft into the ground, spaced according to the pruning system to be followed. Stretch wires between the posts, spaced according to the pruning system.

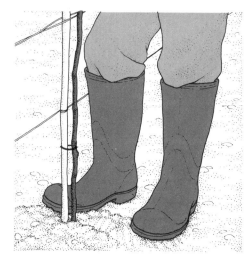

2 In early spring, plant the vine to the nursery depth between posts in prepared ground. Firm the soil and water well. Cut back the vine to one cane and eight good buds.

The first year

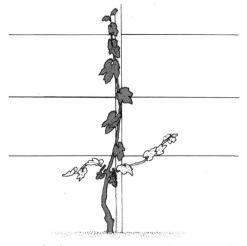

3 For both pruning systems, allow one rod to develop. Pinch back to one leaf any other shoots. Leave two good buds (Kniffen) or three (Guyot).

Grapes 2

'Ontario' Very early white fruit of excellent quality for eating and jelly. Hardy.
'Portland' Large white fruit in big clusters. Best very early variety. Hardy.
'Seneca' Small white fruit in large clusters. Delicious flavor. Early. Not a vigorous variety but hardy.
'Van Buren' Very early 'Concord' type with medium-size blue fruits. Hardy and worth trying in zone 3.
'Worden' Large purplish-black fruit. Descended from 'Concord' but ripens about 10 days earlier. Hardy.

MUSCADINE VARIETIES
'Burgaw' Reddish-black fruits of only fair quality. But the vines are self-fruitful and good pollinators.
'Dearing' One of the best self-fruitful varieties. Very sweet white fruits. Good pollinator.
'Dulcet' Small, sweet reddish-purple fruits. Early. Self-unfruitful.
'Hunt' Large, black grapes of excellent quality. Makes a fine jelly. Early. Self-unfruitful.
'Magoon' Small, early, black fruits of good quality. Self-fruitful.
'Scuppernong' Most famous muscadine variety. Bronze-colored fruits of distinctive flavor. Early. Self-unfruitful.
'Thomas' Very sweet, smallish, red-black fruits of excellent quality. Mid-season. Self-unfruitful.

but increasing the height to 6 ft exposes the vines to more sunlight and is especially recommended for short-season areas.

Use 9-gauge wire at the tops of the posts and 11-gauge at 30 in above ground. The wires can be stapled to the posts or run through holes drilled in the posts. Drilled holes give greater security. If staples are used, do not drive them down tight because it may be necessary to tighten the wires when they sag under the weight of the vines.

Plant the grape vines between posts. If planted at the base of posts, they may be injured by any wood preservative in the treated posts, and would undoubtedly be damaged when the posts had to be replaced.

The first year When the two top shoots on the young plant are about 1 in long, rub off all other shoots.

The second year Select the strongest cane for the trunk and tie it to the top wire. Cut the cane just above the wire and remove all other canes. If no cane reaches the top wire, tie the strongest one to the bottom wire and extend it to the top wire the next year. If no cane reaches either wire, reduce the vine to a single stem with two or three buds and start all over again.

The third year Pick four good canes for the arms; cut them back to approximately 10 buds in length; stretch them out along the top and bottom wires in both directions from the trunk; and tie them. Cut four other canes back to two or three buds for renewal spurs and remove all other canes.

Subsequent years Each year cut off the 10-bud fruit-bearing canes of the previous year and replace them with the renewal spurs (which are shortened to approximately 10 buds). The renewal spurs are replaced with new renewal spurs cut back to two or three buds. All other canes are removed.

The actual number of buds that should be left on fruit-bearing canes each year depends on the variety of grape and the growing conditions. Until the home gardener has raised grapes for some time, the best way to determine how hard to prune is as follows. First rough-prune the vine, leaving a few more buds than needed. Weigh the wood removed. For the first pound of wood, leave 30–40 buds, more or less equally divided between the four fruit-bearing canes, on the plant. For each additional pound of wood removed, leave eight more buds on the vine. (This weighing plan is used not only for the Four-Arm Kniffin training system, but also for all other training systems).

All pruning is done in early spring while the vines are dormant and after danger of severe freezes has passed. If pruning is done too early, heavy frost can compound the winter injury already suffered by the plant, and the gardener cannot be certain which canes are alive and which are dead. Pruning late does no serious damage, but there is a good chance that some of the buds meant to be saved will be destroyed. If the cut canes "bleed", there is no need for worry as this does no great harm.

Munson system This is an excellent system for humid climates because the grapes are carried well above ground where they are exposed to more air currents.

The trellis consists of sturdy and large posts (4 × 6s are recommended) with stout 24 in crossarms 5 ft above ground. Brace the cross-arm. Staple two No 9 wires to the ends of the crossarms on the top edge. Run a third wire through the posts 6–8 in lower.

Train the new vine, as above, to a single trunk extending to the bottom wire. In the third year, prune it to two fruit-bearing canes and two renewal spurs. Tie the canes along the lower wire, and as the young shoots develop, drape them over the upper wires, allowing them to hang down.

Each year thereafter replace the arms with the canes from the renewal spurs and replace the spurs.

Modified Chautauqua system This system is used where tender grape varieties need winter protection. The trellis is made with 4-in posts and three No 9 wires spaced 12, 28 and 44 in above ground.

In the first year, simply let the vine grow upward and tie it to the wires. In the fall of the same year, select the best cane for the trunk, reduce it to 30 in long, and remove all other canes. Lay the trunk on the ground and cover it with about 8 in of soil for a measure of protection.

In the spring, pull the cane out along the bottom wire at an angle and tie it. As new growth develops, tie to the other wires.

Prune the new growth to short two-bud spurs in the fall. Keep the cane closest to the end of the trunk to form an extension of the trunk. Remove the vine from the trellis and bury it as before.

In following years, repeat this procedure. Let the trunk grow to a maximum length of about 7 ft.

Muscadine grapes

Muscadines can be trained by any of the systems described, but the vine is such a strong, rampant grower that it is often cultivated on arbors. In this case, train the young vine to a trunk 6–7 ft long before allowing it to branch out to the sides along wires, spaced about 2 ft apart, forming the arbor roof.

In the Four-Arm Kniffin system, train and prune the vine to form a trunk and four strong arms. Do not cut the arms back until they meet those of the neighbouring vines. Thereafter, annually prune out deadwood, weak canes, and side growth on the trunk and the tendrils. Cut the remaining canes back to two or three buds.

Kniffen system—The second year

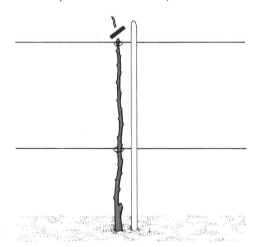

1 In spring, select the strongest cane, tie it in and cut off just above the top wire. Remove all other canes.

The third year

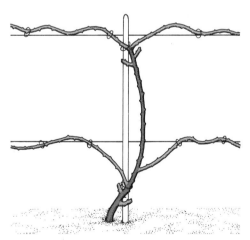

2 In spring, select four vigorous canes and tie them in to form arms. Prune them to ten buds each. Prune four other canes to form four renewal spurs for the next year.

Fourth and subsequent years

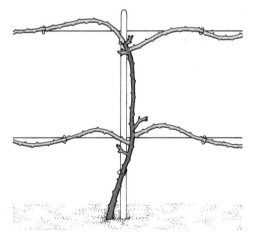

3 In spring, cut off the old fruiting arms. Tie in four new canes chosen from the renewal spurs. Cut each new cane back to six buds. Cut four new canes back to two buds to form renewal spurs.

Grapes 3

'Topsail' Sweetest of all muscadines. Medium-large, greenish-bronze fruits. Mid-season. Self-unfruitful.

VINIFERA VARIETIES
'Baco No 1' Also called 'Baco Noir'. Black grape for making red wine. Early. Hardy.
'Cardinal' Large, dark red fruits with a slight muscat flavor. Early.
'Csaba' Medium-size, yellowish-white fruits with a slight muscat flavor. Very early. Hardier than most.
'Flame Tokay' Very large, red fruits for eating. Mid-season. Tender.
'Johannisberg Riesling' Medium-size, greenish-yellow fruits with russet spots. Early. For making white wine.

'Perlette' Large, yellow to pale green berries in big, compact clusters. Very early.
'Seibel 5279' Pink-white fruits for wine-making and eating. Early. Hardy to zone 6.
'Seyve-Villard 5247' Very large, lavender fruits for making rosé wine. Early. Hardy vines have a bushy habit.

'Thompson Seedless' Famous green to yellow grape. Early. Favorite seedless table grape.
'Zinfandel' Medium-size red to black fruits for making red wine. Medium-early.

In the warmest regions, pruning should be done after the first killing frost in the fall or early winter. Further north, prune in early spring. Muscadines pruned at this time bleed great deal, but there is no damage to the plants.

Vinifera grapes

The Four-Arm Kniffin system is the method generally chosen in warm climates, but a modification called the Spur system is used for varieties such as 'Csaba' and 'Cardinal'. The Spur system allows the fruit-bearing arms to be permanent, that is they are not renewed annually. Each arm has 6–8 vertical fruiting spurs and each spur has 2–3 buds that produce fruit shoots.

In cold climates, where tender varieties need winter protection, the Modified Chautauqua system can be used.
Guyot system This is actually two systems. In the single Guyot system there is one fruit-carrying arm while in the double Guyot system there are two fruit-carrying arms. The double Guyot system is the more popular and is described below.

Double Guyot system—The second year

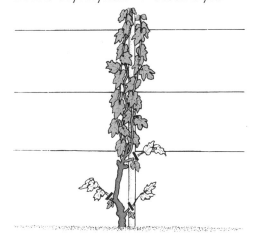

1 In spring, cut the vine down to within 15 in of the ground, leaving three buds. Train the resulting shoots vertically. Pinch back any laterals to one leaf as they develop.

Each year, allow three new main stems to develop. Retain two for fruiting and cut back the others to produce replacement stems for the next year. The fruiting canes are trained close to the ground to take advantage of its radiated warmth.

The trellis consists of 4-in posts spaced 8–10 ft apart. Brace the end posts. Attach a No 12 wire to the posts 15 in above the ground and two No 14 wires so they cross at each post.
The first year At planting, cut the vine down to about 6 in from ground level if the vine is on its own roots or, if it is a grafted plant, 6 in above the graft union, leaving at least two good buds. During the summer following planting, train one shoot up the post and pinch out all others to one leaf.
The second year In the spring, cut the vine down to within 15 in of ground level, leaving three good buds. During the summer, train in three shoots vertically. Pinch back any laterals to one leaf as they develop. In the next spring, the vine should be pruned as for an established vine (below).
Pruning an established vine Each spring

Third and subsequent years

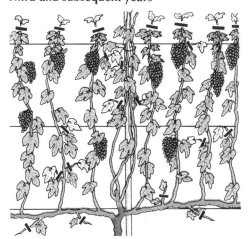

2 From April to August, train three shoots vertically from the center. Pinch back any laterals produced on them to 1in as they develop. Tuck in the vertical fruit-carrying laterals through the double wires. Cut them back to three leaves.

(except the first) cut back the arms that bore fruit the previous summer to the replacement spurs. Do not allow fruit on the plants in the second year after planting, but allow them in the third. Tie down on to the lowest wire one replacement shoot to the left and one to the right. Cut down the remaining spur to three or four buds to provide replacement spurs for the following year. Cut back the immature wood on the replacement spur, leaving about $2–2\frac{1}{2}$ ft of strong growth either side.
Third and subsequent years From April to August, tuck in the vertical fruit-carrying laterals between the double wires. Cut them back to two or three leaves above the top wires, as necessary, and remove any sub-laterals. Train the three replacement spurs from the center for the following year up the post. Pinch back any sub-laterals on the replacement spurs to one leaf and remove any blossom. Remove any surplus spurs coming off the main stem.

Thinning

Thinning of the fruit is recommended for vinifera grapes, but not for American and

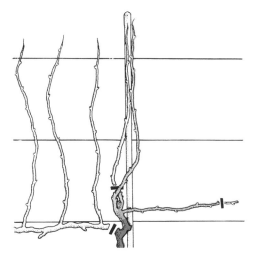

3 In November, cut out the two arms that bore fruit in summer to the replacements. Tie down one replacement shoot to the left and one to the right. Cut back each to leave $2–2\frac{1}{2}$ ft of strong shoot. Cut down the remaining shoot to three buds.

Muscadine grapes. Viniferas are very heavy producers, and thinning is needed to improve fruit size. Thinning of varieties with very large or compact fruit clusters is done by removing individual berries immediately after fruit set. On varieties with loose or straggly clusters, remove some of the immature flower clusters appearing with the new growth in the spring.

In addition, with all vinifera varieties, it helps to remove entire fruit clusters soon after fruit set. The number of clusters left depends on the size and vigor of the vine. Keep about 20–30.

Harvesting

Even when grapes are fully colored, they are not ripe because they need a finishing period for sugars to form. This period can vary from 4–8 weeks. Once picked, grapes do not continue to ripen.

Pests and diseases

Grapes are not greatly bothered by pest and disease problems. But it is advisable to spray the plants in late winter with dormant oil. A general-purpose fruit spray should be applied when the new growth is about 8 in long, just before bloom and two weeks thereafter.

Mildew should be sprayed with a fungicide whenever it appears. Spraying with carbaryl takes care of Japanese beetles, which have a particular liking for grape vines. Repeat treatment as necessary.

It is almost impossible to cover grape vines securely with nets to protect them from birds. But the individual fruit clusters can be enclosed in mesh or with paper bags.

In some years, wasps are even worse than birds, attacking the fruit just as it is ready to harvest and quickly destroying entire bunches. Only paper bags can keep wasps in check.

Disease or pest infestation should not prove a hindrance in viticulture if the grape vines are tended so that they remain in a healthy condition. Soil balance is the greatest determinant influencing grapevine health while weather is the most unpredictable factor. Wet, humid weather usually means mildewed grape vines.

Melons

MELON VARIETIES

'Burpee Hybrid' An outstanding Muskmelon. Heavily netted, ribbed fruits to 6 in across. Delicious, sweet, deep orange flesh. Resistant to mildew.
'Crenshaw' An extremely large winter melon with superior, thick, salmon-pink flesh of finest flavor.
'Delicious 51' Large, oval Muskmelon of excellent flavor, but flesh is rather soft.
'Early Hybrid Crenshaw' Almost exactly like the winter melon but matures in only 90 days so can be grown in areas with fairly short summers.
'Gold Star' Medium-size fruits with juicy, deep-orange flesh. Vigorous vines.
'Hale's Best 36' A famous old melon of fine flavor and good size.
'Harper Hybrid' Very thick-fleshed fruits with an unusual tang. Medium-size.
'Harvest Queen' Large melons of top-quality.
'Heart of Gold' Fruits medium size, long and oval. Orange flesh.
'Honeydew' Winter melon with smooth creamy-white skin and green flesh. Fruits range from medium to huge.
**Delicious to eat.
'Honey Drip Hybrid'** Like a small Honeydew. Matures in only 85 days—almost a month less than 'Honeydew'.
'Persian' Enormous winter melon with superb, bright orange flesh.
'Supermarket' Prominently ribbed fruits with thick orange flesh of musky flavor. Resistant to mildew.

Gray-green or ochre-colored melons with rough, netted skins are known to most Americans as cantaloupes, but the true cantaloupe is a hard-shelled European fruit that is rarely grown in the United States. Gardeners wishing to attempt to grow it usually have to order seeds from a foreign supplier.

Melons Americans grow fall into two categories: Muskmelons and Winter or late melons. Muskmelons mature in roughly 90 days and can be grown in zones 5–10 and even into zones 3 and 4, if the quick-maturing varieties are chosen. Winter melons, including the 'Casaba', 'Crenshaw', 'Honeydew', and 'Persian' varieties, are larger fruits with variously colored skins and most of them take about four months to mature, so they are grown primarily in warmer climates.

Cultivation

A popular misconception about melons is that they cannot be planted with cucumbers, squashes or other members of the cucurbit family because they are cross-pollinated and this changes the flavor and aroma of the melons. This does happen if seeds from melons grown the year before are used. But the use of fresh seed every year eliminates the problem.

Melons are tender and vulnerable and cannot be sown outdoors until the soil is warm and all danger of frost is past. In short-season areas, this makes melon-growing by this common method impossible.

Soil The soil for melons should be reasonably fertile but not too rich, with a pH of 6.7–7.0. Good drainage is essential. Dig the soil well before planting and mix in considerable humus to improve fertility and moisture retention. Also mix in about 24 oz of 5–10–10 fertilizer per 50 square feet.

Sowing the seed In the North, therefore, seeds are sown in flats or peat pots indoors about 3–4 weeks before the mean date of the spring freeze. When the plants have two or three true leaves, they are moved into the garden and grown under cloches or polyethylene tunnels, usually about two weeks after the last frost.

Planting Further south, however, direct sowing in the garden is a simpler and better method. Sow the seeds in $\frac{1}{2}$ in deep drills about 6 in apart and thin them to stand 2 ft apart. In setting out transplants, space them 2 ft apart. The rows should be 5–6 ft wide. The alternative is to sow seeds or plant seedlings in gently rounded mounds (hills) 6 ft wide and a few inches high at the center spaced 4 ft apart. Allow two or three plants per hill.

Furrows about 10 in wide can be dug on the south side of the hills to a depth of about 6 in to allow watering without wetting the foliage. Water well, especially during dry spells, but do not keep the soil soaked.

If nematodes are a problem in the garden, the soil should be fumigated before planting.

Watering and feeding Melons need plenty of moisture throughout the growing season and this should be provided by deep weekly watering in dry spells. Pull out weeds as they appear. Mulching the plants with organic matter or black polyethylene film is a good idea to hold in moisture and keep down weeds. When the vines begin to run, side-dress them lightly with balanced fertilizer or nitrate of soda.

For example, apply 4-8-4 balanced fertilizer carefully at $\frac{1}{2}$ oz to each mound in a circle around each mound after thinning the plants. Keep the fertilizer well clear of the plants and cover the dressing with nearby soil. The dressing should ideally be applied 4–6 in away from each plant.

Harvesting

When melons start to turn their characteristic mature color, they are ripening and will soon be ready for picking. In the home garden, however, actual harvest should not start until the fruits pull away from the stem easily. At this time they are in prime eating condition. Do not leave them on the vine any longer, because they begin to deteriorate within a couple of days. Ripe melons have a strong, fruity scent.

Pests and diseases

Melons are attacked by a few insects, but these are not generally very troublesome and can usually be controlled by spraying with malathion or carbaryl when they appear. But diseases can be difficult, especially in warm, humid weather. The best protection against disease is to plant resistant varieties.

Melons under cloches

1 About four weeks before the expected date of the last spring frost, sow melon seeds in peat pots indoors. Harden off gradually before removal to the garden.

2 Plant out under cloches when the danger of frost is past. Make a hole wide and deep enough for the root ball to fit into comfortably.

Melons in the open

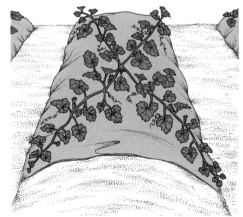

1 Dig soil well before planting and incorporate humus and 5-10-10 balanced fertilizer at 24 oz per 50 square foot. Mound up the soil.

2 Mulch the plants with black polyethylene and water well. Train as usual. Check for dryness at regular intervals thereafter. Mulching will help to warm cold soil.

Tree fruits

Introduction

Tree fruits (also sometimes referred to as top fruits) form a group comprising all the larger growing fruits which, in the natural state at least, attain tree form. The exceptions to this are the fig, elderberry, mulberry and quince, which may have several main stems and be more shrub-like in appearance; they are, however, still generally classified as tree fruits.

Botanically, the most familiar tree fruits are members of the rose family (*Rosaceae*), including the apple, pear, plum, cherry, peach, apricot and quince; the mulberry and fig are outsiders belonging to the mainly tropical family Moraceae. Also included in the tree fruit section are some of the most popular nuts, such as almonds, chestnuts, filberts, hazelnuts and walnuts.

Tree fruits are not difficult to grow provided the soil is well drained but moisture-retentive and of a moderate to good depth (see pages 10–11). The site must be sunny and not prone to severe late spring frosts (see pages 6–7).

Unlike growing soft fruits, cultivating tree fruits in the garden is a long-term project. Full fruiting capacity is reached by the tree only after several years, but with care it will then continue for a lifetime. However, the fruit grower is compensated by the fact that the fruiting season for tree fruits is much longer than that of soft fruits. Furthermore, if fruits such as peaches or figs are grown in a greenhouse the season can be prolonged.

Rootstocks

Apples, pears, cherries and plums can all eventually make sizeable trees if grown on their own roots; some even become too large for most gardens. For this reason they are grafted on to rootstocks which control their eventual size. Usually apples are grafted on to a range of apple rootstocks to produce dwarf or less vigorous trees which are ideal for the small garden (see page 45). Pears are traditionally grafted on to quince rootstocks and this lessens their vigor and ultimate size. A dwarfing rootstock for cherries has proved harder to find but a less vigorous one has now been produced, although it is not as dwarfing as some of the apple stocks that are now widely available.

Pruning and training

For all tree fruits, initial training and subsequent pruning is necessary to keep them in good shape and productive throughout their lives. Methods of training, particularly pruning, can seem daunting to an amateur but this need not be so if the instructions with each fruit entry in this book are followed closely. There is also a companion volume on pruning in this series.

Pruning terms The terms used frequently in fruit tree pruning are defined as follows. Maiden describes a one-year-old, for example, a maiden tree. A scion is a variety grafted on to a rootstock of another tree; the union is where the two join. A branch is a limb that arises from the trunk. Primary branches are the first formed, and secondary branches arise from the primary ones. A leader is a main central stem of a tree or a shoot selected to extend a main branch; a lateral is a side-shoot. Spurs are short laterals that bear flower buds and which can occur naturally or be induced by selective pruning of the laterals. Flower buds, or blossom buds, are unopened flowers, often referred to as fruit buds. Wood buds open to give rise to a shoot, as opposed to a flower. Suckers are shoots that grow from below the ground or below the union.

Choice of site

The site should be chosen with care and the soil cleared of perennial weeds either with a selective herbicide (see page 17) or by hand weeding during digging. If some weeds still persist, herbicide treatment can be given again after the tree is planted, but take care to choose one which will not damage the tree.

Protection against birds

In areas where bird damage is expected (and few rural or suburban districts are exempt), protection is necessary. For small tree forms, such as dwarf bush trees, cordons or espaliers, this can be provided by a fruit cage, ideally one with tubular steel or metal alloy poles and netting, although 7 ft headroom is a minimum (see page 17). It is generally impracticable to protect larger tree fruits against bird damage.

Wall- and fence-trained trees

If there is no room in the open garden for free-standing tree fruits, good use can be made of walls and fences if restricted tree forms such as fans, cordons or espaliers are grown. North-facing walls can be used in this way for Morello cherries. Some plums are even more successful on walls than in the open, ripening well in the sheltered and warmer environment. Figs are often best grown on a warm wall (see pages 8–9).

Pollination

Unlike most soft fruits which will produce an adequate crop even if only one plant is grown, many tree fruits are totally or partially self-incompatible, or self-unfruitful. This means that some varieties cannot produce a good crop of fruit if their flowers are fertilized with their own pollen. In such instances at least two different compatible varieties must be grown close enough for bees to be able to carry pollen from one to the other. Sweet cherries provide the best example of self-sterility, but practically all the tree fruits set heavier crops if two or three varieties are planted together. They must, of course, flower at the same time and produce plenty of good pollen.

Storage

If it is decided to plant enough apples and pears to provide fruit for the late fall to winter period, storage facilities are necessary. This can be provided by a cool but frost-free cellar or shed (see page 90). Late apples and pears finish ripening many weeks after they have been picked, and so they should not be stored with mid-season varieties until this ripening has taken place because the gases given off by the earlier varieties shorten the storage life of the later ones. Deep freezing is suitable for these two fruits only if they are to be used in cooking when thawed.

Fruit under glass

Figs, peaches and nectarines produce luscious fruits under glass in cool areas. Artificial heat is not required although ripening can be hastened by its use early in the season. Wall or roof space not less than 10 ft long is needed for a well developed peach or a fig rooted in the floor of the greenhouse. Alternatively, much smaller trees can be grown in large pots and housed in all but the smallest greenhouse. Space outside should be set aside where hardy potted trees can be kept with the roots protected during the winter after the fruit has been picked. For fruit in the greenhouse, see page 19; for fruit in tubs and pots, see pages 80–81.

Pollination

Pollination is the transfer of pollen from the anthers or male parts of the flower to the stigmas or female parts of the flower. This results in fertilization and the eventual production of fruit. It is usually carried out by bees or other insects or by the wind. Occasionally, it is necessary to pollinate by hand.

The flowers of most garden fruits contain both anthers and stigmas. Some fruits, such as melons and hazelnuts, bear separate male and female flowers on the same plant.

Some fruit trees, such as peaches, nectarines, apricots and certain plums, are self-compatible—that is they can be fertilized by their own pollen. Others, such as nearly all sweet cherries, elderberries and many varieties of apples and pears are self-incompatible (self-unfruitful); they must be grown with another variety of the same fruit that flowers at the same time so that the two varieties can fertilize each other.

Pollination groups

Different varieties of plums, apples, pears and cherries are divided into pollination groups according to when their flowers are open and ripe for pollination. Those varieties in the same pollination group will cross-pollinate because their flowers are open at the same time. Those in adjacent groups are also acceptable because in most years their seasons of flowering overlap. However, a plant that blossoms very early cannot be counted on to cross-pollinate another plant that blossoms very late.

Incompatibility groups

Not all varieties of the same fruit can cross-pollinate, even when they are in the same pollination group. This is called cross-incompatibility. These varieties are divided into incompatibility groups and will not set fruit with their own pollen or that of any variety in the same incompatibility group. They will cross-pollinate with varieties in another group or in adjacent groups (provided they flower at the same time).

Ineffective pollinators

Some varieties of apples and pears, although not strictly cross-incompatible, are ineffective pollinators. This can occur for a number of reasons.

Most varieties are diploid, that is, they have the normal number of chromosomes. A few are triploid, that is they have $1\frac{1}{2}$ times the normal number. Triploids are poor pollinators and should be grown with two diploid varieties to pollinate each other and the triploid.

Some varieties of pears are known to be ineffective pollinators. Also some varieties of both apples and pears flower only every two years (biennially) or, irregularly. These cannot, therefore, be relied upon to pollinate other varieties.

Many triploids, ineffective pollinators and irregular flowering varieties are good varieties in their own right and popular with gardeners. If planting these varieties, remember to plant other varieties near them to provide the necessary pollen.

The following list gives the specific pollination nature of a selection of popular garden tree fruits from apples to sweet cherries.

Specifics

Apples No variety is completely self-compatible, so more than one variety should be grown.

Apricots Usually self-compatible with a few exceptions (for example, 'Moongold' and 'Sungold' should generally be planted together).

Crabapples Self-compatible.

Nectarines Self-compatible.

Peaches The great majority of varieties are self-compatible.

Pears No variety is fully self-compatible. Plant two or more varieties. Most bloom at about the same time.

Plums Most varieties are self-incompatible, and even those that are self-compatible bear more reliably if planted with another variety. European plums cannot pollinate Japanese plums or vice versa. Native plums are pollinated by other native varieties, sandcherry-plum hybrids or Japanese varieties, if a native variety has been crossed with a Japanese.

Quinces Self-compatible.

Sour cherries Self-compatible. Sweet cherries are not suitable pollinators for sour cherries, but sour cherries can pollinate sweet cherries, although most flower too late.

Sweet cherries Self-incompatible. Two or more varieties are needed. However, some varieties, such as 'Bing', 'Emperor Francis', 'Lambert' and 'Napoleon' do not pollinate one another.

STRUCTURE OF BLOSSOM (APPLE)

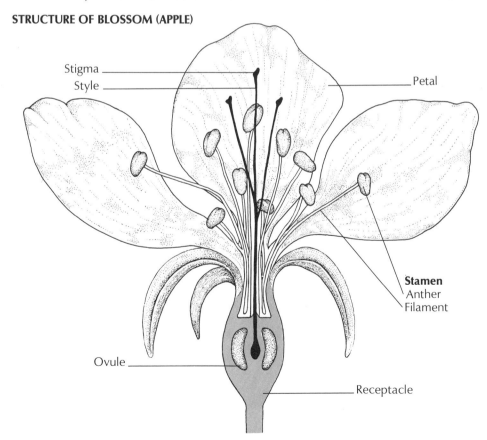

Stigma
Style
Petal
Stamen
Anther
Filament
Ovule
Receptacle

HAND POLLINATION

Some fruits require hand pollination. First draw the finger-tip over the anthers. A deposit of yellow grains on the finger indicates pollen is being shed. Pollinate at midday and when the weather has been warm and dry for two or three days.

Very gently transfer the pollen from the anthers to the stigmas by using a soft camel-hair brush or a piece of cotton wool on a matchstick.

Carry out hand pollination every day until flowering is over.

Planting fruit trees

Good establishment, healthy growth and eventual successful cropping of a fruit tree depend a great deal on how well it is planted.

Preparation

Before planting prepare the ground in early fall as described on pages 10–11. Then, for each tree, prepare an area 3 ft square by single digging clean ground and double digging weedy land. Prepare the ground overall for closely planted trees such as those on dwarfing rootstocks. Apply lime if the pH is less than 5.8 (see page 10).

Just before planting, fork in a balanced fertilizer, such as 10-10-10, at a rate of 3 oz per square yard with bonemeal at 2 oz per square yard.

Time to plant

Plant in the dormant season from late October to April; but spring planting is generally recommended. Container-grown trees can be planted at any time. Do not plant when the soil is frozen hard or very wet.

If the tree arrives from the nursery when the soil conditions are not right, heel it in in a sheltered part of the garden. If the ground is too cold and hard to heel in, keep the tree in an unheated, frost-free place such as a cool basement. Unpack the upper parts of the tree but keep the roots in damp straw wrapped in burlap until planting.

Staking

Mark out the planting position and drive in a stake to a depth of 18 in on heavy soils and 24 in on light. Standard trees require 7½–8 ft posts, semi-dwarfs 6–6½ ft and dwarfs 3½–4 ft. Central-leader trees need a stake as long as the height of the tree plus the depth into the soil. A large-headed standard, such as a sweet cherry, is best supported by two stakes 18 in apart with a crossbar (to which the tree is tied) nailed just below the stake tops. The top of the stake should be 2–3 in clear of the tree's head to avoid chafing the lowest branches. Stakes come in a variety of materials (see pages 12–13).

Trees on very dwarfing rootstocks, for example apples on Malling 9, are best staked permanently. But for trees on more vigorous stocks, the stake can usually be removed after four or five years, depending on the vigor. Before removing the stake, check if the anchorage is sound by rocking the tree.

Planting

If the roots are a little dry, soak them for an hour before planting. Keep them covered.

On the day of planting, dig out a hole deep and wide enough to take the roots fully spread out. Mound the soil in the center. Keep the fertile top-soil separate from the lower layers. Fork the bottom and prick the sides of the hole to allow the roots to develop outwards. Dig in into the base rotted-down sods or a bucketful of well-rotted manure, compost or peat. Trim off with shears any broken or long tap roots. If planting a container-grown tree, gently tease out the soil and roots around the edge of the rootball.

Place the tree on the mound with the stem 2–3 in away from the stake. Ensure that the lowest branches clear the top of the stake. Plant the tree to the same depth as it was in the nursery, indicated by the soil mark. Keep the union between scion and rootstock at least 4 in above the soil surface to prevent the scion from rooting.

Fill in the holes; this is easier if one person holds the tree while another fills it in. Sprinkle a little of the fertile top-soil over the roots first then return the remaining soil a spadeful at a time. Occasionally shake the tree gently so that the soil falls among the roots. Finally, firm the soil and level off the surface.

Next, mulch the tree with well-rotted manure compost or peat over an area 18 in in radius to a depth of 2–3 in, keeping the material 1–2 in clear of the trunk to prevent fungal diseases from infecting the base.

Tie the tree to the stake. A one-year-old can be secured with plastic chainlock strapping using a figure of eight tie, but older trees need a more substantial tie with a cushion between stake and tree to prevent chafing. There are a number of proprietary makes, or one can be made (see pages 12–13).

Dwarfs require one tie placed 1 in from the top of the stake. Semi-dwarfs and standards require two ties, one at the top and one halfway down. Nail the ties to the post to prevent them slipping down.

Where animals are particularly trouble-some, protect the trees with wire netting.

Each year in April, July and October check the tree ties and if necessary loosen to avoid constriction. Re-tie home-made ties.

Planting against a wall

The soil at the foot of a wall can become very dry and poor, especially if it is protected from rain-bearing winds or is sheltered by overhanging eaves.

Where the soil is poor and the drainage is bad, construct a drywell or a single line of tiles 3 ft deep to take the water away (see page 10). Re-soil over an area at least 6 ft × 3 ft wide × 2 ft deep with a fibrous, medium chalky loam, if possible made from sods stacked for six months before use. Add rubble to the loam in the ratio ten soil to one rubble. Two weeks before planting thoroughly mix in base fertilizer at the rate of 8 oz per 2 gal bucketful of soil.

The tree should be planted about 9 in from the wall base. During the growing season, water it whenever the soil is dry, applying 4 gal at a time around the base of the tree.

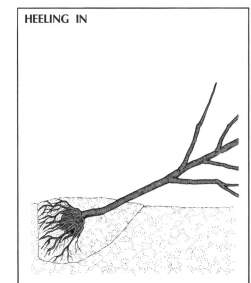

HEELING IN

Take out a shallow trench. Unpack the tree and lay it in the trench at an angle. Cover the roots with moist, friable soil.

1 If the roots are dry, soak them for an hour before planting. Trim off broken or long tap roots with shears.

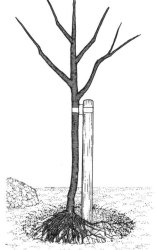

2 Drive in stake. Dig a hole deep and wide enough to take the roots fully spread out. Mound the soil slightly in the center.

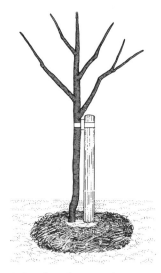

3 Set the plant on the mound 2–3 in away from the stake with the union at least 4 in above the soil surface. Replace the soil, firming gently. Mulch well.

Apples and pears 1

'Baldwin' Only fair eating quality; better for cooking. Dull, red, medium-large fruits. Late. Slow to start bearing. Usually a biennial producer and a poor pollinator.

'Cortland' Big, red, dark-stripped fruits of fine flavor. Mid-season. Reliable.
'Cox's Orange Pippin' Famous English apple generally considered the finest dessert apple grown. Flesh tender, yellow, juicy, aromatic. Fruits medium, round, conical; golden-yellow with brown-red flush and russet. Late. Does not succeed in many areas.

'Dudley' Large, greenish-yellow fruits with red blush. Coarse yellow flesh, but tasty. Mid-season. Hardy.
'Golden Delicious' Medium-sized, conical, yellow fruits. Late. Excellent quality for eating. Biennial bearer.
'Golden Russet' Very old variety. Medium-large fruits highly flavored and of top quality. Russet-yellow. Late.

'Granny Smith' Pure grass-green fruits with shiny skin. Hard, crisp, white flesh. Very late. Excellent for cooking.
'Gravenstein' For cooking and eating. Big, red fruits. Mid-season. Poor pollinator; plant with two other varieties.
'Grimes Golden' Medium-size, yellow-green fruits in mid-season. Good pie apple and also good to eat.

Introduction and rootstocks

The domestic apple (*Malus domestica*) is of complex hybrid origin but it has evolved, under human influence, from various species, all of them belonging to the series Pumilae. It has been estimated that up to 1980 there were at least 6,000 named varieties of apples in the world.

Like the apple, the pear (*Pyrus communis*) has long been cultivated. It is a native of Northern Europe. In the United States, apples are grown in zones 3–8 and pears in zones 5–8. In both cases, however, a very few varieties will grow further north or further south of these zones.

Site

Ideally, the site should be frost-free, in full sun, and sheltered from strong winds. Pears flower in late April to early May and apples in the first half of May, when they are at risk from spring frosts. The gardener in a frost-prone site should consider growing trees on dwarfing stocks or using the restricted forms whose small size makes it practicable to protect them by covering the trees on frosty nights. With apples, the alternative is to plant varieties that flower late, but this is not applicable to pears because even the later varieties flower in the danger period.

Ample sunshine is important, particularly for pears, if the fruits are to develop their full color and flavor. Apples will tolerate some shade, provided they receive at last half a day's sun in the growing season. Where there is a choice, allocate the sunniest position for pears and dessert apples, and the less sunny positions for cooking apples, for which color and flavor are not so critical.

Shelter is essential because both kinds of fruit are insect pollinated and strong winds inhibit the insects' flight, which results in poor pollination. Wind-breaks, either living or artificial, should be provided on exposed sites or, again, choose apples and pears on dwarfing stocks or in restricted form because they are easier to shelter than are taller trees (see pages 6–7).

Soil

The ideal soil for both apples and pears is a medium well-drained loam, not less than 24 in deep and slightly acid (pH 6.7). They are, however, tolerant of a wide range of soils. Pears and dessert apples require good drainage, whereas cooking varieties can be grown in heavy soil and marginally poorer drainage, but the soil must never be waterlogged.

Light sandy soils are acceptable provided bulky organics are incorporated and heavy mulching and watering is practiced. Thin soils over limestone are unsuitable because lime-induced chlorosis and lack of water and nutrients generally occur. Deep soils over limestone can support apples and pears quite satisfactorily.

Soil preparation

In late winter, prepare the soil by clearing away perennial weeds over an area 3 ft square. Fork in a compound fertilizer such as 10-10-10 at 3 oz per square yard.

Planting and staking

In early spring, plant the tree to the same depth as it was at the nursery, spreading the roots out well (see page 44).

Standard trees and semi-dwarfs require stakes and tree ties. The restricted forms are supported by wall or fence wiring.

Selecting the rootstock

Apples and pears are not grown on their own roots for a number of reasons. Some will not root easily, some are prone to root troubles, and some make large unproductive trees. To overcome these problems, apple and pear varieties are grafted by the nursery on to various rootstocks.

The rootstock is the most important influence on the eventual size of the tree. An apple grafted on to a dwarfing stock, for example, will stay small, whereas on a vigorous stock it will eventually become large. It can also affect how long it is before the tree will fruit and its cropping capacity, so it is important to know the rootstock on which the tree is grafted or, when ordering a new tree, to indicate to the nursery what size of tree is required so that the appropriate rootstock is selected.

The stocks most widely used are listed right. The size of the tree quoted under the rootstock is an estimate.

ROOTSTOCKS

Apples

M7: Semi-dwarfing tree that can be controlled by training and pruning and grown to a height of about 15 ft.

M9: Very dwarfing One of the most dwarfing stocks, M9 is widely used, making a tree about 6–10 ft in height and spread. It soon bears fruit, usually from the third year onwards, sometimes even in the second year. It requires good soil conditions and will not tolerate neglect, or competition from grass and weeds. The root system is brittle and such a tree requires staking throughout its life. An excellent stock for the small garden. Used for dwarf, dwarf pyramid and cordon.

M26: Dwarfing M26 makes a dwarf tree 8–12 ft in height and spread. It tolerates average soil conditions. It soon bears fruit, usually within three or four years of planting. It requires staking for the first four or five years, longer on exposed sites. Used for dwarf pyramid, and cordon and occasionally espalier and fan. It is a suitable stock for the small garden.

M27: Extremely dwarfing It is too soon to comment about its suitability for garden use but first reports are that it will make an ideal tree for growing in pots and in small gardens. It needs careful feeding and watering.

MM106: Semi-dwarfing MM106 makes a tree 12–18 ft in height and spread. It is tolerant of a wide range of soils. Trees on this stock soon bear fruit—usually within three or four years—and can produce heavily in later years. Such a tree requires staking for the first four or five years. Used for cordon, espalier and fan.

MM111 and M2: Vigorous The trees on these stocks make trees 18–22 ft in height and spread, but their growth varies according to soil and variety. They make large trees on good loamy soils, but only medium-sized trees on poorer sandy soils. Used by nurseries for half-standard and standard trees, espaliers and occasionally cordons and fans. They are slow to fruit in comparison with the more dwarfing stocks, sometimes taking seven to eight years. They are too vigorous for most gardens except where the soil is poor.

Pears

Pears are usually grafted on to quince rootstocks, which make them small to medium-sized trees. Some pears have a weak and spreading habit, and others are vigorous and upright, therefore the sizes given below are only an approximation.

There are three rootstocks: Quince C, Quince A and Pear. Both Quince C and A are suitable for the garden.

Quince C: Moderately vigorous Quince C makes a pear tree about 8–18 ft tall. It bears fruit in four to seven years. It is suitable for highly fertile soils and vigorous varieties, but not where conditions are poor. Used for cordon, dwarf pyramid and espalier.

Old stocks of Quince C may be infected with a virus, so where possible obtain stock certified as virus-free. If in doubt, use Quince A because there is not much difference in vigor between the two.

Quince A: Medium vigor Slightly more vigorous than Quince C, it is the stock upon which most pears are grafted. It bears fruit in four to eight years. Pears on Quince A make trees between 10–20 ft in height and spread. It is used for all forms of pear tree except standards.

Certain pear varieties are not compatible with quince and these have to be double worked by nurseries. This means a piece of pear graftwood compatible with both the quince rootstock and the pear variety, such as 'Beurré Hardy', is used as an intermediate between the two. Varieties requiring double working include 'Bristol Cross', 'Dr Jules Guyot', 'Doyenné d'Eté' and 'William's Bon Chrétien'. If this is not done, the pear could eventually separate at the graft union.

Pear stock: Very vigorous Pears grafted on to pear rootstock make very large standard trees, and, consequently, are too big for most gardens.

Apples and pears 2

'Haralson' Tart, juicy, medium-size red fruits. Mid-season. Especially popular in Midwest.
'Idared' White, somewhat juicy flesh of fair flavor. Big, ribbed fruits are yellow with red flush on sunny side. Moderately vigorous, spreading tree. Late.
'Jonathan' Mid-season cooking and eating apple. Red fruits are small to medium-size with tart flesh. Susceptible to fire blight.
'Lodi' Big, yellow fruits for cooking and eating. Early. Much planted in Oregon.
'Macoun' Dark red, medium-size, flavorful fruits in mid-season. Excellent flavor. Heavy thinning of fruit required.
'McIntosh' Large, red, beautiful fruits of excellent flavor. Mid-season. Heavy producer. A favorite in the Northeast.
'Melba' Excellent early-season dessert apple; small and red striped. Heavy bearer in alternate years.
'Milton' Tasty, large, often poorly-shaped fruits. Pinkish-red. Mid-season.
'Northern Spy' Fruits large and red-striped. Delicious flavor. Late. May not start bearing until 10 years old. Often a biennial bearer. Very particular about needing well-drained soil. Poor pollinator.
'Red Delicious' (or simply Delicious). Probably most widely grown American apple. Red, conical fruits of excellent eating quality but poor for cooking. Late. The many sports have a richer red color but offer few positive advantages, and often revert permanently to the original.

Selecting the tree form
Just as important as the correct choice of rootstock is the choice of tree form.

There are two basic types of trees, those that are planted in open ground and pruned in the winter, and those that are grown in restricted form, usually against a wall or fence, and pruned mainly in summer. The restricted form of tree is not widely available in the general market and it may be necessary to seek out a nursery specializing in this form.

Where a gardener has plenty of land and a heavy yield is the main criterion, the unrestricted winter-pruned trees planted in the open are the best choice. Where the gardener has little room, or prefers the neat look of well-trained summer-pruned trees, or wants to fill a blank space on a wall or fence with fruit trees, then the restricted forms should be chosen.

Trees in the open
The tree forms commonly grown in the open are the dwarf, semi-dwarf and standard. These are all open-centered trees and they differ only in the length of stem or trunk before the first permanent branch and in the size of the head, or framework.

Dwarf tree The dwarf tree has an open center and is goblet-shaped with a short stem of about 18–24 in. It is used only for apples because there is as yet no truly dwarfing stock for pears. Dwarf apples are grafted on to a Malling 9 rootstock or the equivalent and, because of their small size, are suitable for any garden. The soil must be very fertile, however, and the trees have to be fed and watered regularly or they will be stunted. Gardeners with less fertile soils should choose trees on more vigorous rootstocks.

Dwarf trees are easy to prune, spray and pick, and they soon bear fruit, but obviously their cropping capacity is not as great as that of larger trees. It is best not to plant dwarf bush apples in a lawn because they cannot compete with grass but if this is unavoidable, maintain a grass-free area for at least 2 ft around the base by mulching and water the tree regularly.

Semi-dwarfs The semi-dwarf tree has a clear stem or trunk of about 20–30 in before the first primary branch is reached, and its total full-grown height is roughly midway between the height of a dwarf and a standard tree.

Semi-dwarf apples develop into moderately-sized trees which bear fruit in about three to six years, depending on the rootstock used, the variety of the apple, and the growing conditions.

Semi-dwarf apples and pears are suitable for the medium to large garden and can be planted in a lawn provided the grass does not inhibit the young tree's growth. They are not suitable as shade trees because the head is too low.

Standard The standard has a clean stem of 6–7 ft, and, in the case of a few varieties, may reach an ultimate height of 40 ft. But they should be kept much smaller by pruning, about 20 ft at most. The gardener needs a long ladder for picking fruit and a powerful sprayer for pest and disease control. Vigorous trees are slow to bear fruit but, because of their large size, they eventually yield heavy crops.

Restricted tree forms
The restricted tree forms are used where trees have to be contained in some way, for example, against a wall or fence. They are ideal for the small garden or where space is limited. However, because they are restricted, the yield in comparison with trees in the open is relatively small.

The main restricted tree forms for apples and pears are the cordon, the espalier and the dwarf pyramid. The fan is occasionally used.

The cordon is intended for a low fence. If closely planted, many varieties can be grown in a relatively small space and the gardener can more easily meet the cross pollination requirements (see pages 50–1).

The espalier may be planted against a low or high fence, depending upon the number of arms it is intended to have. Its long horizontal arms require more room than the cordon. It is a handsome form (see pages 52–3).

The fan requires a high wall, the height depending on the kind of fruit grown (see pages 8–9). Unlike the cordon or espalier it cannot be planted against a low fence unless the gardner is prepared to increase the height with trellis work. The fan is used mainly for stone fruits such as peaches, cherries and plums, and for this reason it is described only on those pages.

The dwarf pyramid The dwarf pyramid is a small tree, pyramidal or Christmas tree-like in shape and kept this way by summer pruning. If, like the cordon, it is closely spaced, many trees can be planted in a relatively small area. Close attention to summer pruning is necessary, however, to maintain space between the framework branches and adjoining trees, otherwise a row of dwarf pyramids can soon degenerate into an unproductive hedge.

Although a restricted form, the dwarf pyramid is intended for planting in the open, not against a wall or fence (see pages 54–5).

Varieties
The choice of varieties depends upon the personal preferences of the gardener. Nevertheless, when making the final selection, ensure that the varieties will pollinate each other (see page 43).

Many triploid varieties are very vigorous and are not suitable for growing in restricted form unless grafted on to the dwarfing rootstocks Malling 26 for apples and Quince C for pears.

The description of the apple and pear varieties gives the season when the fruit is mature and fit to eat or cook. The picking date and maturity are not necessarily the same and this varies from locality to locality.

**TREES IN THE OPEN:
SPACING AND YIELDS**

Dwarf tree
Spacing Plant the trees 8–10 ft apart.
Yield A good average yield from an established tree is about 40–60 lb.

Semi-dwarf tree
Spacing Plant 18–20 ft apart.
Yield 70–90 lb.

Standard tree
Spacing Plant 30–35 ft apart.
Yield A good average yield from a well grown standard apple is 60–120 lb and from a pear 40–100 lb.

TREE FORMS

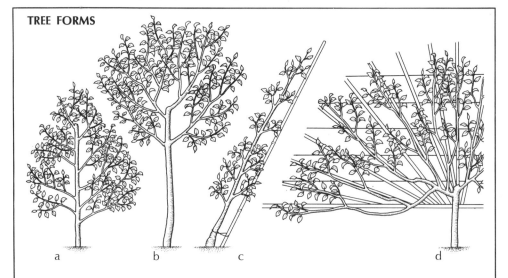

The dwarf tree (a) is made up of the top, an inter-stem of 18–24 in, and the rootstock. The standard tree (b) has a clear stem of 6–7 ft grafted onto a vigorous rootstock. The cordon (c) is planted and trained obliquely. The fan (d) is shaped.

Apples and pears 3

'Rhode Island Greening' Excellent cooking apple. Very large, green and very tart. Late. Extremely productive but often on a biennial basis. Poor pollinator.
'Roxbury Russet' Ancient variety that stores exceptionally well. Pale green with russeting. Excellent cider apple and also suitable for various kinds of cooking. Late.

'Rome Beauty' Splendid cooking apple. Big, red fruits. Very late. Heavy producer. Susceptible to fire blight.
'Sheepnose' Large, oblong, ribbed fruits are deep black-red when fully ripe. Prized for cooking. Late.
'Spitzenburg' Brilliant orange fruits with gray spots. Fine eating apple also used for cooking. Late.

'Stayman Winesap' Big, juicy, red-striped dessert apple. Late. Poor pollinator.
'Summer Pippin' Medium-large, green, very early cooking apple. Productive but likely to bear biennially.
'Summer Rambo' Early cooking apple. Large fruits may be almost entirely green or have red stripes. Poor pollinator.
'Tydeman's Red' ('Tydeman's Early').

Medium-sized red fruits of better quality than most early apples. Popular in Northwest.
'Wealthy' Favorite in northern Midwest. Medium-size, red-striped. Early. For eating and cooking.
'Winesap' Small, red, crisp apple for eating and cooking. Late. Does best in Virginia's Piedmont area. Poor pollinator.

Trees in the open
The dwarf, semi-dwarf and standard tree forms are commonly grown in the open.

Selecting the tree
A nursery can supply one-year-old, two-year-old or three-year-old trees. Trees older than this are not recommended because they may not establish well.

A one-year-old, or maiden, tree consists of a straight stem with or without laterals. A maiden with laterals, sometimes called a feathered maiden, is a better choice because if the laterals are suitably placed they can be used as primary branches, and a year is saved in the formative pruning stage. The maiden is the least expensive type, but it requires initial shaping and takes longer to bear fruit.

Trees of two and three years old will have already been partly shaped by the nursery and, being older, bear fruit sooner.

Soil preparation and planting
Prepare the soil in the late winter (see page 44). Plant the tree while dormant, in March or April, driving in a stake first.

Pruning
Prune in late winter, but not when the air temperature is below freezing.
The first winter The work of forming the head begins with the maiden tree.
Unfeathered At planting, shorten the maiden tree to 24 in for a dwarf bush or to 30 in if a standard is to be formed. Cut back to just above a bud, making a sloping cut away from the bud and ensuring there are three or four good buds beneath it. This cut stimulates the formation of primary branches the next year.
Feathered Cut back the main stem to a lateral at about 24 in for a dwarf or 30 in for a standard, ensuring there are two or three suitably placed laterals just beneath it. Remove all others flush with the main stem. Shorten the selected laterals by about two-thirds to an outward-facing bud.
The second winter (or the two-year-old tree) In the dormant season, select three or four strong leaders to form the primary branches, taking care to select those that are evenly spaced and have formed wide angles with the main stem. The wide angles ensure a stronger joint; a narrow-angled branch may break

off under the weight of the crop later on. Notice the effect of apical dominance, that is, the topmost shoot is the most upright and it is often unsuitable because it is too central and forming a narrow angle with the stem. If this is so, cut it out, heading back to the next branch. Next, shorten the selected primary branches by one-half and shorten the less vigorous ones by two-thirds. Cut each to an outward-facing bud. The remaining shoots are removed altogether. Protect the cuts.

During the summer, the branch growth following the hard pruning should be strong, with secondary branches forming.
In the third winter (or the three-year-old tree) Select about four more widely-spaced branches. The framework now consists of about eight branches. Shorten these by one-half or, if weak, by two-thirds, cutting back to outward-facing buds. Prune back to about four buds those laterals not required for secondary branches and those competing with the leaders. If the tree is growing vigorously, some laterals on the outer part of the tree can be left unpruned to form flower

buds. Shoots crowding the crotch of the tree should be removed. The center should be open, but not completely barren of growth. Growth from the main stem lower than the primary branches should be cut off to maintain the clean leg. Protect the cuts with a tree paint.
The fourth winter The tree is entering the cropping phase of its life, but a little more formative pruning is still necessary, as described for the third winter. Weak varieties may need further formative pruning for the next two or three winters.
Winter pruning the cropping tree By the fourth or fifth year the tree should start bearing fruit. From then the pruning guidelines are flexible, exactly how much is pruned depends on the condition of the tree.

Before pruning an older tree, remember that the harder the tree is pruned, the more growth is obtained, but in consequence the less fruit is produced. Thus, a heavily pruned tree will be vigorous but unfruitful, whereas a lightly pruned tree may crop heavily, but the fruit will be small and the framework weak and badly shaped.

Pruning a feathered maiden

1 In late winter, prepare the soil and drive in a stake. Plant a maiden tree to the same depth as it was at the nursery. Tie to the stake. Cut the main stem back to a bud or lateral at about 24 in for a dwarf, 30 in for a standard.

The second year

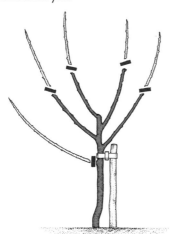

2 In late winter, select four of the primary branches that have formed wide angles to the stem. Cut back vigorous ones by one-half and less vigorous ones by two-thirds. Prune to outward-facing buds. Remove unwanted branches.

The third year

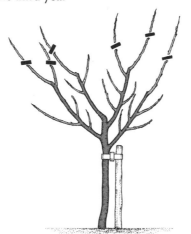

3 In late winter, select a further four well-placed new growths to form permanent branches. Cut back vigorous ones by two-thirds. Prune to outward-facing buds.

Fourth and subsequent years

4 In late winter, the branch framework has now been formed and leader pruning can cease, unless growth is weak. Leave laterals on the outer parts of the tree unpruned. Cut back laterals on the inside to about 4 in.

Apples and pears 4

'Yellow Transparent' Among early apples, probably the best. Used for cooking. Greenish-yellow fruits ripen unusually early; consequently, apple can be grown with reasonably consistent success in Alaska.
'York Imperial' Lopsided red fruits of fair to good eating quality but fine for processing. Late. Bears biennially.

Pruning the cropping tree

Before pruning apple or pear trees that are past the formative stage, it is important to distinguish between the spur-bearing and the tip-bearing varieties. A spur-bearing variety produces fruit buds on the two-year-old as well as on the older wood, where they are carried on short stubby shoots called spurs. Where these shoots become very branched, typically on old wood, they are called spur systems. The spur-bearer is the most common type of apple and pear tree.

A tip-bearing variety produces fruit buds at the tips of slender shoots made in the previous summer. A few spurs are also produced on the older wood, but considerably fewer than on a spur-bearer. The tip-bearer has a more gaunt appearance in comparison. There are also partial tip-bearers, which produce spurs on the older wood as well as fruit buds at their tips. For pruning purposes they are treated as spur-bearers.

There are three basic pruning techniques: spur pruning, renewal pruning, and regulatory pruning.

Spur pruning As mentioned above, spur-bearing varieties form spurs naturally, but they can also be induced to form spurs. Each winter cut back a proportion of maiden laterals to four or five buds. Choose those that have insufficient room to extend as secondary branches.

In the following summer, a lateral so pruned produces one or two shoots from the uppermost buds, but usually the lower buds develop into flower buds by the end of the growing season.

In the second winter, cut back the laterals to the topmost flower bud, thus removing the previous summer's growth. However, where there is room and no risk of the spur overlapping an adjoining branch, extend the spur system by cutting back to three or four wood buds on the previous summer's growth.

After some years, a spur system may become crowded and complicated and, as a result, the fruits are too numerous and therefore small. Then spur thinning is undertaken by reducing the length of the spur systems, cutting away the weakest buds and those buds growing on the undersides of the branches.

Renewal pruning of spur-bearers This also depends upon the tendency of many apple and pear varieties to produce flower buds on unpruned two-year-old laterals. It is best reserved for the strong laterals on the outer part of the tree, where there is room for such growth.

The renewal system of pruning is a method that encourages regular cropping by the removal of fruiting laterals that have passed their peak in growth. Young laterals are trained to take the place of the old laterals. This system is only effective when done by experienced gardeners and so should be practiced with great care.

In the winter, select a proportion of strong, well-placed laterals on the outer part of the tree and leave them unpruned. Prune the others as described in spur pruning. During the following growing season, the terminal bud on each unpruned lateral extends to produce a further maiden shoot, while most of the remaining buds develop into flower buds.

In the second winter, cut back the laterals to the topmost flower bud. In the following summer the cut-back laterals produce fruit.

In the third winter, half the laterals that have fruited can be retained as an elongated spur system. The others are cut back to leave a 1 in stub. This severe shortening stimulates the production of a new lateral from the stub, and so the cycle is repeated.

To sum up, at any one time the tree carries a number of one-year-old laterals unpruned, two-year-old laterals pruned back to a flower bud, and three-year-old laterals which are stubbed back to 1 in after fruiting—or left if there is room.

Regulatory pruning This applies to the tree as a whole rather than to specific parts of it as in spur or renewal pruning. Basically it entails keeping the center open by removing crowding and crossing branches and cutting out dead, diseased and broken wood. There is no need to prune the leaders after the early formative years except with poorly growing varieties, which require the stimulus of hard pruning.

The framework branches, laterals and spurs also should not be crowded. As a rough guide, in an old tree no main branch should directly over-shade another by less than 18 in, nor should branches be closer than 18 in when side by side. Laterals should be spaced about 18 in apart and spurs not less than 9 in along the framework of branches.

If in later years, as a result of light pruning, the tree over-crops (with consequent small fruit) and growth is weak, adopt a policy of harder pruning to reduce the number of flower buds and to stimulate new growth. Simplify some of the over-long spur systems, and where they are crowded cut out some of them altogether. Increase the amount of renewal pruning.

Pruning of tip-bearers In the winter, prune lightly on the regulatory system (see above). Leave any maiden shoots less than 9 in long unpruned because they have fruit buds at their tips. Prune longer laterals back to four buds. This induces short shoots in the following summer with fruit buds at their tips—spur pruning in effect.

Always prune the leaders of tip-bearing varieties because this induces more laterals to bear fruit in the following year.

SPUR PRUNING

The first year

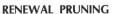
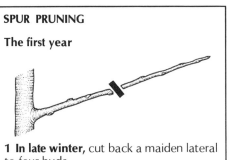

1 In late winter, cut back a maiden lateral to four buds.

The second year

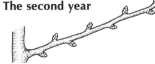

2 In late winter, cut back the lateral to a flower bud.

Third and fourth years

3 In late winter, a spur system begins to be formed.

RENEWAL PRUNING

The first year

1 In late winter, select a strong well-placed lateral and leave it unpruned.

The second year

2 In late winter, extension growth has occurred. Flower buds have formed on last year's wood. Cut back to the junction between old and new wood.

The third year

3 In late winter, cut back the fruited lateral to leave a 1 in stub.

4 In October, at the end of the growing season, a strong new lateral has been produced from the 1 in stub. This is left unpruned to repeat the cycle.

Apples and pears 5

PEAR VARIETIES
Plant two or more varieties together to assure fruiting.
'Anjou' Excellent dessert pears even after long storage. Medium-large, oval. Yellowish-green with slight russeting. Does best in West. Late.
'Baldwin' Tender with good flavor. Early. Can be grown in zone 9.

'Bartlett' Favorite pear for eating and processing. Juicy, sweet fruits. Medium-large. Yellow. Vigorous, productive. Mid-season. Trees susceptible to fire blight. Do not plant with 'Seckel' as that variety does not pollinate it.
'Beurre Bosc' Long-necked, medium-large fruits are yellow overlaid with bronze. Smooth, juicy, rich flavor.

Productive, but very susceptible to fire blight. Late.
'Clapp's Favorite' Symmetrical, medium-large fruits. Excellent quality and flavor. Pick while quite firm, because fruits soften rapidly. Early. Very susceptible to fire blight.
'Comice' Outstanding dessert fruit; juicy, delicious, melting flavor. Medium-

large. Yellow. Late. Grows in zones 5–8, but is by far best at higher elevations.
'Duchess' Very large fruits. Greenish-yellow. Fine flavor. Often self-fruitful, but is more reliable when planted with another variety.
'Flemish Beauty' Grows in zone 4. Spicy-flavored, medium-large, rounded fruits. Mid-season.

The central-leader tree

The success of this form, which is not common in the United States, depends upon producing wide-angled branches off the central leader. Depending on the training method, it is referred to as a vase shape or modified-leader form. Therefore buy a feathered maiden, because the laterals on such a tree are naturally formed at the correct angle. Such a form may be used if the gardener does not desire maximum fruit production, but only wants a specimen of beauty.

Soil preparation and planting

Prepare the soil in the early fall (see page 44). This form requires a long stake to support the central leader. The stake should be 8–8½ ft long by 1½–2 in top diameter.

Drive the stake in first, 18 in deep on a heavy soil and 2 ft deep on a light soil. Plant the tree and tie it to the stake.

Pruning and tying down in the first year (or the one-year-old tree)

During the dormant season from November to February, select three or four laterals to form the first tier of branches starting at not less than 24 in from the ground. Choose strong, well placed laterals coming off the main stem at a wide angle. Prune these back by one-half to an outward-facing bud. Remove the rest of the laterals entirely. Cut back the central leader to the third bud above the topmost selected lateral.

By August the original laterals will have extended and possibly new laterals will have been produced. A new central leader will have grown on. Tie the leader to the stake using a figure of eight tie with soft thick string. Choose three or four good laterals that form a wide angle with the main stem and gently tie the extension growth of each down to 30 degrees above the horizontal with soft

thick string secured to 9 in long wire pegs pushed into the ground. Remove any upright laterals and those directly beneath the central leader.

Pruning in the second winter

Cut back the central leader by about one-third of the previous summer's growth to a bud on the opposite side to that of the previous year. The technique of cutting to an opposite bud is called "zig-zagging" and helps to maintain the more or less straight growth essential in the central leader. Remove any upright laterals and those competing with the leader. Prune each remaining lateral by one-quarter to a downward-facing bud. Check the string ties to ensure there is no constriction and remove any where the branch has set at about 30 degrees.

In August, again tie down suitable new laterals to form branches.

Pruning the cropping tree

In the third and subsequent years a similar procedure is followed. The central leader is pruned by one-quarter (if weak by one-third) to induce the lower buds to produce new laterals. The more vigorous the leader is, the lighter it is pruned. Branches are allowed to grow from the central stem at regular intervals, choosing those with a wide angle. Narrow-angled laterals are removed. The higher placed branches must be kept shorter than those beneath to allow sunlight to reach the lower parts. After the laterals at the very top have fruited, they must be pruned on the renewal system (see page 48). Tying down is discontinued once the branches have set at the required angle.

Each winter cut back the extension growth of the central stem to a weaker side branch once it has reached a height of 7–8 ft. Tie up the side branch to the stake as the new leader.

The second year

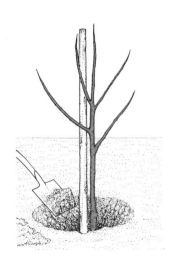

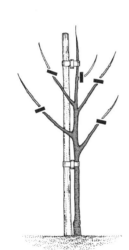

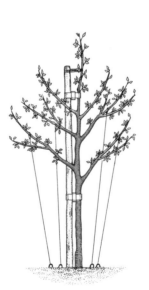

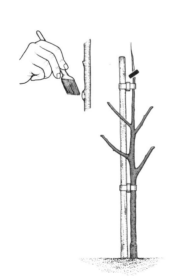

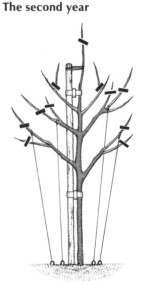

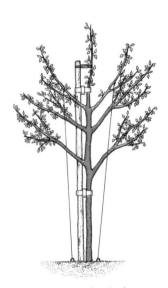

1 In November to March, prepare the ground and drive in a stake. Plant the feathered maiden tree to the same depth as it was at the nursery. Tie it to the stake.

2 At the same time, select three or four laterals to form the first tier of branches at about 24 in from the ground. Prune them back by one-half to an outward-facing bud. Remove remaining laterals entirely.

3 Then, cut back the central leader to the third bud above the topmost selected lateral. Protect the pruning cuts with a wound paint.

4 By August, the original laterals will have extended and a new central leader will have grown on. Tie the leader to the stake. Tie down the extension growth to 30 degrees above the horizontal using soft string.

5 In winter, cut back the central leader by one-third of the previous year's growth to an opposite-facing bud. Remove any upright laterals. Prune remaining laterals by one-quarter to a bud.

6 Every year, check the string ties. Remove the ties where the branch has set at 30 degrees. In August, tie down new laterals. Cut back the leader to a weaker lateral. Tie it up as the new leader.

Apples and pears 6

'Gorham' Fruits large and yellow with light brown russet. Melting, sweet musky flavor. Late. Vigorous, but susceptible to fire blight.
'Kieffer' Grows from zones 4–9. Only fair quality when fresh, but processes very well. Big, yellow fruits. Late.
'Lincoln' Recommended for region around Oklahoma. Large, good-quality

fruits. Mid-season to late.
'Magness' New hybrid descended from 'Comice' and 'Seckel'. Medium-size, sweet, aromatic fruits. Greenish with russeting. Mid-season. Tree resistant to fire blight, but thorny. An unreliable pollinator; plant with two other varieties.
'Maxine' Fruits of only fair quality, but the tree is highly resistant to fire blight,

and is therefore recommended for areas where this disease is a particular problem. Large, yellow fruits. Late.
'Moonglow' Large, smooth, sweet, mild-flavored fruits. Big fruits are yellow with rosy blush. Early. Highly resistant to fire blight. Heavily spurred tree produces at an unusually early age.
'Orient' Very large, rounded fruits in

mid-season. Spreading, vigorous tree resistant to fire blight. Grows in zone 9.
'Seckel' Small, brownish,yellow, red-blushed fruits of delicious flavor. Late. Productive, but slow to produce. Not pollinated by 'Bartlett'.
'Tait Dropmore' Very hardy, growing into zone 3. But medium-size fruits are of only fair quality. Mid-season.

Restricted tree forms: The cordon

A cordon consists of a single straight stem furnished with side-shoots or fruit spurs which are kept short by summer pruning and sometimes by winter pruning. It may be planted and trained vertically or obliquely, usually the latter because it requires less height and its growth is more easily controlled. There are also multiple cordons, with two or more stems.

The single stem apple cordon is not difficult to care for and is an ideal way for the amateur gardener to experiment.

The cordon is a form that, perhaps more than any other, is suited to the small garden. It is closely planted, so many varieties can be grown in a relatively small space and the gardener can more easily meet the cross-pollination requirements of apples and pears. Cordons can be grown against walls and fences or out in the open on a wire fence.

Choice of rootstock

For apple cordons, the dwarfing rootstock Malling 9 is the most suitable where space is very limited and the cordons are to be kept down to a height of 5–6 ft. The soil must be fertile, however. If in doubt about the soil, obtain trees on a slightly more vigorous stock.

For pears, the cordons must be grafted on to Quince A or C rootstocks.

An apple cordon crops high quality fruit early and heavily because it is raised on dwarfing rootstock. Other fruits that can be grown on the cordon system include gooseberries, red currants, sweet cherries, and white currants.

Selecting the tree

Cordons of one, two or three years old can be planted. If selecting a maiden tree, preferably choose one with plenty of laterals because these are the foundation of the fruit spurs to come. Two- or three-year-old cordons will be quicker to bear fruit, but they must be well furnished with spurs and laterals.

Spacing

Space the cordons 2½ ft apart on medium to good soils or 3 ft apart on poor, shallow or sandy soils with the rows 6 ft apart.

Support system

Cordons may be planted against a wall or fence or out in the open on a wire fence. On walls and wooden fences erect horizontal wires every 2 ft as described on pages 8–9. Out in the open drive in wooden posts every 12 ft to hold the wires. The posts may be 2½ in × 2½ in oak or 3½ in top diameter in other woods. Set the posts 2 ft deep or 3 ft in sandy soils. The end posts should be strutted. Alternative materials include iron, steel or concrete posts. Erect the wires at 2 ft, 4 ft and 6 ft and use 10 gauge wire for the upper wire and 12 gauge for the other two. Securely tie 8 ft bamboo canes to the wires at an angle of 45 degrees, with the tops pointing towards the north if the rows run north-south, or to the east if they run east-west. Space the canes at 2½–3 ft intervals to correspond with the planting stations.

Planting and training oblique cordons

Prepare the soil in the early fall (see page 44). Plant in the dormant season, unless using container-grown plants, which can be planted at any time. Against walls and solid fences, the cordon should be planted 6–9 in away from the structure to allow room for the growth of the trunk. Set the cordon at an angle of 45 degrees with the union between stock and scion uppermost, and then securely tie the cordons to the cane using thick soft string or plastic chainlock strapping in a figure of eight. If the one-year-old tree has laterals, shorten those over 6 in long to four buds. Thereafter, prune each summer. Do not prune the leader.

It is not wise to allow a cordon to crop in the first year after planting, so in the spring remove any flowers, taking care not to cut the growing shoot just behind the blossom.

Summer pruning: Modified Lorette System

Summer pruning is necessary to confine the growth to the limited space available. It also induces the production of fruit spurs close to the main stem. The Modified Lorette System is the simplest method.

Summer prune in about mid-July for pears and in the third week of July for apples in

warm climates. Prune seven to ten days laterals arising from existing side-shoots or all mature shoots of the current season's growth that are growing directly from the main stem. Cut back those mature sub-laterals arising from existing side shoots or spurs to one leaf beyond the basal cluster or rosette of leaves. Mature shoots have a stiff woody base, dark leaves and are 9 in or more long. Leave immature shoots until mid-September. Do not prune shoots that are shorter than 9 in because they usually have fruit buds at their tips.

Pruning the cropping tree

Each May, once the cordon has passed the top wire and reached the required height (usually 7 ft), cut back the extension growth to its origin. Each July subsequently, cut the leader to 1 in. From mid-July onwards the remaining shoots on the cordon are pruned on the Modified Lorette System (see above).

If, later on, there are secondary growths from shoots pruned in July, cut them back to mature wood just before leaf-fall. In areas

The first year

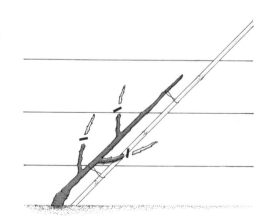

1 In late winter, plant the maiden tree with the union uppermost, against a cane secured to wire supports at about 45 degrees. Do not prune the leader. Cut back any feathers to four buds.

Second and subsequent years

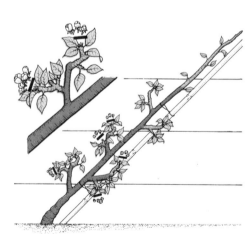

2 In spring, after a further year's growth spurs will have formed on the cut-back feathers. Remove any flowers as they appear, leaving intact the growing shoot behind the blossom.

3 In late July, cut back laterals longer than 9 in arising directly from the main stem to three good leaves from the base, ignoring the basal cluster. Cut back sub-laterals from existing spur systems to one leaf beyond the basal cluster.

Apples and pears 7

where secondary growth is prolific after pruning, for example in high rainfall regions, delay pruning until later in the summer. If much secondary growth still occurs, then stop summer pruning altogether and prune in the winter instead, pruning to one bud from existing spurs and three buds on laterals arising directly from the main stem.

Winter pruning
Normally neither the leader nor the side-shoots are pruned in the winter except when a tree makes too much secondary growth, or makes poor growth, or to renovate it.

When a young cordon does not produce sufficient side-shoots, resulting in bare areas of stem, laterals may be induced by pruning the leader (previous summer's growth) by up to one-third of its length. Treat newly planted tip-bearers in the same way.

Neglected cordons can be brought back into shape by winter pruning. Thereafter prune them in the summer. Overlong or complicated spur systems should be reduced to two or three fruit buds.

Secondary growths

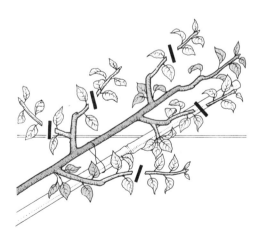

Just before leaf-fall, if further growth has developed from pruned shoots, cut it back to mature wood. In high rainfall areas, where much secondary growth occurs, stop summer pruning and prune from November to March instead.

LOWERING THE CORDON

When the cordons reach the top wire they may be lowered to obtain a longer stem. Lowering also helps to check the vigor of an overvigorous cordon. Lower carefully five degrees at a time and not lower than 35 degrees, so that there is no risk of breaking the stem. Lowering the angle slows down the movement of sap and limits extension growth while encouraging fruit bud protection.

The fruiting cordon

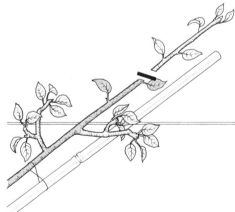

1 In May, when the leader has passed the top wire and reached the required height of about 7 ft, cut back the extension growth to its origin.

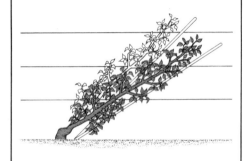

2 Each July, cut back the leader to 1 in. Cut back to three leaves all mature laterals longer than 9 in growing directly away from the main stem and those from existing side-shoots and spurs to one leaf beyond the basal cluster.

MULTIPLE CORDONS

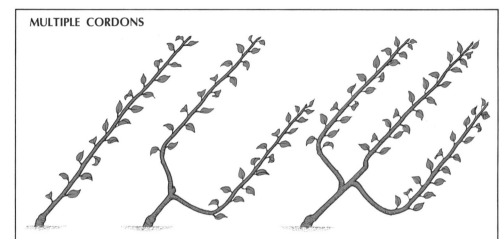

Cordons may also be formed with two, three or more arms, trained either vertically or at an angle. The training of a multiple cordon is initially similar to the formation of the first horizontal arms of an espalier. Thereafter each stem of the multiple cordon is treated as a single cordon. Vertically trained cordons are generally more vigorous and often less fruitful than those trained at an angle of about 45 degrees. The angle can be reduced further (see Lowering the cordon).

OVERCROWDED SPUR SYSTEMS

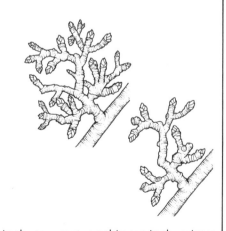

As the tree matures thin out in the winter by reducing overlong overlapping or complicated spur systems to two or three fruit buds. Remove buds that are weak on the underside and shaded parts of the branches.

Apples and pears 8

Restricted tree forms: The espalier

An espalier consists of a central stem from which horizontal fruiting arms (tiers) grow at about 15–18 in intervals. The tree is trained in one plane and makes a handsome boundary marker or can be used to cover walls or fences.

Choice of rootstock and spacing

If a small espalier apple is required, for example, against a low fence, the tree should be on the Malling 9 rootstock. This means obtaining a maiden tree and shaping it, because pre-formed espaliers on this stock are not usually available. For more than one espalier, plant 10 ft apart.

Where more vigorous trees are required, to clothe a large wall for example, they should be on vigorous rootstock and spaced 15–18 ft apart. Pears should be on Quince A or C rootstock.

Selecting the tree

The number of horizontal arms or tiers required depends upon the height of the wall or fence. Most nurseries that sell trees for espaliering supply two-tier and three-tier

espaliers and further arms can be trained in if required. A formed espalier is much more expensive but crops sooner.

Support system

On walls and fences erect the horizontal wires to coincide with the espalier arms (as described on pages 8–9); usually each tier is 15–18 in apart. Out in the open, drive in posts to hold the wires every 12–18 ft, depending upon the spacing of the espaliers. The end posts should be strutted. Plant the espaliers centrally between the posts. Use 10 gauge galvanized wires and strain tight with straining bolts on the end posts.

Soil preparation and planting

In late winter, prepare the soil (see page 45). Plant in March or April. To allow room for the trunk to grow when sited against a wall or fence, the espalier should be planted 6 in away.

Formative pruning

Formed espaliers may be obtained or the gardener may prefer to start off with a maiden

tree. The formative pruning steps in the first, second, and subsequent years are described below in as much detail as possible.

The first year Plant an unfeathered maiden tree in late winter or early spring. Cut back the stem to within 15 in of ground level, making sure that room for a short leg is left, together with three good topmost buds. The two lower ones should point in opposite directions.

In spring carefully direct the shoot from the top bud vertically up a cane and the others to the right and the left. It is difficult to obtain horizontal shoots in the first year without a check to growth and it is best to train the two shoots initially at angles of about 45 degress to the main stem. This can be achieved by tying them to canes secured to the wire framework.

During summer the angle can be varied so that a weaker shoot is encouraged to catch up by raising it a little towards the vertical.

In November, at the end of the first growing season, lower the two side branches to the horizontal and tie them to the wire supports. Prune back the central leader to within 18 in of the junction, with the lower arms to

coincide with the next wire. The intention is to promote a further three growths—one to continue the central axis and the other two to form a second tier of side branches. Shorten surplus laterals from the main stem to three buds. Prune the two horizontal leaders to downward-pointing buds, removing about one-third of each shoot. If growth has been particularly satisfactory, perhaps because of a good growing season, the leaders can be left unpruned.

Second and subsequent years The next years are a repetition of the first, with subsequent tiers of branches being trained in. In late winter lower the side branches to the horizontal and secure them to the wire supports. Cut back the central leader to within 18 in of the last tier of arms at the next wire. Cut back unwanted laterals from the main stem to three buds. The horizontal leaders should be cut back by one-third, cutting to downward-pointing buds, if growth has been quite poor.

Cut back competing growths from the main stem to three leaves during the summer from July to September.

The first year

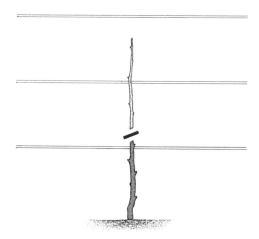

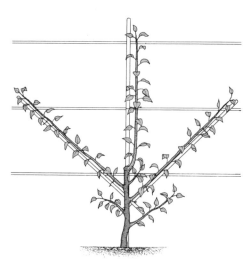

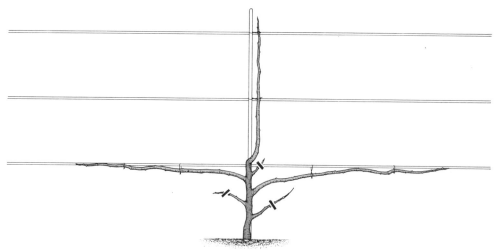

1 In late winter, plant an unfeathered maiden tree. Cut back the stem to within 15 in of ground level. Leave room for a short leg and select three good upper buds for training.

2 From June to September, train the shoot from the top bud vertically up a cane. Train the shoots from the two lower buds at an angle of 45 degrees to the main stem. Tie them to canes fixed on the wire support.

3 At the end of the growing season, lower the two side branches to the horizontal and tie them carefully to the wire supports with soft string. Cut back surplus laterals on the main stem to three buds.

Apples and pears 9

There is a tendency for vertical shoots to grow from the horizontal arms. These laterals are pruned in summer, cutting each back to three leaves above the basal cluster. Do not tie the extension growth of the horizontal arms until the end of the summer because early tying checks growth. In winter train and prune both the horizontal and vertical leaders in the same way as before. This regime of winter and summer pruning should continue until the desired number of tiers has been built in.

The number of tiers finally achieved depends on soil, site and inherent vigor, but four or five is usual. Eventually both the central axis and the horizontal arms fill their allotted space. From then onwards cut back the new terminal shoots to their origin each May and summer prune subsequent growth.

The fruiting stage

Each summer The fruits are carried on spur systems on the horizontal arms. The spurs are formed by the summer pruning of laterals on the Modified Lorette System in exactly the same way as for cordons. Regard each arms as a horizontal cordon (see pages 50–1).

Winter After a few years of fruiting, the spur systems may become complicated and should be simplified by removing clusters of weak buds and by cutting back some of the spurs to two or three fruit buds.

Second and subsequent years

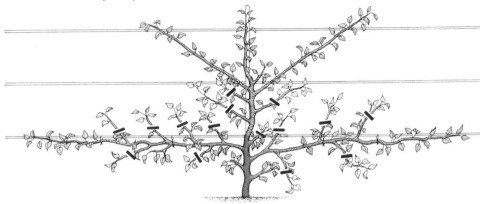

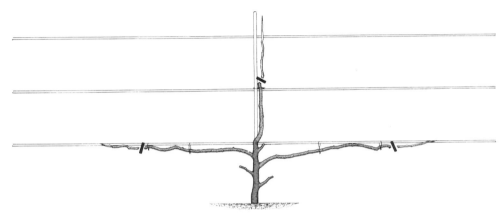

4 At the same time, cut back the central leader to within 18 in of the lower arm at the next wire, leaving three good buds to form the central leader and two new horizontal arms. If growth is weak, prune back the horizontal leaders by one-third, cutting to downward-pointing buds.

5 From July to September, train the second tier of branches in the same way as in the previous years (see caption 2). Cut back competing growths from the main stem to three leaves. Cut back laterals from the horizontal arms to three leaves above the basal cluster.

Mature tree

6 In winter, cut back the central leader to within 18 in of the lower arm, leaving three good buds to form the new central leader and two new horizontal arms. Cut back surplus laterals on the main stem to 3 buds. Tie down the extension growth of each arm to the horizontal. If growth is poor, prune back the leaders by one-third.

7 In May, when the final number of tiers is produced and the tree has filled its allotted space, cut back the new terminal growths of the vertical and horizontal arms to their origins. From now on prune them each summer as if they were cordons.

Apples and pears 10

The dwarf pyramid
The dwarf pyramid was evolved by commercial fruit growers as an easier method of producing apples and pears intensively. The pear, in particular, when grown on Quince rootstock, responds well to this method of training and in recent years the technique has been extended to plums. With apples and pears the aim is to produce a central-leader tree some 7 ft high with a total branch spread of about 4 ft through the tree, tapering to the top to form a pyramid.

It is essential to keep such a closely planted and compact tree under control. This control is exerted by a combination of summer pruning, early cropping, the complete removal of any vigorous upright shoots, and the choice of a rootstock capable of sustaining the required balance between steady cropping and the renewal of bearing wood.

Choice of rootstock
Malling 9 and Malling 26 rootstock are suitable for apples in most gardens and either Quince A or the re-cloned Quince C (when generally available) can be used for pears.

Planting and staking
In early fall, prepare the soil (see page 45). Plant in the dormant season from November to March. Individual stakes are not necessary unless planting only one or two trees. With a row of trees, support them by erecting two posts at the ends of the row, and stretch two horizontal wires between them, one at 18 in and the other at 36 in. Tie the trees to these, using string or strapping.

Spacing
Space apples on M9 rootstocks at 4–5 ft apart, and apples on M26 rootstocks and pears 5–6 ft apart. Allow the wider spacing on fertile soils. The rows should be 7 ft apart.

Pruning and training
The first year A start is made with a maiden tree, which is cut back to about 20 in on planting during the dormant season in early spring. Prune to a bud on the opposite side to the graft. The result of this initial pruning is the production of four or five strong shoots. The uppermost shoot, which will become the leader, grows vertically.

The first year

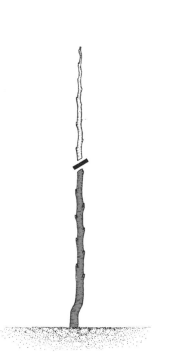

The second year

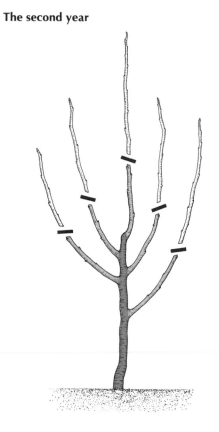

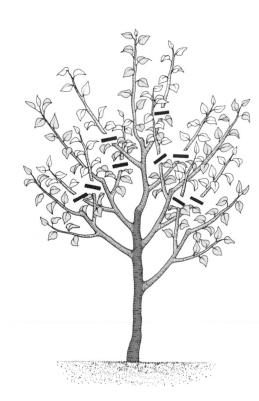

1 In early spring, at planting cut back the maiden to a bud within 20 in of ground level.

2 From July to August, four or five strong shoots will have been produced. No pruning is necessary.

3 In late winter, cut back the central leader to leave 9 in of new growth. Cut to a bud that points in the opposite direction to the last pruning. Cut back side branches to downward-pointing buds to leave 8 in of the maiden extension.

4 In late winter, cut back laterals not required for the framework to three leaves or 3–4 in and sub-laterals to one leaf beyond the basal cluster. Leave leaders unpruned.

Apples and pears 11

The second year In the following winter prune the central leader to leave about 9 in new growth, taking care to cut to a bud that points in the opposite direction to the last pruning. This is aimed at keeping the successive stages of the central stem as straight as possible, in a series of zig-zags. It would be easier not to prune the leader at all because the stem would be straighter if left untouched, but such pruning is necessary to stimulate the annual production of side branches during the formative stages. These side branches, perhaps four in number and evenly spaced around the tree, are pruned back to within 8 in of the maiden extension, cutting each to a downward-pointing bud to maintain the horizontal direction.

During the following summer begin summer pruning, starting in mid-July for pears and about the end of July for apples. Cut back laterals (the current season's growth) longer than 9 in arising directly from the side branches to three leaves, and laterals from existing spurs to one leaf beyond the basal cluster. Leave immature shoots until September and then prune them in the same way.

Do not prune the leaders in summer.

Third and subsequent years Prune the central leader in winter. Aim to leave about 9 in of new growth, cutting to a bud that is pointing in the opposite direction from the bud to which the stem was pruned in the previous winter. This stimulates the production of new side branches. Cut back any secondary growth that may have occurred as a result of summer pruning to a mature bud.

Every summer, prune the current season's growth on the side branches using the Modified Lorette System (see page 56), treating each side branch as if it were a cordon. Prune the branch leaders to six leaves.

When the tree reaches 7 ft, further extension growth should be stopped by cutting back the leader to its origin each May. Prune any other shoots that need restriction, such as vigorous upright shoots at the top or branch leaders growing into adjacent trees.

In winter it is occasionally necessary to shorten branches to a downward-pointing shoot in an attempt to maintain the essential horizontal position of the fruiting arms. Trim overcrowded spurs at the same time.

Third and subsequent years

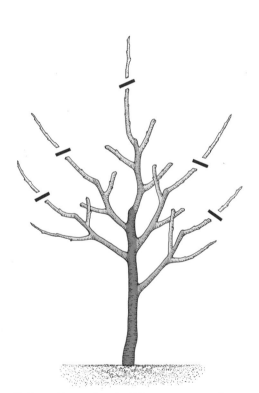

5 From November to February, prune the central leader to leave about 9 in of new growth, cutting to a bud on the opposite side to the previous pruning.

6 From July to August, throughout summer cut back laterals to three leaves or 3–4 in and sub-laterals to one leaf beyond the basal cluster. Prune the leaders of the side branches to six leaves.

7 In late winter, prune the central leader to leave 9 in of new growth. Remove entirely any over-vigorous shoots. Shorten branches to downward-pointing buds as necessary to maintain the horizontal position of the fruiting arms.

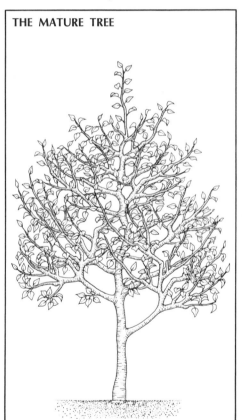

THE MATURE TREE

When the tree has reached the required height of about 7 ft, cut back the leader to its origin each May. Thin fruiting spurs as necessary. Maintain the central stem and retain the pyramid shape by close pruning and removal of vigorous shoots.

Apples and pears 12

Cultivation

Feeding and mulching Apply fertilizers as a top dressing over the rooting area, which is roughly equivalent to the spread of the tree and slightly beyond. Inorganic fertilizers can scorch grass, therefore brush well in and water the grass if the weather is dry. If the soil tends to be acid, with a pH lower than 6.7, sulfate of ammonia should not be applied because it makes the soil more acid. Instead use an artificial fertilizer containing calcium carbonate and ammonium nitrate. It does not affect the pH.

In early March, mulch newly planted and young trees with well-rotted manure, compost or peat to a depth of 2 in over a radius of about 18 in, but keep the mulch just clear of the stem.

Dessert apples In mid-winter apply sulfate of potash at $\frac{3}{4}$ oz per square yard. Every three years, in mid-winter apply superphosphate at 2 oz per square yard. In late winter apply sulfate of ammonia or the fertilizer mentioned above, at 1 oz per square yard.

Dessert apples in grass See cooking apples.

Cooking apples The same rates and timings given for dessert apples apply except that extra nitrogen is necessary, so double the application of sulfate of ammonia or the fertilizer mentioned above. This also applies to dessert apples grown in grass.

During heavy rainfall in spring and summer, and in high rainfall areas, some apple varieties suffer from magnesium deficiency (see pages 14–16). At the first signs, apply three foliar sprays at 14-day intervals, using 8 oz magnesium sulfate in $2\frac{1}{2}$ gal water, plus a spreader ($\frac{1}{4}$ fl oz washing-up liquid). To avoid a recurrence, apply the magnesium sulfate as a top dressing in April, at 2 oz per square yard over the rooting area.

Pears, dessert and cooking Pears benefit from additional nitrogen, but if too much is given, vigorous growth is encouraged which, in turn, encourages fire blight. In the first year, therefore, apply only a few handfuls of balanced fertilizer such as 10-10-10. From the second year until the tree starts to bear, apply 8 oz of ammonium nitrate. Then increase the application to 16 oz and then, when the tree is about 10 years old, apply 24 oz. Thereafter, apply 32 oz per year.

Watering To ensure good establishment and strong growth, young trees (especially newly planted ones) need to be watered in the growing season whenever the soil is dry. As a guide, apply 4 gal per square yard every ten days throughout dry periods.

Cropping trees also respond to irrigation by producing heavier crops of larger and better quality fruit. Lack of water may induce a biennial bearing pattern (see page 58). The total amount of water needed is about 4 in (18 gal per square yard) in July, 3 in (13$\frac{1}{2}$ gal per square yard) in August and 2 in (9 gal per square yard) in September.

Obviously, in cool wet regions these totals will be met by natural rainfall, but in dry areas some water must be applied, the actual amount depending upon the rainfall. Apply 2 in (9 gal per square yard) at a time under the trees, starting in early July. Use a slow-running hose as a soaker and keep the water on the ground rather than on the foliage, irrigating over the rooting area.

Fruit thinning The main purpose of fruit thinning is to obtain larger and better quality fruits. In heavy cropping years if the fruits are not thinned, the resultant crop will consist of small, medium to poor quality apples or pears and, as with lack of water, the strain imposed upon the tree might put it into a biennial habit. Much depends upon the condition of the trees: trees with healthy foliage and a strong framework can carry more fruit than can weaker trees. Young trees should not be allowed to crop so heavily that the branches are bowed down and the tree cannot make the essential strong growth needed for its framework.

Some varieties naturally shed some of their fruitlets in late June or early July which is called the June drop, but this may not be sufficient. Start lightly thinning before this in mid-June by removing the malformed fruits, and then complete the task after the June drop in about mid-July.

Cooking varieties should be thinned harder than the dessert fruits.

Use sharp scissors or press the fruitlet with the thumb and finger, leaving the stalk behind. In the final thinning, dessert apples should be spaced on average 4–6 in apart with about one fruit per cluster and occasionally two where there is a good show of supporting leaves. Cooking apples should be spaced on average 6–9 in apart.

With apples, sometimes the "king" or "crown" fruit produced in the center of a cluster is virtually stalkless and malformed. If this is the case, remove it, but if the apple is well shaped, leave it because the king fruit can be the best in the cluster.

Pears need less thinning than do apples. Start thinning after the natural drop in late June, but not until the fruitlets turn downwards. Thin to two fruits per cluster and occasionally to one where the foliage is poor or sparse.

Supporting heavily laden branches Prop up heavily laden branches well before there is a risk of the branches breaking. Use forked poles or stakes but place a cushion of soft material such as a piece of rubber tire between the prop and the branch.

Weak branches can be tied to stronger ones with rope or webbing. Small trees can

Manuring

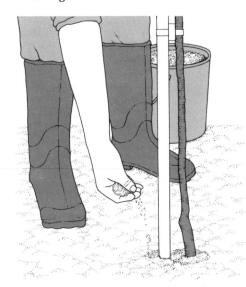

1 In mid-winter, apply sulfate of potash at the recommended rates. In late winter apply sulfate of ammonia.

Mulching

2 In early March, mulch newly planted and young trees with a 2 in layer of well-rotted manure or compost over a radius of 18 in.

Watering

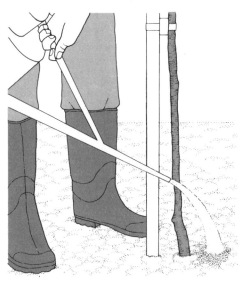

3 In summer, apply 4 gal per square yard every ten days in dry periods.

Apples and pears 13

be supported by "maypoling". This involves driving a tall stake into the ground near the stem of the tree and tying rope or thick string from its top to each branch that will benefit from support.

Protection from wasps and birds

Apples and pears (especially the early varieties) sometimes need protection against wasps and birds. The trees can be netted or collars placed around the fruit stalks against birds (see page 17) but wasps are more difficult to combat. One remedy is to find and destroy the wasps' nests. They can also be trapped in jam jars partly filled with beer and sugar. However, these two methods guarantee only partial control, and the most positive (if tedious) protection against wasps is to enclose each fruit, or cluster of fruits, in a muslin bag or piece of nylon stocking.

Harvesting and storing

The time for picking apples and pears varies according to the season and the locality so it is not possible to give exact picking dates. As a guide, the earliest varieties of apples are ready for picking in late July to early August.

Apples A good test for ripeness is to lift the fruit in the palm of the hand and if it leaves the spur easily with its stalk intact, it is ready. Another sign is the first windfalls (discounting drops from strong winds and codling moth attack). With the later ripening varieties, the color of the pips is an indication. They should be beginning to change color from white to straw-coloured and eventually to brown. With dessert apples in particular the skin of the fruits becomes more brightly colored.

Early varieties are best picked when slightly immature because they soon go mealy. Pick those apples that have colored rather than clearing all the apples in one go. Usually those apples in full sun are ready first and those in the middle of the tree last. Handle the fruits very gently because bruised fruits do not keep. Put the fruits carefully into a picking container lined with soft material and transfer them just as gently into their final container.

Late apples reach maturity in storage sometime after picking, depending upon the variety. Most should be off the tree by about the third week of October, but there are a few varieties which keep better and acquire more flavor if left on as long as possible, birds and winter gales permitting. These include 'Granny Smith' and 'Idared'.

Store only sound fruits (see page 90 for details of storage).

Pears The correct time for picking pears is harder to assess than it is for apples. The best test of readiness is to lift the pear in the palm of the hand and with a slight twist and tug, it should leave the spur with its stalk intact. There is also an almost imperceptible change in the ground color of the skin from dark green to lighter green.

Early and early mid-season pears (August to September) must not be left on the tree until they are fully ripe otherwise they may go "sleepy", that is very soft, mealy and brown at the center. Pick them when they are almost ready but still firm, and then let them mellow in storage. Their storage life can be extended considerably by keeping them under cool conditions (3°–7°C/37°–45°F).

Late pears should be left on the tree until they leave the spur easily; the first sign of windfalls is an indication. The fruits are hard at this stage but will mellow in storage. Keep them under cold conditions and bring the pears into room temperature to finish ripening whenever required. (See page 82 for details of storage).

Pests and diseases

Apples The most troublesome diseases are scab, mildew and canker and the most troublesome pests are aphids, leaf-eating caterpillars, sawfly and codling moth larvae.

Scab and mildew can be controlled by regular spraying with benomyl or captan starting at bud burst and finishing in July. If canker occurs, cut out the rotting wood and paint the clean wounds with a canker paint. In bad attacks also apply liquid copper sprays after harvest and at 50 per cent leaf-fall, and the following year at bud burst. Check that the soil is not badly drained (see pages 10–11).

Use a systemic aphicide against aphids.

Thinning

4 In mid-June, thin the fruits using sharp scissors or press the fruitlets off with the thumb and finger, leaving the stalk behind.

In mid-July, thin again to leave one or two dessert apples per cluster 4–6 in apart, cooking apples 6–9 in apart. Pears need less thinning; leave two fruits per cluster.

Maypoling

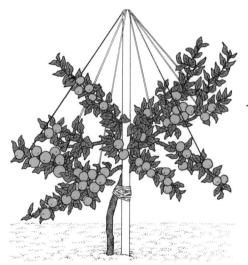

5 On small trees, to support branches with a heavy crop, drive a tall stake into the ground near the stem of the tree. Tie a rope from its top to each branch.

Grassing down the orchard

6 After four or five years, sow grass in the orchard. Sow a fine lawn mixture at 2 oz per square yard, leaving a grass-free area of 2 ft radius around the base of each tree.

Apples and pears 14

Spraying with dimethoate one week after petal fall controls sawfly larvae. Use a general-purpose fruit spray against codling moth caterpillars in mid-June and again at the end of June.

Pears The most troublesome disease of pears is scab and the most troublesome pests are aphids and leaf-eating caterpillars.

For scab spray with captan or benomyl at bud burst, repeating every two weeks as necessary until late July.

The whole business of pest control can be greatly simplified if a general-purpose fruit spray containing an insecticide and fungicide is used on a systematic schedule throughout the growing season.

In winter, during dormancy, spray with a dormant oil. Then use the general-purpose spray (1) just before blossoms open, (2) when three-fourths of the flower petals have fallen, (3) two weeks after petal fall, and (4) every 10–14 days thereafter until about three weeks before harvest.

Adding a "sticker" (a gluey liquid) to the spray keeps it from being rapidly diluted by the rain. If the "sticker" is not used, it may be necessary to increase the frequency of spray in wet or very humid weather to every seven days.

Propagation

Apples and pears do not come true from seed nor are they satisfactory from cuttings, so they are propagated by budding or grafting on to suitable rootstocks, a task normally performed by the fruit tree nursery.

Biennial bearing

Biennial bearing or the carrying of a heavy crop one year and little or none in the next, is a common problem with apples and pears. Certain varieties are prone to it, although almost any variety can fall into this habit. It is more likely to happen to trees which are starved or receiving insufficient moisture, which makes them unable to carry a heavy crop and at the same time develop fruit buds for the following year. Frost destroying the blossom one spring can sometimes be the start of biennial bearing. Once the tree is into this cropping pattern it is difficult to correct, although there are certain techniques the

---

BIENNIAL BEARING

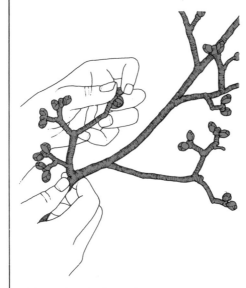

1 In spring, before a heavy crop year, rub one-half to three-quarters of the fruit buds from the spurs, leaving one or two per spur.

2 Each March, apply 4 oz per square yard of a balanced fertilizer, such as 10-10-10, and sulfate of ammonia at 2 oz per square yard. Mulch small trees with a 2 in layer of well-rotted manure over a radius of 2 ft.

3 In late August, apply a further 2 oz per square yard of sulfate of ammonia. In dry weather water copiously, giving at least 1 in of water ($4\frac{1}{2}$ gal per square yard) over the rooting area every ten days until rain restores the balance.

---

gardener can try which sometimes improve the situation.

In early spring before an expected heavy crop year, half to three-quarters of the fruit buds are rubbed off the spurs, leaving about one or two per spur. This lessens the burden of too heavy a crop in that year and may enable the tree to develop fruit buds for the next year.

In conjunction with bud rubbing, a policy of more generous feeding and watering should be adopted in "on" and "off" years. But remember the danger of over-feeding pears.

First, clear away grass or weeds from the base of the tree over a radius of at least 2 ft.

Each March apply a balanced fertilizer such as 10-10-10 at 4 oz per square yard and sulfate of ammonia at 2 oz per square yard. Small trees should also be mulched with well-

rotted manure or compost to a depth of 2 in over a radius of 2 ft but keep the material clear of the stem.

In late August apply a further 2 oz per square yard of sulfate of ammonia. Throughout the growing season, whenever the conditions are dry, the tree should be irrigated copiously by applying at least 1 in of water ($4\frac{1}{2}$ gal per square yard) over the rooting area every ten days until rain restores the balance.

If bud rubbing does not work, an alternative technique is to induce the tree to crop biennially over half the tree by removing half the blossom. Alternate branches are selected and marked in some way. Half the branches are designated to crop in the even years (1980, 1982, and so on) and half the branches are designated to crop in the odd years (1981, 1983, and so on). Each spring, those branches not selected to crop in that par-

ticular year must be rigorously deblossomed. At first this deblossoming represents quite a task, especially with a large tree, but after the third or fourth year it should be found that the branches have accepted this alternate pattern and very little blossom removal is necessary. However, a careful watch should be kept to see that the tree does not slip back into the full biennial cropping. As with the first technique, generous feeding is recommended.

Grassing the orchard

After four or five years, sow grass seed throughout the orchard. Grass checks the vigor of the trees and promotes color in the fruits, so grass down dessert fruits, but not cooking apples or cooking pears for which size is more important than color. Delay grassing if the trees are growing poorly.

Plums 1

EUROPEAN PLUM VARIETIES
'Fellemberg' Large, oval, purple fruits with sweet firm flesh. Mid-season. Hardy, productive tree. Self-fruitful.
'French damson' Large, dark blue fruits of excellent quality. Remain on trees for a long time without too much deterioration. Mid-season to late. Self-fruitful.

'Green gage' Excellent flavor. Small, yellow-green fruits with russet dots and pink flesh. Juicy. Freestone. Mid-season. Self-fruitful.
'Imperial Epineuse' Very large prune-plum with reddish-purple skin. Semi-clingstone. Mid-season. Self-fruitful. Brown rot is troublesome.
'Oneida' Reddish-black prune-plum of

good size and quality. Freestone. Self-fruitful.
'Shropshire' Small, blue, very tart fruits in mid-season. Self-fruitful.
'Stanley' Large, bluish-purple fruits. Juicy, rich flavor. Mid-season. Reliably self-fruitful.
'Yellow Egg' Large, oval yellow fruits of quality. Juicy and sweet. Late. Self-fruitful.

A classification of plums

Plums grow in varieties of color, shape, and size and are known by different names in various parts of the world. Understandably, therefore, confusion often occurs among gardeners and botanists over names in the plum family.

The plum is a deciduous tree ranging in height from 15–30 ft when mature. It bears small fruit and is popular with gardeners. For reasons of simplification, the plum can be classified into three broad categories or groups: European, Japanese and native. But there are several other fruits which are also called plums, and these will be described briefly at the end of this section.

The European plum, primarily a blue fruit growing in zones 5–7, is further sub-classified simply as plum, or as, for example, gage, damson, or bullace. These fruits are recognized in the United States as plums, but a varietal name, such as green gage plum, damson plum, or Stanley prune plum, is appended for more precise identification.

The Japanese plum is a red fruit somewhat larger than the European plum, and grows in zones 5–9. Native plums, the best of which are for the most part hybrids, are the results of crosses with Japanese plums. The fruits are red or yellow and fairly small. These trees grow in zones 3–7.

All plums can be canned or made into jams or jellies, but not all are ideal for immediate consumption. The Japanese plum is generally the best of the many plums available for eating when ripe and fresh, but many of the European plums are also excellent eating.

Since the plum does not form a very large tree, it is generally grown as a free-standing tree in the open. Standard, semi-dwarf and dwarf specimens are available. Some of the European varieties can be fan-trained against a warm wall or a fence, or as a pyramid, a very good form for the small garden. It is not suited to such restricted forms as the cordon or espalier.

Pollination

As a rule of thumb, plums are self-unfruitful. The numerous exceptions to this rule are noted in the lists of varieties (above). A general safeguard, however, is to plant any variety of plum in the proximity of another variety to ensure a good set of fruit. But it should be realized that European and Japanese plums cannot pollinate each other. Native plums are pollinated either by other native varieties, by sandcherry-plum hybrids or, in the case of crosses between native and Japanese plums, by Japanese varieties.

Cultivation

The cultivation of all the various types of plums is broadly the same. The major variations are in pruning.

Yield A good average yield from a fully-grown plum tree in the open ranges from 30 to 120 lb.

Soil and situation Plums require a deep, moisture-retentive, well-drained soil with a pH from 6.5 to 7.2. Shallow soils over light, sandy subsoils are unsuitable. The plums grow best in clean soil. Control grass and weeds around the tree by shallow hoeing. Avoid too deep cultivation because this encourages suckering. Plum varieties on vigorous rootstocks can be surrounded with grass, but a clean area 2 ft square should be maintained right around the base of the tree.

Plums flower early, and so a sheltered, frost-free site must be chosen because this is essential to avoid irregular cropping. Japanese plums, which bloom very early, should be planted on a north-facing slope or the north side of a building or wall in order to retard blooming and thus protect the plums from late frosts.

Soil preparation In the fall or early spring, prepare the ground by thoroughly clearing away perennial weeds over an area 3 ft square. Fork in a balanced fertilizer such as 10-10-10 at 3 oz per square yard and bone-meal at 2 oz per square yard just before planting. If the soil is light, also fork in well-rotted manure or compost at one 2-gal bucketful per 2 square feet.

Planting and spacing Plant bare-root trees in March or April while the tree is dormant. Container-grown trees can be planted at any

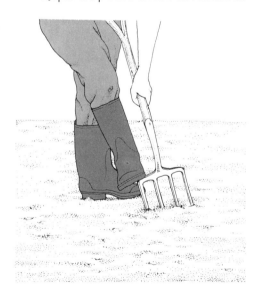

1 In autumn, prepare the ground, clearing away perennial weeds. Lightly fork in 3 oz of a balanced fertilizer and 2 oz of bonemeal per square yard.

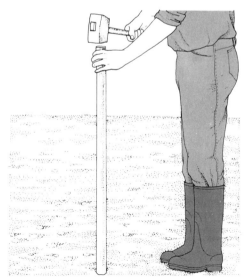

2 For trees in the open, drive in a stake. For fan-trained trees construct a system of wires on the wall. Plant the tree and tie it to the stake or to the wall wires.

3 In February, apply a balanced fertilizer at 4 oz per square yard. One month later, apply sulphate of ammonia at 1 oz per square yard. Mulch the tree with a 1–2 in layer of compost or manure.

4 Thin the fruits when they are the size of hazelnuts and once the stones have formed within the fruits. Repeat when the fruits are twice this size to leave them 2–3 in apart on the branches.

Plums 2

JAPANESE PLUM VARIETIES

'Abundance' Big, red fruits. Sweet and juicy. Extremely susceptible to brown rot.
'Elephant Ear' Big, red fruits with red flesh of outstanding flavor. Mid-season. Does best in dry western areas.
'Methley' Purple-red fruits with delicious red flesh. Very productive, but inclined to bear bienially. A good variety for warm climates.
'Queen Ann' Large, heart-shaped fruits of a dark mahogany color. Tree is weak.
'Santa Rosa' Large, red fruits changing to reddish purple when fully ripe. Excellent flavor. Mid-season. Widely grown and prolific.
'Shiro' Golden-yellow fruits ripening in early August.

time. Dig a hole wide and deep enough to take the roots fully extended. For trees in the open, before planting drive in a stake to reach just below the lowest branch. For fan-trained trees, construct a system of supporting, horizontal wires spaced 6 in apart (see pages 8–9). Plant the tree to the same depth as it was in the nursery. Return the soil and firm it well. Tie to the stake with a tree tie and cushion or tie in the branches of a fan to the wall wires. Water well. Trees in the open require staking for the first two or three years.

Space trees grown in the open 20 ft apart. Fan-trained trees are spaced 15–20 ft apart.

Pruning
Since Japanese and native plums grow more vigorously than European varieties, they require more pruning. This includes cutting back the head to some extent almost every year.

The first year In late winter, cut back the central stem of the maiden tree to a bud at about 2–3 ft for a dwarf, or 4–5 ft for a standard. It may be necessary to grow the tree on for another year to acquire the needed height for a standard before cutting it back. Shorten all laterals to about 3 in to help thicken the stem.

In July or August, select four to five evenly spaced primary branches around the stem at the top. Pinch out the growing points of all others at four or five leaves, including those lower down the main stem.

The second year In late winter, select four branches that have formed wide angles with the stem. Cut back each leader of those selected by one-half to outward-facing buds. Remove the remainder, including the lower laterals of the last year to thicken the stem.

In the summer, remove any suckers that appear from the ground as well as shoots on the main stem below the head.

The third year Repeat the procedures adopted in the previous spring and summer, but allow more secondary branches to develop to fill the increased space, providing up to eight strong, well-placed outward-growing branches. In late winter, cut these back by one-half to two-thirds of the maiden growth to outward-facing buds. Leave shoots on the outer parts of the head not required for leaders. Prune back unpruned laterals on the inside of the tree to 3–4 in.

Little pruning of European plums is necessary in subsequent years. Generally, all that is needed is to cut out dead, broken, rubbing and crossing branches and to thin out the head when it becomes crowded. Japanese and native plums require the same general treatment, but, as noted above, may need some heading back.

Pruning the fan-trained tree Starting with a maiden tree, the framework of a fan-trained plum is built up in the same way as a fan-trained peach (see pages 67–9). Thereafter, the pruning is different because, unlike the peach, the plum fruits on short spurs on three- and four-year-old wood as well as on growth made in the previous summer. However, the older wood tends to become bare with age and from damage by frost or birds. The aim in pruning is to encourage spur formation and, when necessary, to replace worn-out branches.

In the early years, extend the framework, as with the peach, to fill in the wall space; then follow the steps below.

In the spring of later years, cut out a proportion of the old, worn-out wood back to young replacement branches. Paint the wounds.

Feeding and watering
In early spring, apply a balanced fertilizer, such as 10-10-10, at 4 oz per square yard. Mulch young trees with a 1–2 in layer of well-rotted manure or compost over a radius of 18 in, keeping the mulch clear of the stem.

Water well and regularly in dry weather during the growing season, applying 1 in of water ($4\frac{1}{2}$ gal per square yard) every ten days until rain corrects the balance. Avoid irregular heavy watering because this can cause splitting of the fruits, especially near the ripening stage.

Thinning the fruits
Thin the fruits (if the tree carries a heavy crop) after the stones have formed within the fruits

The pyramid plum: the first year

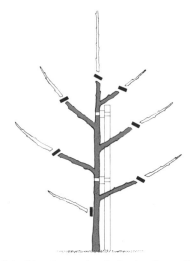

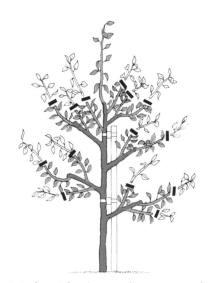

Second and subsequent years

1 In March, cut back the leader to 5 ft. Cut back to the stem all laterals up to 18 in from the ground. Cut back the remaining laterals by one-half.

2 In late July, shorten the new growth of the branch leaders to 8 in to downward-facing buds. Shorten the current season's laterals on the branches to 6 in. Do not prune the central leader.

3 In March, shorten the central leader by two-thirds of the previous summer's growth until the tree has reached about 9 ft, then shorten the central leader to 1 in each May to keep the tree at this height.

4 In late July, shorten the current season's growth of each branch leader to eight leaves. Shorten the laterals to six leaves. Cut out any vigorous shoots at the top of the tree.

Plums 3

NATIVE PLUMS
'Red-coat' Medium-size dark red fruits not very good for eating, but fine for cooking. Freestone. Mid-season.
'South Dakota' Medium-size, red fruits. Very sweet. Mid-season.
'Superior' A Japanese-native hybrid. Large, red fruits of superior quality. Mid-season. Not so hardy as true natives, but hardier than Japanese varieties. Very productive.
'Tecumseh' Medium-sized, juicy, red fruits. Early.
'Underwood' Excellent quality. Big, dark red fruits. Early.

to avoid loss of flavor and the possibility of a biennial pattern of bearing. Thin once when the fruits are about the size of hazelnuts, and again when they are twice this size. On most European and native plums, fruits left on the tree to ripen should be 2–3 in apart; however, allow 4 in in the case of very large varieties. Japanese plums should be thinned to 3–4 in apart. Do not tug the fruits off because this may tear away the following year's fruit buds; cut the fruit stalk with scissors or shears.

Supporting the branches

It is essential to support very heavily laden branches because they may break and spoil the shape of the tree. Such wounds also increase the risk of bacterial infection. Support individual branches with a clothes prop or forked stake driven into the ground at an angle. Wrap the branch with burlap where it meets the crotch of the support. Alternatively, the branches of dwarf trees can be supported with ropes tied to a central stake in maypole fashion (see illustration 5 on page 57).

Protection against birds

The fruit buds of the plum are susceptible to bird damage in winter and the ripe fruit is also at risk in the summer. Where necessary and practicable, protect the tree with netting (see page 17).

Harvesting and storing

Plums ripen from midsummer on. They do not ripen simultaneously and it is necessary to go over the tree several times. Pick fruits intended for canning, jam and cooking while still slightly under-ripe. Pick all fruits with the stalks intact.

Plums cannot be stored for prolonged periods, but they will keep for two to three weeks if picked when a little under-ripe and kept in a cool place, at about 6°–7°C/42°–45°F.

Propagation

Plums are propagated by budding or grafting, a task normally carried out by the nursery. For details see the companion volume in this series, *Plant Propagation*.

Pests and diseases

Spray trees with dormant oil in late winter. Then apply a general-purpose fruit tree spray when the petals fall and at 10–14 day intervals until approximately a month before harvest. Brown rot is a problem if the weather is warm and humid at time of bloom or in the three-week period before harvest. To control it, spray with captan at 3–4 day intervals.

Sandcherry-plum hybrids

These small ($\frac{1}{2}$ in to $1\frac{1}{4}$ in diameter) plums are also known as cherry plums. They are the result of crossing native sandcherries with plums, usually native but sometimes Japanese. Accordingly, the deciduous plants range from shrubs no more than 4 ft high to trees about 25 ft high. The fruits have purple, red or green skins and yellow to purple flesh. Sandcherry-plum hybrids are most commonly grown in zones 2–6, where true plums do not thrive.

The many varieties all fruit from mid-August to September.

Cultivation

The sandcherry-plums are grown like plums and in dry regions require about as much space. In wetter areas, however, spacing can be reduced considerably. The best fruit is borne on young growth, so the plants must be pruned rather hard every year. A good procedure is to remove entire branches after they have fruited for about three years. The plants are self-unfruitful; plant two or more varieties.

Beach plums

The beach plum is generally associated with Cape Cod, where it grows wild in profusion, but it can be grown throughout zones 6–8 near the ocean.

Cultivation

The beach plum grows in indifferent soil so long as it is well-drained, but needs full sun. A little balanced plant food can be applied in early spring, the plants can be mulched with leaves, and then pretty well forgotten. Watering is required only in long dry spells.

The plum fan

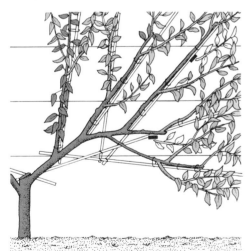

1 For the first three years, follow the formative pruning steps for the peach fan (see pages 69–70), extending the framework to fill in the wall space. Prune only in spring or summer.

Fourth and subsequent years

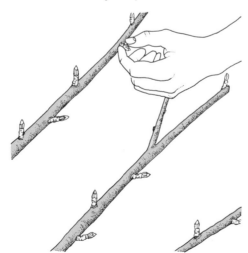

2 Each spring, as growth begins, rub out shoots growing directly towards the wall and breastwood.

3 From late June to late July, as new shoots are made, pinch out the growing points of shoots not wanted for the framework when they have made six or seven leaves. This begins to form the fruit-bearing spur system.

4 After cropping, between mid-August and mid-September, cut back the pinched-out shoots to three leaves to encourage fruit buds to form at the bases of the pinched-out shoots the following year.

Sweet and Duke cherries 1

SWEET CHERRY VARIETIES
'Bing' Undoubtedly the best known. Large fruits in mid-season are very deep red, almost black, with firm, sweet flesh. But subject to cracking. Mid-season.
'Black Tartarian' Excellent purple-black fruits of medium size. Semi-early.
'Early Rivers' Very large crimson-black fruits of excellent flavor. Vigorous,

somewhat spreading tree. Early.
'Emperor Francis' Big red and yellow fruits. Mid-season. Juicy and of excellent flavor. Productive.
'Giant' Very similar to 'Bing' and considered to be better by some gardeners.
'Lambert' Large, purple-red fruits. Very sweet. Late. Unusually hardy: the variety

The cultivated sweet, or dessert, cherry is a hybrid between *Prunus avium* and *P. cerasus*. It is a hardy deciduous tree which is cultivated in many areas of Europe and western Asia. It bears clusters of attractive, white flowers in spring and bears fruits, ranging in color from yellow and pink to almost jet black, from June onwards in cool temperate areas. It grows in zones 6 and 7, and in protected locations in zone 5.

The Duke cherry is thought to be a cross between the sweet and sour cherry and it is intermediate in character between the two.

'May Duke', 'Olivet', 'Reine Hortense' and 'Royal Duke' are good varieties, but are difficult to find.

Cultivation

Although this delicious fruit merits a place in any garden, it has one serious drawback—its extreme vigor. Despite the introduction of increasingly dwarfing rootstocks, the cherry remains quite vigorous and is therefore not suitable for a small garden. It is often grown as a fan on a wall, but the wall must be fairly high. In the open it is grown as a standard. By using the less vigorous rootstock Colt, it could be grown as a pyramid. Treat Duke cherries in the same way as sweet cherries.

Yield The yield from the different kinds of cherry can vary enormously depending, of course, on the size, age and form of the tree and the climate. A good average from a fan is about 30 lb and from a well-grown standard 100 lb.

Soil and situation Cherries grow in any good, well-drained soil but it must be deep, ideally more than $2\frac{1}{2}$ ft. The pH should be between 6.7 and 7.5. Light, sandy and shallow soils are not suitable.

Cherry blossom is susceptible to frost and young trees to wind damage so the site should be sheltered from winds, in full sun and not in a frost pocket.

Soil preparation In the spring clear away weeds over an area 3 ft square, single digging clear ground and double digging weedy ground. Just before planting, fork in a balanced fertilizer such as 10-10-10 at the rate of 3 oz per square yard with bonemeal at

2 oz per square yard.

Planting and spacing Plant when dormant in March or April. Container-grown trees can be planted at any time. Dig a hole wide and deep enough to take the roots fully extended. For trees in the open, before planting drive in a stake to reach just below the lowest branches. Standard cherries require two stakes and a crossbar. For fan-trained trees, erect a system of horizontal wires on the wall using 14 gauge wire and spaced 6 in or two brick courses apart (see pages 8–9).

Plant the tree to the same depth as it was at the nursery. Return the soil and firm it well. Tie to the stake with a tree tie and cushion, or tie in the branches of a fan to the wall wires. Space fan-trees 18–25 ft apart; half-standards and standards at 30–40 ft apart and dwarfs 25–35 ft apart.

Pruning the fan-trained tree

The sweet cherry fan is pruned as shown in the step-by-step instructions below. Prune in spring as the buds burst and not in winter because of the risk of bacterial canker. If the

maiden tree is well feathered use two strong laterals, one to the left and one to the right at the first wire to form the initial ribs. Tie these to canes fixed to the wires at 35 degrees.

Pruning dwarf, semi-dwarf or standards

The first year: the maiden tree Prune in the early spring just as the buds begin to open. The head is formed by cutting back to three or four suitably placed buds in the same way as for the apple (see page 47). The objective is to obtain three or four well-placed primary branches by the end of the summer. Pinch out any flowers that are produced. Shoots lower down on the main stem should be pinched back to four leaves. These help to stiffen the stem and should not be removed until the cherry is four years old. Protect the pruning cuts.

The second year In spring, prune each leader by one half to an outward-facing bud. Summer prune the pinched-back shoots on the main stem by pinching out the growing points. Weak or diseased branches should be entirely removed.

Pruning the fan-trained tree: the first year

The second year

1 In spring, prepare the soil. Dig a hole wide and deep enough to take the roots fully extended. Plant the tree against a wired wall for fan-training (or with two stakes and a crossbar for standards).

2 Each April, apply a top dressing of balanced fertilizer at a rate of 3 oz per square yard over the rooting area. Mulch with a 2–3 in layer of well-rotted manure over a radius of 18 in.

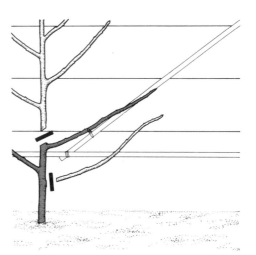

1 In spring, tie two strong laterals to canes fixed to wires at 35 degrees. Head the center stem back to the uppermost of the selected laterals. Remove all other laterals and protect the cuts.

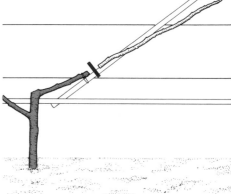

2 In spring, select suitable buds and shorten each leader to about 12 in. This encourages shoots to develop in the summer which are used as the ribs of the fan.

Sweet and Duke cherries 2

is grown commercially in Montana.
'Napoleon' Also called 'Royal Ann'. A favorite among fruit packers, but likely to be difficult for the home gardener because fruits crack in wet weather and are often afflicted with brown rot. The tree is also only semi-hardy and demands perfect soil. Mid-season fruits are red and yellow

'Seneca' Probably the best of the early cherries. Soft, juicy, purple-black fruits.
'Windsor' Large purple-red fruits with yellow flesh. Very late.

The third year By the third spring six to nine well-spaced leaders should have been formed. Prune them lightly, leaving about 24 in of the previous summer's growth. Prune laterals competing with the leaders back to three buds. Upright laterals in the center should be cut out because these may grow too vigorously and spoil the shape of the tree. Where there is room, leave other laterals unpruned.

Fourth and fifth years No more leader pruning should be necessary. In the fourth spring clean up the trunk by removing the pinched-back shoots. Protect the wounds by sealing them with bituminous paint.

Pruning an established tree
Very little pruning is necessary while the tree is well furnished with cropping wood and of manageable height. Each year cut out dead, broken, crowded or crossing branches, cutting them flush to avoid any snags. Prune in the spring and protect the wounds by sealing them with bituminous paint.

Grassing down For the first four or five years the soil around trained trees must be kept clear by maintaining a 3 ft wide border along the length of the wall over the spread of the tree. The border may then be planted to grass if the tree is developing in a satisfactory manner.

Dwarf and standard trees should also be grassed down after five years. For the grass mixture (see page 57). Keep the grass clear of the trunk of the tree, as not to do so will encourage pests or diseases.

Feeding and watering In March or April apply a balanced general fertilizer, such as 10-10-10, at 3 oz per square yard as a top dressing over the rooting area. Young trees, both fan-trained and in the open, should also be mulched to a depth of 2–3 in over an overall radius of 18 in.

Cherries against walls require watering in dry spells during the growing season. Once a good set of cherries has been achieved, water the border soil copiously in times of drought. Apply 1 in (4½ gal per square yard) over the rooting area every seven days (ten for the sour cherry) until rain falls. Keep the tree accustomed to moist soil conditions. Do not suddenly give heavy applications of water after the soil has become dry because this may cause the fruits to split and so spoil the subsequent crop.

Pollination
With one exception (the variety 'Stella') sweet cherries are not self-compatible, in fact, cross-incompatibility occurs. Most Duke cherries are self-compatible and can be planted singly but a few are not.

Protection against frost and birds
It is feasible to protect the blossom of a fan-trained tree against frost, but hardly practicable with a tall standard. Drape the fan with burlap or netting (see page 7). Other birds destroy the buds in the winter while starlings and blackbirds eat the ripe fruits. Protect the tree by covering it with adequate netting.

Harvesting
Leave the cherries on the tree until ripe unless they start cracking. Pick with the stalk on using scissors or shears: if fruits are pulled off and the stalk is left hanging it encourages brown rot. Cherries should be eaten as soon as possible after picking as they can deteriorate quite quickly.

Propagation
Cherries are propagated by budding, or by grafting on to rootstocks, tasks normally carried out by the nursery but which can be done by keen amateurs if great care is taken in the exercise.

Pests and diseases
Tent caterpillars, cherry slugs, and brown rot are the most troublesome problems. Cherry slug and tent caterpillar as well as most other problems can be controlled by a regular spray program. The program should include the application of a dormant oil in late winter or early spring followed by consistent use of a general-purpose fruit spray after petal fall. To prevent brown rot, spray the plants with captan during periods of warm and humid weather conditions.

The third year

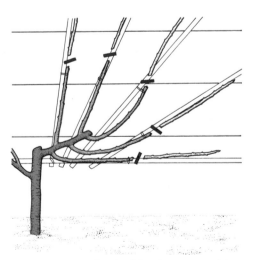

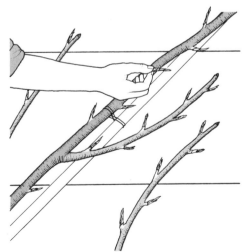

3 In spring, cut back all leaders to suitable buds, leaving 18–21 in of new growth.

Fourth and subsequent years

4 In spring, when most of the wall space has been filled, rub or cut out any breastwood or laterals growing directly towards the wall.

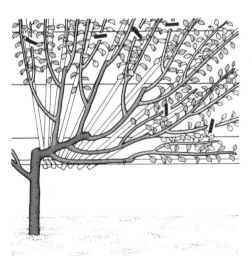

5 In late July, cut back to six leaves any laterals not wanted for the framework. When growth reaches the top of the wall, cut back to a weak lateral just below. Or, bend and tie down the shoots.

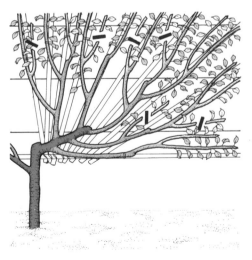

6 At the end of September, cut back to three leaves the laterals that were pinched out in July to encourage fruit buds to form at the base of the shoots in the following year.

Sour cherries

'Early Richmond' Very early soft fruits of medium quality.
'Meteor' Big, light red fruits. The tree is very hardy and does not grow much over 12 ft.
'Montmorency' Most widely grown sour cherry. Unusually large, attractive, crack-resistant fruits that may be eaten fresh when fully ripe but tart enough to make excellent pies and jams.
'Morello' (or 'English Morello'). Most widely planted sour cherry in England, but much less common in the United States. Large, dark red, almost black fruits with a bittersweet flavor when fully ripe. Tree is hardy and small, but not overly productive.
'North Star' Only 8 ft tall, this Minnesota variety is hardy yet grows even into the cooler areas of zone 8. Fruits are big and juicy.

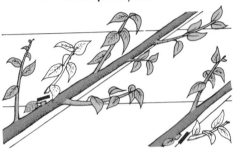

The sour cherry is a culinary fruit derived from *Prunus cerasus*. It is a hardy deciduous tree that is much less vigorous than the sweet cherry and can be grown in a small garden. There are two types of sour cherry: the Morello with dark red, almost black fruits and red juice; and the Amarelle, with red fruits and colorless juice. Both are self-compatible and can be planted singly in zones 4–7.

Cultivation
Usually grown as a small tree in the open, or as a fan on a wall, the sour cherry can also be grown as a central leader tree in pyramid form.

The sour cherry begins to bear fruit in its third or fourth year. A maiden tree can be planted but a few years are gained if a two- or three-year-old tree already partly shaped by the nursery is obtained.

Soil and situation Provided the soil is well drained, the sour cherry is tolerant of a wide range of soils but it prefers one that is neutral to slightly alkaline (pH 7.0).

The sour cherry flowers early in spring and so should not be planted in a frost pocket. It will tolerate partial shade and can be grown as a fan on a north-facing wall.

Planting and spacing Plant the tree when dormant in early spring. Prepare the soil and plant, stake and tie as for the sweet cherry (see page 62). Bush and central-leader trees should be staked for the first four or five years. For fan-trained trees, erect a support system of horizontal wires on the wall before planting. Use 14 gauge wire and stretch the wires at every 6 in or two brick courses (see page 9).

Space trees grown in the open 20–25 ft apart. Fans are spaced 12–15 ft.

Control weeds and grass by shallow hoeing or use weedkillers (see page 17). Leave a border of uncultivated soil around the tree.

Pruning the fan-trained tree
The formative pruning and training is the same as for a peach fan (see page 67), taking care to cut the leaders back hard in the first three years of training so that a head with plenty of ribs arising close to one another is formed.

Pruning the cropping tree is based on the fact that the sour cherry fruits almost solely on the growth made in the previous summer. As with the peach, the aim is to obtain a constant supply of strong new shoots to carry the next season's cherries.

In spring and early summer, thin out the new shoots to about 4–6 in apart along the framework branches. Leave one replacement shoot at the base of each fruit-carrying lateral. Tie the young shoots to the wires while they are still flexible. Do not pinch out the growing points of the young shoots, but let them extend where there is room.

After harvesting in mid-summer, cut out the laterals that have fruited back to the young replacement shoots.

Some sour cherries are relatively weak growing and the fruiting laterals do not readily produce replacement shoots near the base. If these fruiting laterals are left unpruned and no replacements form, they become extremely long with the base and center of the fan bare and the crop carried only on the perimeter. When this happens, in March, cut out a proportion of the three- and four-year-old branches back to younger laterals to stimulate the development of new growth.

Pruning the bush and pyramid
The initial training for these forms is the same as for the open-centered bush and pyramid plum. The leaders are cut back in early spring as growth begins to establish the framework.

Mature trees bear fruit along young wood formed in the previous season. In March cut back a proportion of the older shoots to one-year-old laterals or young shoots so that the old growth is continually replaced.

As the trees become older, the center may become bare and unproductive. Each year after harvesting, cut back one-third of the main branches to within about 3 ft of the head to produce vigorous young replacement branches. Protect the cuts with a wound paint.

Routine cultivation
For feeding, watering, protection, thinning, harvesting, propagation, pests and diseases see Sweet and Duke cherries (pages 62–3).

Fan-trained tree

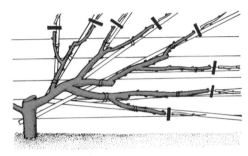

1 For the first three years, follow the eight steps for formative pruning of a peach fan (see pages 67–70), cutting the leaders back hard.

3 After harvesting, cut out the laterals that have fruited back to the young replacement shoots.

The mature tree

2 In March, cut back some of the older shoots to one-year-old laterals or young shoots to replace the older growth.

Fourth and subsequent years

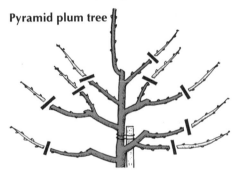

2 In spring and early summer, thin out new shoots to 4–6 in apart along the framework branches. Tie in young shoots to the wires.

Pyramid plum tree

1 For the first three years, follow the steps for the initial pruning of a pyramid plum. Cut back the leaders in early spring.

3 After harvesting, if the tree is bare and unproductive, cut back one-third of the main branches to within 3 ft of the head.

Figs 1

'Brown Turkey' Also called 'Southeastern Brown Turkey'. This is not the same 'Brown Turkey' variety grown in California. Medium-size, bronze fruits in summer and fall. Recommended for colder areas because it sets a good crop even after freezing.

'Celeste' Small violet to light brown fruits in mid-summer. Will not bear the same year it has been frozen.

'Green Ischia' Green, medium-size fruits. Midsummer. Very seedy. Will not bear in the same year it has been frozen.

'Hunt' Medium to small fruits. Dull bronze skin, white flecked. Mid-summer. Will not bear in the same year it has been frozen.

'Kadota' Also called 'Dottato' and

The fig (Ficus carica) is a deciduous tree considered to be native to the area ranging from Afghanistan to Syria. It has since spread and is now widely grown, and sometimes naturalized; in all the tropical, sub-tropical and warm temperate regions of the world. In the United States, the fig is grown in zones 8–10, but can also be cultivated in zones 6 and 7 if the trees or shrubs are given excellent winter protection.

The figs grown in cool temperate regions are parthenocarpic—that is, they will develop fruit without fertilization, so single trees can be grown.

Cultivation

In the Tropics the fig can yield three crops a year, in sub-tropical regions two, and in cool temperate areas only one.

Soil and situation The fig is tolerant of a wide range of soils provided they are well-drained. If nematodes are a problem, fumigate the soil before planting. Figs trained as trees should be spread 20 ft apart; those grown as shrubs require only 10 ft spacing. In colder climates where the plants cannot survive the winter, the bushes are often planted in containers. The containers should be at least 14 in across so that they can be moved into a frost-free spot in winter.

Figs are also grown in greenhouses, but this is not a common practice in the United States.

The fig requires warmth to ripen and so must be planted in the sunniest position possible. This means, for preference, on a south- or south-west-facing wall as a fan. It may also be grown as a bush in a sunny corner bounded by walls or in the open as a standard.

Preparing the site Before planting, fork into weed-free ground 2–3 oz per square yard of a balanced fertilizer, such as 10-10-10.

Planting the fan-trimmed fig Prepare the site for planting by digging a trough about 6 ft long, 2 ft wide by 2 ft deep. This will allow the tree to cover an 8 ft wall with a spread of 15 ft. Make a 2 ft square box if the tree is to cover a 6 ft high by 10–12 ft wide fence. Paving slabs 2 ft square are ideal for the purpose. The slabs of the sides of the container should protrude 1 in above the surrounding soil. For good soil drainage leave the base of the trough open but, to prevent the fig forming strong tap roots, tightly pack the bottom with broken bricks, mortar rubble or lumpy chalk to a depth of 9 in; then fill it up with a good fertile loam.

Plant the tree in the dormant season from February to April (see page 44), 9 in away from the wall.

To support the branches construct a system of horizontal wire supports on the wall using galvanized 14 gauge wire, spaced 12 in apart. Tie the branches to the wires with strong cord.

Planting a bush or tree in the open In a small garden and in zone 8 northward, a bush tree is best. The standard is more suitable for the large garden, and zones 9 and 10, because in such places it is unlikely to be damaged by the occasional freeze. Where possible, buy a two- or three-year-old tree with the framework partly formed by the nursery.

Standard trees should be planted to a stake. Drive in the stake, then plant the tree 2 in deeper than it grew at the nursery (see page 44). Secure the tree to the stake with a tree tie and cushion. Bushes are planted 4 in deeper than they previously grew and need not be staked unless in a very windy location.

Feeding and watering To maintain fruitfulness, each spring apply 2 oz of balanced fertilizer, such as a brand name like 8-8-8, as a top dressing over one square yard around the tree base, followed by a light mulch of stable mature rotted compost or peat. Apply a second feeding about 6–8 weeks later.

Irrigation is important because a growing fig needs a uniform supply of moisture. Frequent watering is required for plants in containers. Lack of moisture is a frequent cause of fruitlet drop in the spring.

Figs should not be fertilized in summer or watered heavily in late summer, thus forcing the plants into growth easily killed by frost.

Pruning a cropping tree It is important to understand the cropping habit of the fig grown in cool temperate areas because this governs the pruning. The fig bears two crops but only one ripens. The fruits that are successfully harvested are those which develop at the apex of the previous summer's shoots and extend back 6–12 in from the tip. They are carried over the winter as embryo fruits about the size of peas. Provided the

Formative pruning

1 Plant the tree to the same depth as it was at the nursery, spreading the roots well out. Firm the soil. If grown against a wall, plant it 9 in away from the wall.

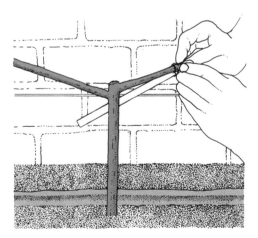

2 Construct a system of horizontal wire supports on the wall 12 in apart. Tie the branches to the wires with jute or other strong string.

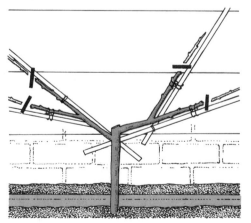

3 After last frost, prune back the leaders by about one-half to a bud. This encourages some of the remaining buds to break and produce more shoots for framework branches.

4 From June to July, select and tie in those shoots growing parallel with the wall so that they radiate out from the center like a fan. Rub out shoots growing towards the wall. Pinch back breastwood to three leaves.

Figs 2

'Florentine'. Large, yellow fruits in mid-summer and early fall. May sour in wet weather. Best grown in warmest regions. Fruit set is fairly good in the same year after freezing.
'Magnolia' Also called Brunswick. Bronze, medium-size fruits with white flecks. Mid-summer. Fruits sour and split badly in wet weather. Will produce fruit in the same year it has been frozen.
'Mission' Best home garden fig for California. Purple-black fruits in midsummer. Little pruning required.
'San Piero' Also called 'Thomson' and 'California Brown Turkey'. Very large, purplish-green fruits in summer and early fall. Fruits sour and split badly in wet weather.

embryo figs are not destroyed by cold, they develop in the following spring and summer to ripen in August and September. The second crop is produced on the growth made in the current season. These fruits develop throughout the summer but, if the growing season is not long or hot enough, they are still green by the autumn. They should then be removed. Their removal helps to divert the energies of the plant into developing embryo figs for the next summer.

Fan-trained tree: formative pruning

In the formative years the fig is pruned in the same way as the peach (see page 68), and the aim is to fill in the wall space with strong framework branches. When the hardest frosts are over, prune back each leader—there may be five or six—by about one-half to a bud. This is repeated every year until the wall is covered, which should take three or four years. Thereafter prune as for the cropping tree.

Pruning a mature fan-trained tree The aim is to produce each year a plentiful supply of shoots well ripened by the fall.

Pruning a mature fan-trained tree

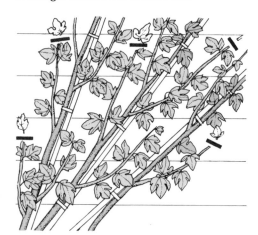

4 At the end of June, pinch out the growing points of about one-half of the young shoots carried by the main framework branches. As the shoots develop, tie them to the wires.

At the end of June pinch out the growing points of every other young shoot carried by the main framework branches. This encourages the lower buds to break and produce more shoots which will be hardy and produce their own embryo figs by the fall. As the shoots develop, tie them to the wires. In November prune back to 1 in half the shoots that carried fruits. This encourages new growth from the base in the following spring. All the remaining shoots should be tied in parallel with the wall. Aim for a 9–12 in spacing between the shoots, cutting back to source any growth in between. Do not overcrowd the framework because it is important that plenty of sunlight reaches the young growth, as well as the figs, in summer.

Standard tree: formative pruning

The first year With a very young tree where the framework branches have not been formed, select and leave one stout shoot to form the main stem, cutting the remainder back to their point of origin after frost danger is past. In the following growing season, train the chosen shoot up a stout cane driven into the ground 2 in away from the stem.

Next year cut the shoot to a bud at about 6 ft (it may be necessary to grow the tree on for a further year before this height is reached).

As a result of heading back, the lower buds should break to form the primary framework branches the following spring. Retain 4–6 well-spaced shoots close to the apex of the stem to form the framework. Cut out any shoots that appear below this.

The third year (or the first year if planting a two- or three-year-old with the framework partly formed). After frost danger is past, cut back the leader of each branch by about one-half to an outward-facing bud.

Subsequent pruning Very little pruning is necessary after the main framework has formed except to remove any badly placed branches. To rejuvenate an old fig where the branches have become rather gaunt and bare, each February cut out a proportion of the older wood back to a young shoot where these exist. In their absence leave a 1 in stub from which new growth will spring the following season.

Standard trees: the first year

1 After last frost, on a two- or three-year-old tree, cut back the leader of each branch by one-half to an outward-facing bud. Thereafter, little pruning is necessary after the main framework has formed except to remove any badly placed branches.

5 In November, prune back to 1 in half the shoots that carried fruits. This encourages new growth from the base in the following spring. All the remaining shoots should be tied in parallel with the wall 9–12 in apart. Cut back to source any growth in between.

Bush: First year Cut the plant back to half of height attained since planting. Allow the new growth to develop unchecked.

Second year Remove all but 4–6 strong, widely spaced stems in late winter. Cut these stems back to within 1 ft of the base.

Succeeding year The growth attained in the previous year, after frost danger is past, should be about 50 per cent. Entirely remove low-growing branches, suckers and deadwood.

Winter protection

Without protection the young shoots and embryo figs are likely to be damaged by frost. Protect them by thatching them loosely in bracken or material of a similar open nature. Use 6 in square plastic netting to retain the thatch. Remove the protection after the last of the hard frosts (see page 7).

In zones 6 and 7 and the colder parts of zone 8, prune bushes growing in the open to the desired height after the leaves have fallen. Tie the branches together and wrap in loose bundles covered with burlap and filled with straw and soil. The loose burlap bundles can then be wrapped tightly with polyethyelene film and the seams sealed.

More reliable protection can be had, especially in cold climates, by digging around the fig rootball and turning the plant on its side on the ground. The plant should then be covered with straw and soil in loose bundles of burlap, tightly wrapped with polyethylene film that has the seams sealed, and covered with soil.

Harvesting

Picked carefully and kept cool (but not in a refrigerator), figs will keep for 2–3 weeks but they are best eaten fresh.

Pests and diseases

Spray fig plants with Bordeaux mixture to control fig rust and leaf blight after the leaves are fully developed, then four weeks later, and again after the final harvest. The best method of controlling insects is to keep the plants clear of fallen leaves and fruit as well as cutting out deadwood. Plants with mites can be sprayed with a miticide as necessary.

Peaches and almonds 1

highest quality. Mid-season. Brown rot is a problem.
'Golden Jubilee' Large freestone fruits susceptible to bruising. Early.
'Halehaven' Large, delicious fruits. Freestone. Ready for picking about three weeks before Elberta. Tree is hardier than most.
'JH Hale' Famous variety but now used mostly for commercial canning. Large, freestone fruits in mid-season. Must be planted with another variety to ensure fruiting.
'Keystone' Grown in deep South. Freestone. Early.
'Redhaven' Excellent peach for eating out of hand. Semi-freestone. Fruits of medium size are all-over pink and have very little fuzz. Hang on trees even when fully ripe. Early. Very productive.
'Rio Oso Gem' Large, firm freestone fruits. Mid-season.
'Southland' Medium-size freestone fruits especially good for canning and freezing. Flesh does not turn brown when exposed to air. Early.
'Sun Haven' Medium to large fruits are

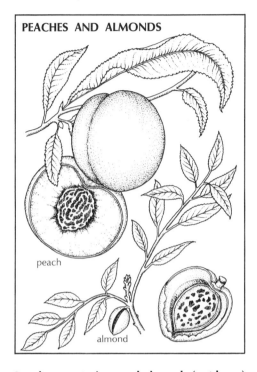

PEACHES AND ALMONDS

peach

almond

Peaches, nectarines and almonds (outdoors)
The peach (*Prunus persica*) is a small deciduous tree with long, tapering light green leaves and attractive pink flowers borne singly in the early spring. Despite its name, the peach did not originate in Persia, but almost certainly in China where it was cultivated for many centuries before being introduced to Europe. The peach is grown throughout the warm temperate regions of the world (zones 6–8).

The nectarine is a smooth-skinned sport, or mutation, of the peach. Generally the fruits are smaller than peaches and often considered to have a better flavor. For most cultural purposes, however, it is treated in exactly the same way as the peach.

The almond tree is similar in size, habit, leaf form and flower to the peach, but it blossoms even earlier and therefore in cooler areas the blooms are frequently destroyed by frost or affected by cold. For this reason in northern latitudes (zone 7) it is grown largely for its beautiful blossoms. The almond tree is a reliable producer of nuts in zone 8 and especially in zone 9. It does best in the hot Sacramento and San Joaquin valleys of California.

Cultivation
The peach and the nectarine are self-compatible and single trees can be planted. The almond is only partly self-compatible and two or more varieties should be planted.

Yield The yield from a peach or a nectarine can vary enormously depending upon the size of the tree and the environment. A good average. yield from a fan is about 30 lb and form a bush 30–100 lb.

Soil and situation The peach is tolerant of a wide range of soils but it is essential that they are well drained. To improve the drainage of a heavy soil place brick and stone rubble and chopped sods in the bottom of the planting hole. The ideal soil is a medium to heavy, moderately limey loam, not less than 18 in in depth with a pH of 6.7–7.0.

The peach is quite hardy, preferring a cold winter and a sunny dry spring rather than a warm, wet winter which causes the buds to open only to be damaged by subsequent frosts. The site must be in full sun and sheltered from cold winds and ideally not in a frost pocket. The peach flowers very early so it is ideally grown as a fan on a wall or fence with a southerly aspect where it can be protected against frost at flowering time and benefit from the warmth of the structure. When planted in the open, as it generally is, the peach can be placed on a northern slope or the north side of a building so that it will bloom late after frost danger is past.

Soil preparation Where there are poor soils at the base of a wall, it is worth while preparing the border specially (see page 44).

On good soils, however, it is sufficient to fork in a balanced fertilizer such as 10-10-10 at the rate of 3 oz per square yard with bonemeal at 3 oz per square yard over an area of two square yards.

Selecting the tree For a tree to grow in the open buy a well-feathered maiden tree. For a fan obtain a fan that is already partly formed. Choose one with 5–12 shoots (depending upon the age of the tree) that are evenly spaced to form the first ribs of the fan.

Planting Plant during the dormant season, usually in March or April. If planting a container-grown tree, it can be planted generally at any time. In the prepared soil, dig a hole wide and deep enough to take the roots fully spread out. Plant the tree to the same depth as it was at the nursery. Give each tree grown in the open a space of about 20 ft in diameter.

A fan must be planted 6–9 in away from the wall or fence to allow for growth, with the stem inclined slightly towards its support structure (see page 44).

After planting, apply a 2–3 in mulch of well-rotted manure, compost, peat or mushroom compost for 18 in around the tree.

A system of horizontal wires is necessary to support the fan. Fix the wires to the wall or fence every 6 in or two brick courses apart, starting at 12 in above the ground (see pages 8–9). Tie canes to the wires where needed with thin wire.

Pruning and training
Stone fruits such as the peach are pruned in late winter or early spring.

The fan-trained tree
The first year In March, starting with the feathered maiden tree, cut back to a lateral at about 24 in above the ground, ensuring that there are two good buds, or laterals, beneath it, one to the left and one to the right. Cut all remaining laterals to one bud. If there is not suitable lateral, cut back to a wood bud which is slender and pointed. If in doubt, cut to a triple bud which consists of two round flower buds and one wood bud.

In the early summer select three strong shoots. Train the topmost shoot vertically and of the other two, train one to the left and one to the right, choosing those that come from just below the bottom wire. Remove all other buds or shoots entirely.

As the two side-shoots lengthen, tie them to canes at an angle of 45 degress. When both these shoots are about 18 in long, in June or July, cut out the central shoot entirely. Protect the wound with a wound paint to prevent disease or pest infection.

The second year In March, cut back the two side-shoots to a wood or triple bud at 12–18 in from the main stem. This will induce new shoots in the coming summer. Protect the cuts with wound paint.

In summer, select four strong shoots from each arm. One to extend the existing rib, two equally spaced on the upper side and one on the lower side of the branch to give the tree a total of eight ribs by the end of the season. Pinch back all other shoots as they develop to one leaf.

Carefully train each new shoot to a cane to extend the wings of the fan. Keep the center open at this stage.

The third year In March, shorten each leader by about one-third, cutting to a downward-pointing wood bud. Paint the wounds.

In the summer, allow the leading shoot on each of the eight ribs to extend. Also select three more shoots on each branch and train these outwards, tying them to canes on the wires, to fill in the remaining space on the wall or fence. Rub out buds growing directly towards the structure and breastwood. Of the remaining buds, allow young shoots to grow every 4 in on the upper and lower sides of the ribs. Pinch back to one leaf any surplus shoots. Repeat this process as and when necessary throughout the summer. When the selected laterals have made 18 in of growth, pinch out the growing points, unless they are required as part of the framework. In late summer tie them to canes on the wires. Fruit will be borne on these laterals in the following summer.

Fourth and subsequent years From this point onwards the tree must be regarded as a cropping tree. The wall or fence should now be more or less completely covered with framework branches on which every 4 in are fruit-bearing laterals.

The peach carries its fruits on shoots made during the previous summer so pruning is aimed at a constant and annual renewal of young shoots. It follows also that the shoots which have borne fruits are cut out to make room for the new young ones.

Each late spring, about May, remove shoots growing directly towards and away from the wall or fence but leave one or two leaves or shoots which have flower buds at the base. Next deal with the previous summer's laterals which should be carrying both blossom and

Peaches and almonds 2

PEACHES
'Elberta' Standard variety by which others are usually judged.
'Freestone' Large, yellow fruits with a bright blush. Sweet yellow flesh, but a little coarse. Mid-season. Large, productive tree, but fairly tender.
'Blake' Large, yellow fruits of fine flavor and texture. Freestone. Mid-season.

'Bonanza' This dwarf starts bearing when only 3 ft tall and never grows over 7 ft. Good for container growing. Large, yellow fruits of fair quality.
'Champion' Old, white-fleshed variety of good flavor. Large fruits in mid-season. Freestone.
'Crawford' Most famous of the peaches grown in the United States almost 200

years ago. Fruits almost entirely red and of fine flavor. Clingstone. Late.
'Dixired' Best very early variety. Moderate-size fruits of nice flavor. Semi-freestone.
'George IV' Excellent freestone peach with white flesh of rare flavor. Mid-season.
'Georgia Belle' Freestone. White flesh of

side-shoots. Select one side-shoot at the base as the replacement, one in the middle as a reserve and one at the top to extend the fruit-carrying lateral. Pinch back the remaining side-shoots to two leaves. When the basal side-shoot and the reserve lateral are 18 in long and the fruit-carrying lateral has a further six leaves, pinch out the growing points of each.

Pruning the standard tree The formative pruning is the same as for an apple (see page 47).

In the cropping years the objective is to encourage plenty of strong new growth each year to carry fruit in the next summer. This new growth is then cut back 50 per cent or more in the early spring of the year if it is to bear fruit. Long branches at the top of the tree should be removed at the same time. It is occasionally necessary to cut back some of the older wood which has become bare to young healthy replacements. Avoid, however, making large wounds because peaches are susceptible to bacterial canker.

Feeding and watering In early spring each year apply a balanced fertilizer such as 10-10-10 at the rate of 3 oz per square yard as a top dressing over the rooting area. Replenish the mulch if necessary.

Trees over the age of three years need nothing more than nitrate of soda or ammonium sulfate unless a soil test indicates the soil has a potassium or phosphorus deficiency.

Keep the soil moist at all times until just before the fruit begins to ripen. Ample water is essential to good production. But it is also important to keep the tree accustomed to moist soil conditions at all times. In other words, do not suddenly apply a lot of water near ripening time because there is the risk of splitting the fruits. Because the soil at the base of a wall tends to dry out rapidly, fan-trained peaches must be watered with special care. Direct water at the base of the tree so that moisture gets to the roots. Do not wet the foliage.

Frost protection
Protection of the blossom against frost is also essential from pink bud stage until the danger of frost has passed. Drape the fan-trained tree with burlap or bird netting (see page 17). Remove during the day.

Planting

1 Before planting, fork in 3 oz per square yard of a balanced fertilizer, such as 10-10-10, with 3 oz bonemeal. Repeat every March.

2 In March or April, plant during the dormant season. A fan should be 6–9 in away from the wall or fence with the stem inclined towards it.

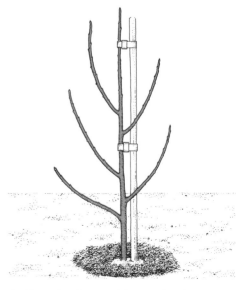

3 After planting, mulch to a depth of 2–3 in with manure or compost for 18 in around the tree. Replenish every year in late winter.

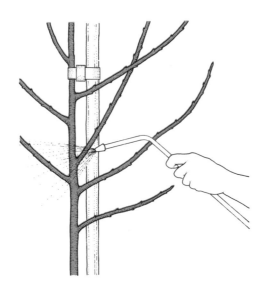

4 In March, spray with a copper fungicide or Bordeaux mixture against peach leaf curl. Also spray with dormant oil.

Thinning

5 From early May to July, thin the fruits, starting when they are the size of large peas.

Harvesting

6 From August onwards, pick the fruit when the flesh feels soft at the stalk end. Hold the fruit in the palm of the hand, lift and twist it slightly.

Peaches and almonds 3

bright red with yellow cheeks. Freestone. Ripen 40 days before Elberta. Very hardy.
'Springtime' White-fleshed, clingstone fruits grown in the South. Ripen two months before 'Elberta'.
'Vedette' A freestone originated in Canada and suitable for zone 5. Early.

NECTARINES
'Cavalier' Small fruits with firm, aromatic flesh. Freestone. Vigorous.
'Cherokee' Large, semi-clingstone of excellent quality. Very early.
'Lexington' Freestone. Tree is unusually hardy and vigorous.
'Pocahontas' Mild, good quality, semi-clingstone fruits. Less troubled by brown

Thinning

To obtain good-sized fruits it is essential to thin the fruits. Thin over a period, starting when the fruitlets are the size of large peas and stopping when they are the size of walnuts. Peaches should be 9 in apart and nectarines 6 in aprt after the final thinning.

Harvesting peaches and nectarines

The fruit is ripe when it has a reddish flush and the flesh feels soft near the stalk end. Hold the peach in the palm of the hand, lift and twist it slightly. It should part easily from the tree. Store the fruits in a cool place until they are to be eaten. They will keep for only up to a week and for long-term storage they must be canned or frozen without the stones.

Pruning the fan-trained tree after harvesting

Immediately after cropping, not later than the end of September, cut out the laterals which carried the fruits back to the replacement shoots. Tie in the young shoots and cut out any dead or broken branches.

Once the peach has reached the required height and spread, remove any unwanted extension growth by cutting to a lateral further back along the branch. Cut out bare wood back to strong young replacements. Protect the wounds with a wound paint.

Harvesting and storage of almonds

Harvest the nuts when the husks split and the nuts fall naturally. Remove the nuts from the husks and dry them thoroughly in well-ventilated conditions: in sunshine is ideal, or in an airing cupboard. Keep the nuts off the ground by laying them on wire netting to allow air circulation. Once dry they should be kept in cool and dry conditions.

If squirrels are troublesome, harvest the nuts slightly earlier and dry both husk and nut initially before splitting them open.

Propagation

Peaches, nectarines and almonds are propagated by budding or grafting, a task normally carried out by the nursery, but it can be performed by the keen amateur.

Pests and diseases

Peaches and nectarines are attacked by a number of diseases and insects but this need not cause worry if a consistent spray program is followed faithfully. A dormant oil can be sprayed on in late winter. Then, after about 75 per cent of the petals have fallen, apply a general fruit-tree spray and continue with this at about two-week intervals for the next wo months, or even up to within a month of harvest. Such treatment will take care of most problems.

To control brown rot, especially troublesome on nectarines and, in some years, just about as bad on peaches, spray with captan. Do this every three days if there is a spell of hot, humid weather at the time of bloom. Captan spraying can also be carried out in the three-week period prior to harvest as well as during a hot and humid spell.

Leaf curl causes first leaves to thicken and curl as well as tinting them red and yellow. To control this, apply a liquid copper fungicide before the buds open in the spring. Bordeaux misture can also be employed, and, if so, it is mixed and applied with dormant oil. Almonds require regular spraying with a general-purpose fruit spray.

The fan-trained tree: the first year

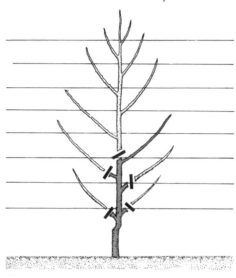

1 In March, cut back a feathered maiden peach to a lateral about 24 in above the ground, leaving one good bud on each side beneath it. Cut remaining laterals to one bud.

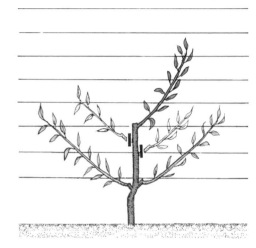

2 In early summer, select three shoots. Train the topmost vertically, and one to the left and one to the right. Remove all other buds or shoots.

The second year

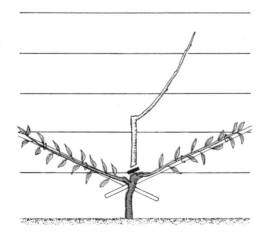

3 In June or July, tie the lengthening side-shoots to canes set at an angle of 45 degrees. Later that summer, cut out central shoot and protect cut with wound paint.

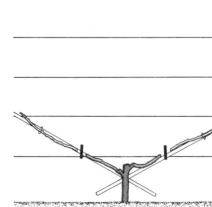

4 In March, cut back the two side-shoots to a wood or triple bud at 12–18 in from the main stem. Protect the cuts with wound paint.

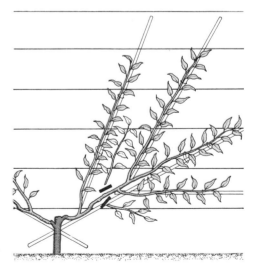

5 In summer, select four shoots on each arm, one to extend the existing rib, two spaced equally on the upper side and one on the lower. Stop other shoots at one leaf.

Peaches and almonds 4

spot than the majority of nectarines.
'Redbud' Early freestone with white flesh.
'Redchief' Bright red fruits with strongly
flavored white flesh. Medium-size.
Freestone. Mid-season. Better-than-
average resistance to brown rot.
'Rivers Orange' Small freestone fruits
covered all over with a red blush.

ALMONDS
'Hal's Hardy' Self-fruitful variety with
hard-shelled nuts of medium quality.
Does best in zones 7 and 8.
'Nonpareil' Most common variety and
most widely planted. Early nuts with
paper-thin shells, uniform and excellent.
'Texas Prolific' (or simply 'Texas'). Late
hard-shelled variety of good quality.

The third year

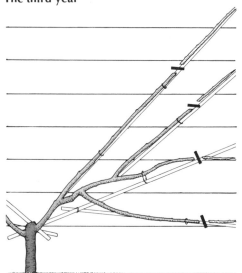

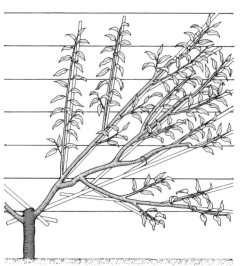

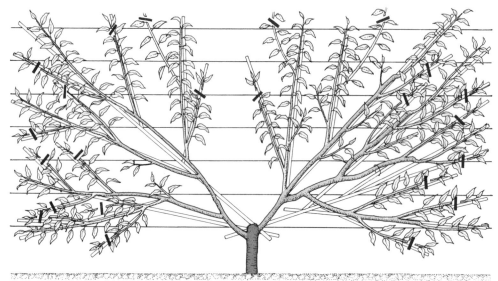

6 In March, shorten each leader by one-third by cutting to a downward-pointing wood bud. Protect the cuts.

7 In summer, allow the leading shoots on each rib to extend. Train three shoots on each branch outwards, tying them to canes. Allow shoots to grow every 4 in.

8 In late summer, when the selected laterals have made 18 in of new growth, pinch out the growing points of each and tie them to canes on the wires. These laterals will bear fruit the following summer.

Fourth and subsequent years

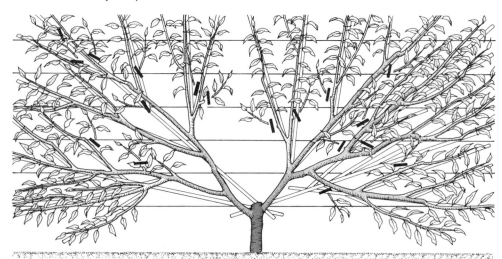

9 Each year in about May, remove shoots growing directly towards and away from the wall or fence. Leave shoots with flower buds at their base one or two leaves.

10 Select two replacement laterals on each leader: one at the base and a reserve in the middle. Allow a lateral to extend the fruit-carrying lateral. When the basal and reserve laterals are 18 in long and the extension has six leaves, pinch out the growing points. After harvesting, cut the fruited laterals back to their replacements.

Apricots

'Alfred' Good flavor. Fruit medium to large, round and flattened, orange with pink flush; flesh orange and juicy. Ripens late July to early August. Tends to biennial cropping. Flowers early.
'Early Moorpark' Rich flavor. Fruit round to oval, yellow with crimson flush and darker mottling; flesh deep orange and juicy. Ripens late July. Heavy cropping.

'Farmingdale' Very good flavor. Fruit medium, roundish, orange-yellow with red flush; flesh orange and moderately juicy. Ripens late July. Heavy cropper. Vigorous, fairly disease-resistant tree.
'Moorpark' Very popular variety. Rich sweet flavor. Fruit large, uneven round, pale yellow with reddish-brown flush. Ripens late August. Regular.

'Moongold' Sweet, firm, slightly flattened, yellow freestone fruits in mid-July. Hardy to zone 4, sturdy and vigorous. Plant with 'Sungold'.
'Riland' Grown mainly in West. Medium-size fruits with excellent flavor. Red-blushed skin. Early.
'Royal' Popular old variety widely grown in California. Medium-big, fine textured

fruits with orange skin. Mid-season.
'Sungold' Medium-size round fruits colored gold with orange blush. Ripens a week later than 'Moongold' with which it should be planted to ensure pollination.

The apricot (*Prunus armeniaca*) is a hardy deciduous tree. It is a native of China and is widely grown in California and Washington, but can be raised successfully elsewhere in zones 5–8.

Cultivation

A dwarf tree is best for the garden where space is limited. Even this can reach a height of 8 ft and a span of 15 ft. Buy a two- or three-year-old tree.

Soil and situation The apricot needs a well-drained but moisture-retentive and slightly alkaline soil with a pH range of 6.5–8.0. Light, sandy soils are not suitable.

Warmth in summer is essential and, although the apricot can be grown in the open in warm temperate areas, it thrives best fan-trained against a south- or west-facing wall in the cooler regions. It can also be grown successfully in containers.

Shelter the tree from frost and wind to encourage pollinating insects and to protect the ripening fruit. Keep the soil around the tree clear of weeds and grass so that ample moisture can reach the roots.

Planting In all but the mildest climates, where fall planting is safe, apricots should be planted only in the spring. To prepare the ground, clear away perennial weeds over an area 3 ft square. Dig in well-rotted manure or compost at a rate of one 2-gal bucketful per square yard. Plant the tree, water well, and mulch lightly.

Plant fan-trained trees 15 ft apart and 6 in from the wall or fence. Plant bush trees 15–20 ft apart.

Formative pruning and training The formative pruning of the fan-trained apricot is the same as that of the fan-trained peach. The formative pruning of the bush apricot is the same as that of the bush plum, but prune it in early spring before growth begins.

Pruning the cropping tree Mature fan-trained apricots are pruned in the same way as are fan-trained plums. Mature bush apricots are pruned in the same way as sour cherries (see page 64).

The apricot carries the best quality and most abundant crops on short spurs on two- and three-year-old wood. Extensive pruning is not necessary because it results in a poor crop. Every four to six years, cut out the older shoots that have fruited to make room for new young ones. This means cutting out some of the lateral and sub-lateral branches of a fan-trained tree. Retain and tie in the same number of new shoots to replace them. Do not prune or pinch back these shoots until the second season, but only if required.

Thinning Thin the fruits at intervals from the time they are the size of cherries until they are almost full size. First remove misshapen fruits and those growing towards the wall. Later, thin pairs and clusters so that those left to ripen have 3–4 in between them.

Feeding Root dryness is a common problem with wall-trained trees. Water generously until the root area is soaked, especially if the weather is dry when the fruit is setting or when it starts to swell.

In late winter, sprinkle an artificial fertilizer containing calcium carbonate and ammonium nitrate around the tree at a rate of 1 oz per square yard and apply a general fertilizer, such as 10-10-10, at a rate of 2 oz per square yard. Every four years, if necessary, apply ground limestone to maintain the pH at a little above 7.0. In late spring, mulch the root area to 1 in.

Pollination Most apricots are self-compatible but, because the flowers open early in spring when few insects are about, hand pollination is sometimes necessary (see page 43). The new and very hardy 'Moongold' and 'Sungold' are not self-fruitful and must be planted together.

Protecting the blossom The apricot is highly susceptible to frost damage. Protect it with polyethylene or netting (see pages 6–7).

Harvesting

Depending on the variety, apricots ripen from midsummer to early fall. Pick the ripe fruit carefully and try not to break the skin.

Pests and diseases

Spray trees on the same schedule and with the same materials as peach trees. The trees are very susceptible to brown rot if the weather is humid and warm at the time of bloom and in the three weeks before harvest starts. To control this, spray frequently with captan during these periods.

1 In early spring, in prepared ground dig a hole large enough for the roots. Plant at the same depth as at the nursery. Mulch well.

The first year

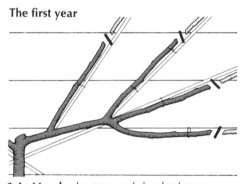

3 In March, shorten each leader by one-third, leaving about 30 in of growth.

The second and subsequent years

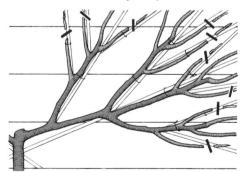

5 In spring, rub out buds pointing towards or away from the wall or fence. Prune the leaders by one-quarter.

A three-year-old fan-trained tree

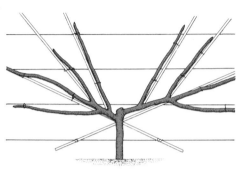

2 Erect supporting horizontal wires 9 in apart on the wall or fence. Tie in the young branches to the canes on the wall wires.

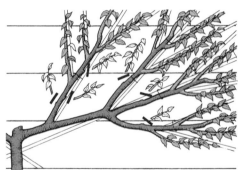

4 In July/August, select and tie in three additional shoots from each pruned leader. Pinch out all remaining shoots.

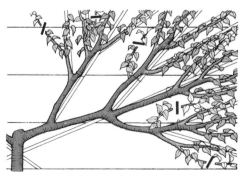

6 Early in July, pinch off the tips of side-shoots at six leaves. After cropping, cut back these laterals by one-half.

Mulberries

'Large Black' Good sub-acid flavor. Fruit oblong, crimson ripening to purplish-black. Very juicy. Suitable for culinary and dessert use. Ripens in September. Attractive spreading tree.
'Red' Good piquant flavor. Fruit cylindrical, bright red ripening to reddish purple. Suitable for dessert and culinary use. Ripens September.

The common or large black mulberry (*Morus nigra*) is a deciduous tree native to western Asia. In the United States it grows from zone 6 southward. The red-black fruits resemble loganberries and have a sharp but sweet flavor particularly suitable for cooking.

Cultivation
The mulberry is long-lived and decorative. It is self-compatible and so will fruit if grown as a single plant. When mature it reaches a height of 20–30 ft.

Soil and situation The mulberry is tolerant of a variety of soils but thrives best planted in rich, fertile well-drained but moisture-retentive soil with a pH of 5.5–7.0.

It should be planted in a sheltered, warm and sunny position. In the coldest areas it is best grown against a south-facing wall or fence.

Planting In early spring prepare the ground thoroughly, clearing away perennial weeds over an area 3 ft square. For planting in the open, drive in a stake to reach just below the lowest branches. For wall- or fence-trained trees, construct a system of supporting horizontal wires, spaced every 9 in (see pages 8–9).

Dig a hole wide and deep enough to take the roots fully extended. The roots are brittle and so take care not to damage them at planting. Never dig near a mulberry tree.

Plant the tree to the same depth as in the nursery, spreading the roots out well. Return the soil and firm it carefully. Tie the tree to the stake with a tree tie and cushion. For wall-trained trees, tie in the branches to the wall wires. Water well and mulch with well-rotted manure or compost.

Pruning and training The mulberry is slow growing, taking eight to ten years to begin cropping, so a three- to five-year-old tree already shaped at the nursery is best.

Prune mulberries grown in the open in winter. Cut back to four or five buds any strong laterals longer than 12 in that are not required as framework branches. Remove or shorten any which spoil the shape of the head. Protect the cuts with a wound paint.

Prune wall-trained mulberries in summer. Train in the main branches 15–18 in apart to cover the wall. Tie down the leaders at the end of the summer and once they have reached the required length stop them by cutting back each leader to one bud on the previous year's growth in April. Prune side-shoots to four or five leaves in late July to encourage fruit spurs to form.

The branches of mature trees become crooked and brittle and may need supporting with a forked stake. Wrap the branch with burlap where it meets the crotch.

Watering and feeding Watering is necessary in extremely dry weather.

In April, apply a balanced fertilizer, such as 10-10-10, at a rate of 2 oz per square yard. In spring, mulch with well-rotted manure or compost.

Propagation
Propagate from cuttings. In early October, after leaf-fall, remove a one-year-old stem with all the year's growth. Make a sloping cut just above the proposed top bud and a horizontal cut about 6 in below it. Dip the basal cut only in rooting hormone. Heel in several cuttings, in bundles of ten, into a sandbox almost to their full depth. Label them and leave for the winter.

Just before the dormant buds break in spring, dig the propagation bed thoroughly. Make a furrow 5 in deep. Lift the cuttings and plant vertically 4–6 in apart. Firm back the soil leaving about 1 in of the cutting exposed. The following fall, lift and transplant the rooted cutting.

Harvesting
The fruit ripens from late August over a period of about three weeks. Pick fruit for cooking when it is slightly unripe. Fruit for eating is almost black.

Pests and diseases
The mulberry is generally free of pests and diseases but protect the ripening fruit against birds (see page 17).

Trees in the open

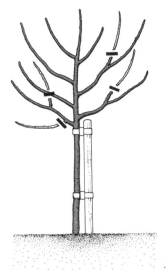

1 In spring, clear the ground of perennial weeds. Dig a hole wide and deep enough to take the roots. Drive in a stake.

2 Plant the tree, spreading the roots out. Return and firm the soil. Tie the tree to the stake. Water well. Mulch with manure or compost.

3 In winter, cut back to four or five buds laterals longer than 12 in not required for the framework. Cut out branches spoiling the head.

Wall-trained trees

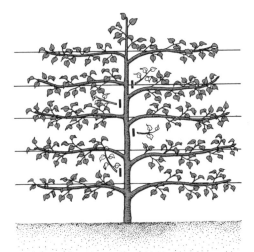

1 In summer, train in the main branches 15–18 in apart. Tie down the leaders at the end of summer. Cut out breastwood and any branches growing into the wall.

2 In April, once the leaders have reached the required length, stop them by cutting back to one bud on the previous year's growth. In late July, prune the side-shoots to four or five leaves.

Elderberries

The common elder (*Sambucus nigra*) is a deciduous tree native to Europe, western Asia and parts of northern Africa and now grows wild over much of the USA and Canada. The shiny purple-black blue or red berries are widely used in preserves, and both the fruit and flowers are popular for making wine. The plant grows as a large shrub or small tree and is often considered too wild and vigorous for the garden. Its new woody growth gives off an unpleasant smell and was used in the past as a fly-repellent. In the northern USA, the American or sweet elder (*S. canadensis*) is widely grown and several improved clones are available. They have an extremely high Vitamin C content. Depending on the variety, they grow from zones 3–9, but are not common in zones 5–8.

Cultivation
Only elders with black berries are grown for their fruit. The red-fruited kinds are inedible.
Soil and situation The elder is tolerant of a wide variety of soils, including those with bad drainage, and a wide range of soil pH. It is lime-tolerant.

The elder will grow in most situations but it fruits most freely in a sunny position. Common elder is hardy to zone 6; *S. canadensis* in zone 3.
Planting The elder may be grown as a standard on a single stem but it is more usually grown as a large rounded bush with a number of branches from near ground level.

Plant a one- or two-year-old tree in early spring. Four weeks before planting prepare the ground, clearing away perennial weeds over an area 3 ft square. Fork in a balanced fertilizer, such as a brand of 10-10-10 at a rate of 3 oz per square yard.

Dig a hole wide and deep enough to take the roots fully extended. For standards, drive in a stake to reach just below the lowest branches. Place the plant in the hole at the same depth as at the nursery and then fill in the soil gradually, firming it at the same time. Tie the standard to the stake with a tree tie and cushion. The bush does not need staking.

The American elder is not self-compatible. For cross-pollination to occur there should be a minimum of two varieties, planted about 10ft apart.

Pruning After planting, cut out weak and damaged growth and cut back main shoots by a few inches to a good, outward-facing bud. This ensures that during the first growing season the plant's energy is concentrated on producing a strong basic framework of branches. Cut back any unwanted suckers to ground level. Little flower is produced in the first year.

In subsequent years, in late winter, cut out dead and congested branches to maintain a good shape. Cut out about a quarter of the old wood back to base each year to encourage new growth. Cut back unwanted suckers to ground level and protect the cuts with a wound paint.
Feeding In dry spring and summer weather water well and mulch the root area with well-rotted manure or compost. If growth is weak or slow, feed with a balanced fertilizer at a rate of 2 oz per square yard.

A 5-20-10 balanced fertilizer or ammonium nitrate can be applied each spring. Ammonium nitrate may be applied at 1oz per year of shrub age up to a maximum of 16 oz, and 5-20-10 fertilizer at 16 oz per year up to a maximum of 64 oz.

Propagation
In late October take a 9–12 in cutting from a sturdy one-year-old stem. Plant in open ground 6 in deep. Alternatively, in July, take 4–6 in cuttings of semi-hard wood stems. Insert them 2 in deep in a cold frame 4–6 in apart. In October in the following year, lift the rooted cuttings and re-plant them in a permanent position.

Harvesting
Pick fruits when dark in color with a noticeable bloom. It is preferable to use them as soon as possible, but they will keep in a refrigerator for about two weeks.

Pests and diseases
The elder is generally free of pests and diseases, except for the elder borer, which deposits its eggs under the bark of old canes. This pest can be controlled by burning annual prunings. If mites become troublesome, spray with a miticide. Plants may need to be netted to keep off birds.

The first year

 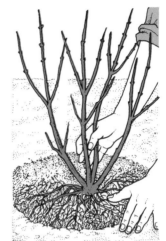 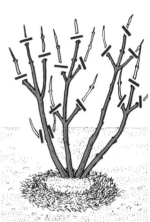

1 Four weeks before planting, clear away weeds over an area 3 ft square. Fork in a general fertilizer at 3 oz per square yard.

2 In spring, plant the elder at the same depth as it was in the nursery, spreading the roots out. Firm the soil. Water well.

3 After planting, cut out all weak growth and cut back the main shoots a few inches to a good outward-facing bud. Mulch well.

Second and subsequent years

4 In April, if growth is slow, feed with a balanced fertilizer at a rate of 2 oz per square yard.

5 In winter, cut out dead and congested branches. Cut out about a quarter of the old wood back to base. Seal the cuts with a wound paint.

Quinces 1

'Champion' Fruit round, 4 in diameter, yellow; flavor delicate. Tree very productive, starting to bear freely when young.
'Orange' Most popular. Fruits resemble orange apples. Early.
'Pineapple' Rounded, light yellow fruits have a flavor suggestive of the pineapple. Popular variety in California. Mid-season.

'Van Deman' Descendant of 'Orange'. Large fruits. Early.

QUINCES

Quince blossom

Apple-shaped quince

Pear-shaped quince

The true quince (*Cydonia oblonga*) is a native of central to south-western Asia. It has been cultivated since ancient times. It is related to the pear, for which it is often used as a rootstock to induce a more dwarfing effect on the vigor of the pear tree. The true quince is often confused with its distant relatives the oriental quinces (*Chaenomeles* spp), referred to as "Japonicas", which are grown as garden shrubs. "Japonicas" have light pink to deep red flowers, spines and edible fruits.

The true quince is a low, deciduous, thornless tree with a crooked irregular mode of growth. When fully grown it is about 15 ft in height and spread, although it can be half as tall again on fertile soils. It may also be grown as a fan against a warm wall in much the same way as a pear. This method is particularly suitable for more northerly areas where it would not thrive in the open.

The tree's natural form is attractive and it can serve an ornamental purpose in the garden. It often lives to a great age and, once established, requires little attention. It comes into cropping in the fourth to fifth year. The flowers are large (1½–2 in), solitary, white to very light pink and most attractive, resembling the wild dog-rose. It has a pale grey bark and dark green oval leaves with downy white undersides.

Quince fruits are apple- or pear-shaped, mostly with a grayish-white down on the skin; when ripe they are pale or deep, clear, golden-yellow. The flavor is acid and astringent, and the texture rather gritty—they are too harsh, in fact, to be eaten raw when grown in northern climates. When grown in warmer, sunnier areas (such as Turkey), the fruits become much sweeter and are eaten raw. Quinces are not grown commercially in cool temperate areas, but they can be cultivated fairly easily by the amateur, providing an interesting alternative to the more conventional tree fruits.

Quinces make a delicious orange-colored jelly, marmalade or preserve; and a slice or two of quince in an apple pie provides a subtle aromatic taste to the dish.

Cultivation

The tree is hardy in zones 5–8, but, as mentioned above, warmth is necessary for the fruits to ripen properly. Quinces can be raised from seed but this is a lengthy process so buy a plant from a nursery or garden centre and ask advice.

Soil and situation The quince succeeds in most soils but grows best in a deep, light, fertile and moisture-retentive soil.

It does well planted near a pond or stream. In warmer areas, it can be grown in the open, but in a sunny, sheltered position. In more northerly areas, extra protection is needed, the best situation being a sunny corner where two walls meet, with the plant grown as a fan or bush tree.

Planting and spacing Since it grows rather crooked, the quince tree needs support for the first three or four years of its life until the stem has acquired sufficient strength to support the head.

Plant in early spring during the dormant period. Container-grown plants can be planted at any time of the year. Prepare the ground thoroughly in the fall before planting, clearing away perennial weeds over an area 3 ft square. Fork in 4 oz per square yard of a balanced fertilizer such as 10-10-10 and a

Planting the tree

1 Between November and March, prepare the ground, clearing away perennial weeds over an area roughly 3 ft square. Choose the planting position carefully.

2 Fork in 4 oz of a balanced fertilizer such as 10-10-10 and a handful of bonemeal over the area where the tree is to be planted.

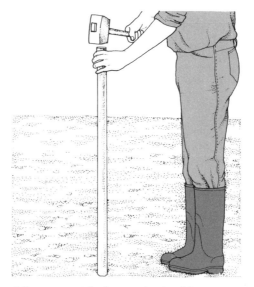

3 Prepare a stake by coating it with bituminous paint. Drive it about 1½–2 ft into the ground. Be sure it is not loose.

4 Dig the planting hole deep and wide enough to accommodate the tree's whole root system with tendrils well spread out.

Quinces 2

handful of bonemeal. Drive the supporting stake in first so that it will just clear the lowest branches. Dig a hole deep and wide enough to take the whole root system with the roots spread well out. Plant with the main stem about 2 in away from the stake and the tree at the same depth as it was in the nursery, ensuring that the union between the root-stock and scion (grafted stem) is not less than 4 in above soil level. Firm the soil well. Tie the tree to the stake with a tree tie and cushion.

Dwarf trees should be spaced about 10–12 ft apart, semi-dwarfs at about 15 ft, and standards about 20 ft apart.

Pruning and feeding The quince is a difficult tree to train in the first year, and so it is best to obtain a tree already partly shaped by the nursery. Buy a two-year-old for a dwarf tree or a three-or four-year-old for a standard or semi-dwarf.

The aim is to achieve a goblet-shaped tree with an open but by no means barren center. Prune during winter for the first three or four years by cutting back the leaders of the main framework branches by one-half the previous

summer's growth, to an outward-facing bud. Prune back to two or three buds any side shoots that compete with the leaders and those crowding the center. Leave other side shoots unpruned to fill in the framework where there is room. Twist off any suckers around the base and cut off unwanted shoots on the main stem back to their point of origin. After the fourth year, little pruning is necessary apart from the removal of shoots that cause crowding, low-lying branches, or suckers at the base. The quince bears its fruit on spurs and on the tips of the previous summer's growth, therefore prune only to keep the head tidy. Cut back any vigorous or badly placed laterals but do not prune every lateral otherwise a large number of fruit buds will be lost.

Each March apply a general fertilizer such as 10-10-10 at 3 oz per square yard, and in early April apply sulfate of ammonia at 1 oz per square yard. On poor soils, mulch the trees in the early spring with well-rotted manure or compost. Maintain a weed-free area over an 18 in radius around the base of the tree.

Harvesting and storing

The fruits should be left on the tree as long as possible to develop their full characteristic flavor, provided there is no danger of frosts. They usually ripen from the middle of September on, depending on the locality. Once gathered, they should be stored in trays or apple boxes in a cool dark place and allowed to mellow for about a month before use. Quinces are strongly aromatic and should be stored by themselves because their aroma will affect the taste of any other fruits stored in the same container.

Pests and diseases

Many of the insect pests such as aphids, codling moth, slugworm and various caterpillars that attack apples and pears also attack quinces. If these pests prove troublesome, a spray program similar to that for apples and pears may be used.

The only diseases that may occur are leaf blight (*Entomosporium maculatum*) and brown rot of the fruit. To prevent them, spray with Bordeaux mixture in mid-June and again two or three weeks later.

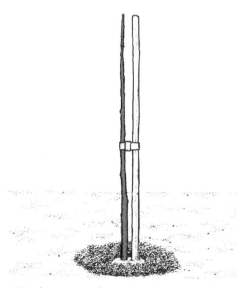

5 Then, plant the tree to the same depth as it was at the nursery, about 2 in away from the stake, firming well during planting.

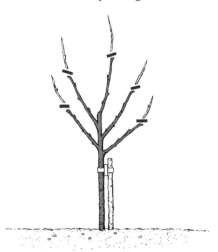

6 Tie the tree to the stake using a tree tie and cushion. In the second year, it may be necessary to prop the tree up if the crop is heavy.

The first winter after planting

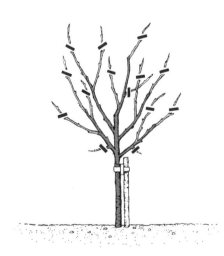

7 Cut back the leaders of the main framework branches by about one-third, pruning each to an outward-facing bud. Cut back to 2–3 buds weak lateral shoots.

In the second and third years

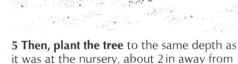

8 In winter, cut back the leaders of the main framework branches by about one-third to an outward-facing bud. Cut back weak lateral shoots to 2–3 buds.

Hazelnuts

FILBERT
Filberts are self-unfruitful. Plant two or more varieties together.
'Barcelona' Standard variety grown in the Northwest. Medium-large nuts. Tree spreading and productive but tends to biennial bearing.
'Bixby' Hybrid filbert widely planted in East. Hardy, prolific producer.

'DuChilly' Another European variety popular in Northwest. Long, large nuts. Medium producer.
'Davianna' European variety. Medium-size, thin-shelled, good quality nuts. Light producer.
'Medium Long' Unusually hardy European variety can be grown to zone 6. Medium-size nuts of good flavor.

'Nooksack' Another fairly hardy European variety. Popular in Washington State.
'Potomac' Hybrid producing a great many large nuts of fine flavor.
'Purple Filbert' Excellent flavor. Medium nuts in purple-red husk. Long, dark red catkins. Moderate cropper. Vigorous and ornamental tree. Requires a pollinator.

'Red Filbert' Excellent flavor. Small, long and narrow nut with a reddish husk. Catkins sparse, long, claret-red. Moderate cropper. Vigorous and ornamental tree. Requires a pollinator.
'Reed' Hybrid. Tasty, medium-size nuts.
'White Filbert' Similar to 'Red Filbert' but with a white husk over the nut.

Botanical authorities have recently decreed that the small shrubby nut trees belonging to the *Corylus* genus should all be called filberts. To many people, however, they are still, and always will be, hazels or hazelnuts. They are frequently found growing wild in the Northeast of the United States. Cultivation is most common in zones 8 and 9 in the Northwest; but the plants do fairly well in zones 6 and 7 more or less everywhere.

In the Northwest, most filberts grown are European varieties. American varieties are hardier, but produce smaller nuts and smaller crops. Consequently, filberts grown in the eastern and central United States are crosses between American and European filberts.

Soil and situation The trees will grow on almost any soil from light gravel to heavy loam, but they require moderately good drainage. They are lime-tolerant and do best on a medium loam over limestone with a pH of 7.5–8.0. Rich soils tend to cause vigorous leafy growth at the expense of the nut yield.

As these are woodland plants by nature, they tolerate light shade but usually produce heavier crops in an open sunny position. Plant them out of the wind.

For good crops, keep the ground clean between the trees. Fork the soil in fall and hoe regularly in spring and summer.

Planting Plant two- to three-year-old trees. In the Northwest, planting is done in early winter; elsewhere in early spring.

Before planting, prepare the ground thoroughly, clearing away perennial weeds over an area 3 ft square. Lightly fork in lime at the rate of 7 oz per square yard.

Dig a hole wide and deep enough to take the roots fully extended. Drive in a stake to reach just below the lowest branch. Plant the tree to the same depth as at the nursery. Return the soil, and firm it in. Tie the tree to the stake with a tree tie and cushion and water well. If planting more than one tree, allow 15 ft between them.

Pruning The filbert is best grown in bush tree form with a 15 in tall stem and six or seven good main branches, giving a cup shape.

Prune during the latter part of flowering (about late February). For the first four to six years, cut back the leaders by about half to an outward-facing bud. Keep the trees at a height of 6–7 ft and, if necessary, cut back to a lateral at the required height. Cut back vigorous laterals to three or four buds. Do not prune the laterals that bear the tiny red female flowers (these are usually carried on the weaker shoots). Pull out suckers.

In August, break off by hand strong lateral growths to about half their length (six to eight leaves from the base) and leave them hanging. This is called brutting and allows air and light into the tree to help ripen fruit buds. It is the brutted side-shoots which are usually shortened back a further 2–3 in in winter.

Feeding In March, apply a balanced fertilizer, such as 10-10-10, at a rate of 3 oz per square yard. In April, apply an artificial fertilizer containing calcium carbonate and ammonium nitrate to old trees making poor growth, at a rate of 1 oz per square yard.

In fall, on light soils, lightly fork in well-rotted manure or compost at the rate of one 2-gal bucketful per square yard.

Every third winter, on acid soils, to keep the soil alkaline, lightly fork in lime at a rate of 7 oz per square yard.

At all times maintain a heavy organic mulch, not only to control weeds and hold in moisture, but also to improve the fertility of the surrounding soil.

Propagation

The most usual methods are by layering or by removing suckers.

For layering, select a young vigorous stem in spring and mark its position on the soil 9 in behind its tip. Dig a hole with one straight side 4–6 in deep. Peg the stem down against the straight side, and return and firm the soil. Keep the soil moist.

In late fall, after leaf-fall, sever the layered stem from the parent plant. In the early spring, cut off the growing tip. Lift and transplant the layered stem.

Harvesting

Filberts come into production about three years after planting. Harvest the nuts from the ground after they drop, and remove husks that remain. Spread the nuts out in a cool place to dry.

Pests and diseases

Spray with derris to combat nut weevil two or three times in May and early June. Spray in late summer with Bordeaux mixture to control filbert blight. Hazelnut trees are on the whole disease-free.

The first four to six years

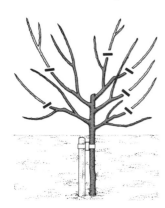

In subsequent years

1 After preparing the soil, dig a hole large enough to take the roots spread out well. Drive in a stake. Plant the tree, firming the soil. Tie the tree to the stake.

2 In late February, cut back the leaders by about half to an outward-facing bud. Cut back vigorous laterals to three or four buds. Twist and pull out suckers.

3 In March, apply a balanced fertilizer at a rate of 3 oz per square yard. Every third winter, on acid soils, fork in lime at a rate of 7 oz per square yard.

4 In August, break off by hand strong lateral growths to about half their length (six to eight leaves from the base) and leave them hanging.

5 In February, cut back previously brutted laterals to three or four buds. Do not prune laterals carrying female flowers. Twist out suckers around the base and cut out dead and crowded growths.

Chestnuts/Walnuts

CHINESE CHESTNUTS
'Abundance' Small nuts but excellent in flavor.
'Crane' Large, dark red nuts that can be stored better than other varieties. Tree may start to bear only one or two years

BLACK WALNUTS
'Myers' Good nuts with exceptionally

thin shells. Vigorous, heavy producer.
'Ohio' Unusually large nut kernels that are more likely to crack out whole than is the case with other varieties. Tree resistant to anthracnose.
'Thomas' Most common variety. Large, flavorful nuts. Inclined to biennial bearing. Highly susceptible to anthracnose.

CARPATHIAN CHESTNUTS
'Broadview' Excellent producer but nuts tend to be a little bitter. Very hardy.
'Hansen' Small tree with small, thin-shelled nuts. Large kernels. Needs good protection against frost since growth starts early. Reliably self-fruitful.
'Lake' Big, very flavorful nuts that crack fairly easily. Very productive.

ENGLISH CHESTNUTS
'Ashley' Large, light-colored, meaty nuts. Early. Produces so heavily that it requires regular and often hard pruning to prevent over-bearing.
'Eureka' Top-quality, large nuts. Old variety widely grown.

Chestnuts

Big, productive American chestnut trees have been wiped out by blight, and although there is some hope that agricultural scientists have finally come up with a solution to the problem, it will undoubtedly be a long time before this once-prized tree is again widely grown.

The sweet Spanish chestnuts that are cultivated throughout Europe for both nuts and timber are equally susceptible to chestnut blight and therefore are not grown in the United States.

This leaves the Oriental varieties. Of these, the Chinese chestnut is the most reliable. An attractive deciduous tree growing to 50 ft and spreading just as wide, it is resistant to the blight and produces masses of good nuts. It grows in zones 5–8. Because it is essentially self-unfruitful, two varieties must be planted together to assure nut production.

Cultivation

Although chestnuts bloom late, the swollen buds may be killed by frost, so locate the trees accordingly. Allow plenty of space for them and, since the branches hang low, do not plant them near a terrace or in other areas where headroom is needed.

The chestnut does well in light, well-drained soils with a pH of 5.5–6.5, but shallow, clay, waterlogged, and alkaline soils are unsuitable.

Planting

Prepare the ground thoroughly, clearing away perennial weeds over an area 4–5 ft square. Dig in well-rotted manure or other humus at a rate of about one 2-gal bucketful per square yard. Dig a hole wide and deep enough to take the roots fully extended and drive in a stake to reach just below the lowest branches.

Grafted trees are generally preferred to those grown from seed because they produce bigger nuts at an earlier age. In any case, plant the trees to the same depth as at the nursery, spreading the roots out well. Firm the tree to the stake, and water well.

Feeding and pruning

Fertilize the trees after they are established in early spring with about 1 lb of balanced fertilizer per inch of trunk diameter. If grafted specimens are used, however, cut the application in half until it is certain the tree will survive the winters.

Cut back by half the laterals produced during the first growing season when they reach 9–12 in. A few of the upper laterals produced later in the season may be left unpruned. In early winter, cut back the pruned laterals flush with the stem. Repeat this training process each year until the required length of clear trunk has been produced.

Little pruning is required after the main branch system has been formed. Where there is congestion, cut out thin shoots in summer. Prune lightly in winter.

Pests and diseases

To control chestnut weevils, the worst pests, spray three or four times in August with carbaryl.

Harvesting

Nuts are borne in the current season's growth. Grafted specimens start bearing after 4–5 years; seedlings take a little longer. Harvest nuts when they fall to the ground after the burrs surrounding them open. Since the nuts deteriorate if left on the ground in the sun, gather them daily and place them in open trays in a dry, airy place to cure until they feel a little soft. The nuts can be stored for a long time if mixed with slightly damp peat in plastic bags and kept under cover at just above freezing.

Walnuts

Despite its name, the English walnut (*Juglans regia*) is native to China, Iran, the Himalayas and south-western Europe and is more properly called the Persian walnut. It is hardy in zones 8–10 and most widely grown in central California valleys.

The rather widely advertised Carpathian walnut is an unusually hardy strain of Persian walnut and grows in zones 5–8. In actual fact, however, it is likely to be a disappointment in all zones except 6.

The eastern black walnut (*J. nigra*) is widely grown in the eastern and central parts of the United States. It is hardier and bigger than the English walnut. It grows in zones 4–8. The nuts have a distinctive rich flavor. All walnuts are self-fruitful, but nut production is more reliable if two different varieties of the same species are planted together.

Cultivation

Usually grown as a central-leader standard, the walnut reaches a height of about 25 ft in 20 years and a final height of 60–70 ft. It is therefore suited only to large gardens. It is slow to crop, taking five to ten years before beginning to bear fruit.

Soil and situation The walnut grows well on a wide variety of soils provided they are deep, fertile and well-drained. The ideal soil is a heavy loam, at least 2 ft deep, over limestone, with a pH of about 7.0.

An open position with shelter from spring frosts is best because both the young growths and flowers are prone to frost damage.

Planting For fruiting purposes, it is best to obtain a three- or four-year-old grafted tree of a named variety. Before planting, lightly fork in ground lime at a rate of 7 oz per square yard on acid soils. Clear away perennial weeds over an area 4–5 ft square. Fork in a balanced fertilizer, such as 10-10-10, at the rate of 3 oz per square yard.

Dig a hole wide and deep enough to take the roots fully extended. Drive in a stake to reach just below the lowest branches. Plant the tree at the same depth as at the nursery. Return the soil. Tie the tree to the stake with a tree tie and cushion. Water well.

If planting more than one tree, allow a space of 40–50 ft between them.

Pruning Once the head of the tree has formed, very little pruning is required. Cut out any dead or awkwardly placed branches in August. Protect the cuts with a wound paint.

Pests and diseases

To control walnut blight on English and Carpathian walnuts spray with Bordeaux mixture when leaves begin to develop, after pollination and during spells of wet weather. For anthracnose on black walnut, spray with zineb when leaves are 12 in long and three times after that at two week intervals. Use malathion or carbaryl to discourage such insect pests as may appear.

Harvesting

English and Carpathian walnuts start bearing in 4–5 years; black walnuts take a little longer. Harvest the nuts as they drop. Remove the husks (wear rubber gloves so the hands are not indelibly stained); wash the nuts; and spread out in a dry place to dry for a few days before storing.

The first year

Second and third years

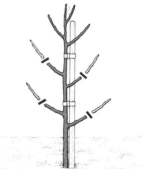

1 In prepared ground, dig a hole large enough for the extended roots. Drive in a stake and plant the tree. Tie to the stake.

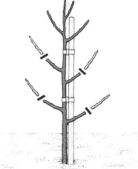

2 Cut back by half all lower laterals produced during the first growing season when they reach 9–12 in.

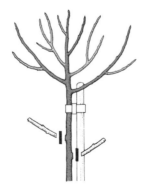

3 In late fall or early winter, cut back the pruned laterals flush with the stem.

Renovation of neglected trees 1

Neglected or mutilated fruit trees are common and many gardeners inherit them when moving to a new house and garden.

Apart from its untidy appearance, a neglected tree may produce many small or misshapen fruits or it may be unfruitful; it may also be stunted or, conversely, over-vigorous. If the tree is very old (say over 30 years old) and producing little or no fruit, it might not be worth taking a lot of trouble to restore it, especially if it is also suffering from such diseases as canker and fire blight, which can destroy many branches or even kill the whole tree. It is better to dig it up and plant a new young tree.

However, most gardeners are unwilling to give in without a struggle and, provided the tree's basic framework is sound, with time and care a neglected tree can be restored to a fruitful and healthy condition.

Neglect A tree that has not been pruned at all may produce plenty of blossom but the fruit is often small and disease- or pest-ridden. First of all, of course, treat any pests or diseases present (see pages 14–16). Then carry out remedial pruning. Remove all dead, diseased and damaged wood completely. Cut any crossing or rubbing branches and any that spoil the shape of the tree. Finally, thin out overcrowded side-shoots on the main branches. Feed and mulch well.

The stunted tree

If the tree is unfruitful and stunted it may be because of starvation resulting from poor feeding, competition for nutrients and water from weeds or neighbouring trees, unsuitable soil conditions, damage to roots through wind-rock, excessive shade or weakening by pests and diseases.

To remedy starvation, remove weeds and other vegetation, including grass, over an area 4 ft square around the tree. Remove overhanging branches if possible. Mulch the tree heavily with well-rotted manure or compost to a depth of 3 in over a 2 ft radius, keeping the material clear of the trunk. To help to prevent root breakage of small trees during gales, drive in a large stake to reach just below the lowest branch and tie the tree to it with a tree tie and cushion. Check the soil depth and drainage and, if necessary, install

a drainage system (see page 10).

There is usually very little new wood to prune but if the tree bears a dense mass of complex spur systems, thin these out and severely shorten any new wood. This admits light and air to the remaining spurs and encourages the formation of shoots which will replace the old framework.

For one or two years, thin out the fruitlets or, preferably, remove them all. This relieves the tree of the strain of reproduction.

Once the tree is restored, maintain it by correct pruning, feeding and mulching, and control of pests and diseases.

The over-vigorous and unfruitful tree

An extremely vigorous tree is usually the result of severe pruning over a number of winters, or of being grafted on to a vigorous rootstock. There are other causes; the soil may be very fertile, the tree may have been given too much nitrogen, or scion rooting may have occurred which destroys the dwarfing effect of the rootstock.

The first step is to grass down the orchard (see page 56) and moderate the supply of

Bark-ringing apples and pears

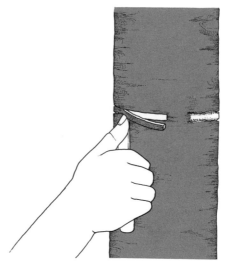 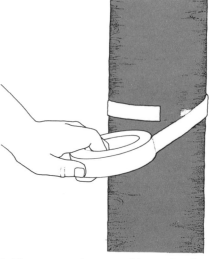

1 In May, mark out a ring $\frac{1}{4}$ in wide on the trunk. Remove a nearly complete circle of bark using a sharp knife. Leave 1 in of the ring uncut.

2 Then, cover the wound immediately with several overlapping circles of adhesive tape. Smear petroleum jelly on the edges of the tape to exclude air, pests and diseases.

The stunted tree

1 Remove weeds and grasses over an area 4 ft square around the tree. Mulch with well-rotted manure or compost. Drive in a stake and tie the tree to it with a tree tie.

2 In winter, thin out overcrowded spurs and severely shorten any maiden wood.

3 In spring, for a year or two, remove most or all of the fruitlets. Feed with fertilizers and mulch well annually. Control pests and diseases.

Renovation of neglected trees 2

nitrogenous fertilizers until the tree is once again fruitful.

More drastic methods of reducing the vigor are by bark-ringing or root-pruning. Root-pruning is recommended for stone fruits such as plums which cannot be bark-ringed because of the risk of silver leaf disease. Surface root-pruning may be necessary for the tree that has scion rooted.

Renovation of severely-pruned apple and pear trees The most common cause of over-vigorous growth is severe over-pruning. The tree becomes out of balance and over-vegetative, and simply cutting back branches only perpetuates the problem. Renovation treatment must be spread over a period of two or three winters in order to minimize the shock to the tree.

From November to March, thin out crossing, broken, diseased and congested branches. Leave healthy, well-placed branches which are spaced 2–3 ft apart. Over a period of two or three years, unpruned branches will produce flower buds and eventually fruit.

When taking off a limb, always cut back to the point of origin or to a replacement branch not less than half the diameter of the sawn-off branch. Never leave a stub, because this might lead to die-back, with subsequent canker. Where it is necessary to remove a heavy branch, undercut it first and then complete the cut from the top so that when it parts, the branch does not tear the bark. Protect all pruning cuts larger than $\frac{1}{2}$ in dia.

Winter pruning stimulates growth but summer pruning checks it. Starting with the longer laterals in early August and finishing in late September, cut back to five leaves any unwanted laterals of the current season's growth that have become woody at the base and are longer than 12 in.

Shoots growing horizontally tend to be fruitful, whereas those growing vertically tend not to be. Avoid, where possible, cutting horizontally-inclined shoots and branches. Tie down young upright shoots or loop one over another to form arches, which encourages the production of fruit-bearing spurs.

Bark-ringing apple and pear trees In May, mark out a ring $\frac{1}{4}$ in wide on the main trunk. With a sharp knife, remove almost a complete circle of bark but leave 1 in of the ring

uncut. Cover the wound immediately with several overlapping circles of adhesive tape. Smear petroleum jelly on the edges of the tape to exclude air, pests and diseases. Bark-ringing, which is also known as girdling, temporarily interrupts the passage of carbohydrates and foodstuffs to the roots and encourages a better crop of fruit.

Scion rooting Sometimes the soil becomes heaped up around the trunk, burying the union with the rootstock, which results in the scion rooting and vigorous growth. To establish if this is the case, remove the soil, weeds and other vegetation for a 4 ft square around the tree. Inspect the trunk and sever any

roots coming from above the union. Paint the wounds. If the union is below ground level or not visible at all (and this may be difficult to detect in old, knotty trunks) drastic action such as bark-ringing may be needed on over-vigorous apple and pear trees (see above).

Root-pruning The roots are pruned to reduce the vigor of the tree and to encourage fruit buds to form. In November or December, mark out and dig a trench around the tree about 5 ft from the trunk (further away if the tree is large). Fold back the thin fibrous roots to expose the thicker woody roots. Cut back the thicker roots with a pruning saw. Retain the thinner fibrous roots and spread them

back into the trench. Cover the soil and firm the ground. Drive in a supporting stake to reach just below the bottom branch. Tie the tree to the stake with a tree tie and cushion. Mulch the root area with well-rotted manure or compost. Water well during the summer.

If the tree is old and very badly neglected, spread this process over two winters.

An over-vigorous tree less than five years old may be lifted to prune the roots. In winter, dig up the tree and cut back the deeper and wider-ranging roots. Replant it in the same position or in a different, more suitable site if appropriate. Support the replanted tree with a stake. Water in dry weather in summer.

RENOVATION OF PLUMS

Old neglected plum trees, especially those on vigorous rootstocks, are particularly likely to become very unkempt and unmanageable. However, plums are not quite as tolerant of poor growing conditions as are apples and pears so renovation is not always successful. If the tree is too badly infected with silver leaf, it is best to dig it up and burn it.

First, clear the ground, removing weeds and other vegetation over an area 4 ft square around the tree and mulch heavily. Treat the tree for any pests and diseases present (see pages 14–16).

Avoid severe pruning and spread the renovation process over three years. The principles of pruning are basically the same as for a neglected apple or pear tree. The

main difference is that plums are pruned in July to August when the danger of infection by silver leaf is small. The aim is to return to a tree with a more or less symmetrical branch system.

Once the tree has been restored to a healthy fruitful condition, maintain it with correct pruning, feeding, and control of pests and diseases.

The first year

1 In June to August, cut out any large branches that upset the symmetry. Cut out any dead or damaged wood. Remove suckers and twiggy growths on the trunk.

2 At the same time, thin out lateral branches and twigs where they are badly overcrowded. Protect all cut surfaces with a wound paint.

Second and subsequent years

3 In June to August, remove any over-vigorous growth that spoils the symmetry. Thin out remaining overcrowded branch systems. Cut out any suckers.

Fruit in tubs and pots 1

Lack of space to grow fruit trees and bushes can be turned from a drawback into an advantage. Most fruits can be grown in containers such as pots, tubs, boxes and troughs.

Pot-grown fruits can be more easily protected against frost, high winds and birds and given the exact type of soil they prefer and need. Although container-grown fruits never give very large yields per tree or bush—their small size sees to that—the quality of the fruit can be very high because extra attention can be given.

Types and sizes of container

The container must have good drainage and be of a shape and construction to allow the plant to be removed when required. Within these constraints, the choice of material and shape is considerable. Remember, however, that it is not worth investing in an expensive pot until the plant has reached its final size. Strawberries, for example, can be grown in perforated barrels or specially designed containers.

The tree's first pot must be large enough to accommodate the root system, and up to 3 in wider but no larger. This usually means a container 9–12 in in diameter and depth.

Cultivation

The principle behind container growing is to limit the size of the plant by constricting the root system. Starting with a maiden, a two- or a three-year-old tree, the gardener adjusts the pot size, re-potting until the tree reaches the required size. Maiden trees are preferable if the gardener wishes to train the tree in a particular way.

Site Container-grown fruits should be sited in a sunny corner where they are protected from high winds, which can damage plants by battering and by cold. Beware of eddies produced by walls and fences. Temporary shelter with plastic sheeting or netting can be erected at such critical times as blossoming and fruit formation or, better still, take the containers into a greenhouse if possible. Avoid frost pockets.

In cool climates, south-facing walls provide an extra source of radiated heat—excellent for the warm temperate fruits. The reflected warmth from the stone or brick often creates a warmer microclimate than the open ground. Walls also cause a rain shadow effect which helps to protect plants from storms, but containers in such rain shadows need extra watering.

Soil An advantage of container growing is that the soil can be more easily tailored to each plant's needs. Stone fruits, for example, thrive best in a slightly alkaline soil whereas pip fruits such as apples, need a slightly acid soil. The potting mix can be modified to suit the plant concerned.

Soil-less mixes, growing mediums of peat and sand with necessary nutrients added, are useful for short-term crops such as strawberries. They are light and clean to handle but there is little buffer action against excessive salts, so feeding and watering are more critical. They are not suitable for long-term fruit such as apples or peaches.

Potting If the plant is bare-rooted, soak the roots of the tree for one hour before planting. If the tree is already container-grown, the existing root ball should be retained but the perimeter roots should be very gently teased outwards to avoid any pot-bound effect.

Whatever the age of the tree, large, thong-like roots should be cut back so that the root ball fits the pot. Trim broken roots using a clean sloping cut with the face of the wound downwards. This trimming induces the tree to create a more fibrous root system. Place a few pieces of broken pot or stones in the bottom of clay pots to ensure good drainage. Plastic pots are usually well equipped with drainage holes, but, if in doubt, also use broken pieces of pot or stones in such pots.

Place the plant in the center of the pot at the same depth as it was previously. Fill the container, firming the soil well as filling proceeds; very firm planting is essential. Level off 1 in below the rim to leave room for watering. Stand the container on bricks so that drainage is not impeded. Water well and leave the pots in a cool but frost-free place for the winter.

Watering and feeding Fruit plants in pots must be watered carefully, avoiding the two extremes of waterlogging and desiccation. The former causes root death and both result in fruitlet drop. Check the top inch of soil regularly: it should be damp but not sodden.

Daily watering is necessary during hot sunny spells. In really hot weather, place moist burlap around the pots to protect the roots. Little watering is necessary in the winter.

No matter how good the potting mix, liquid feeding is necessary in the growing season. A pot-grown plant cannot seek out nutrients as can a plant in open ground. Most fruit trees require a high potassium fertilizer, particularly when they are carrying a good fruit crop. Apply a proprietary liquid fertilizer to the manufacturer's instructions once a fortnight when the plant begins to grow and every 7–10 days when it is in full leaf. Stop liquid feeding when the fruits begin to ripen.

Re-potting In the late fall or early spring gently knock the plant out of its pot. Trim the roots by about one-tenth, particularly any thong-like roots. Cut the aerial parts of the plant by an equivalent amount to balance the root loss. Tease out the perimeter roots to avoid the fruit becoming pot-bound. Take a little of the old soil out of the root ball. Re-pot into a larger container each year while the plant is growing to its final size. Remember the larger the container, the bigger the tree will grow.

Planting

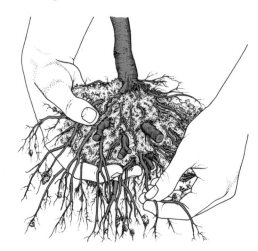

1 Soak bare rooted plants for one hour before planting. Gently tease out the perimeter roots on container-grown plants. Cut back any large thong-like or broken roots using a clean sloping cut.

2 Crock the pot. Place the plant in the pot to the same depth as it was previously. Fill the container, firming well. Level off 1 in below the rim. Water well and stand on bricks to allow excess water to drain away.

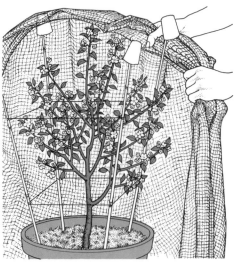

3 In spring, give the plants a top dressing of a 1 in layer of peat or well-rotted manure. Replace each year. Protect blossom from frost with netting over a framework of canes or wire.

Fruit in tubs and pots 2

As a guide, gooseberries grow quite satisfactorily in a final pot of 15 in diameter, black currants in an 18 in pot and trees in an 18–20 in diameter container. Thereafter plants can stay in the same container, except for a change of mix each fall. An easier but less efficient technique is to leave the plant undisturbed and merely to change the top 4–6 in of mix each fall.

Protection In the spring, to protect the blossom against frost, cover the plants with netting or take them inside. Keep the netting off the blossoms by inserting canes or a wire framework into the pot around the plant. Netting should be used to keep birds away from the buds in the winter and from the fruit in the summer.

As with all early-flowering fruit trees, frost is a greater danger in spring than in winter, but container-grown fruits are also sensitive to heavy frosts that can freeze the entire root system and kill the tree. In winter in warmer climates, the containers should be buried in a well-drained ground up to its rim, or moved to a sheltered position. In cold climates, the container must be brought indoors.

Top-dressing In the spring, just as growth commences, the plants should be top-dressed with a 1 in layer of peat or well-rotted stable manure. This helps to conserve soil moisture. Trees requiring extra nitrogen (for example, stone fruits) should be given a dressing of dried blood $\frac{1}{2}$–1 oz at a time, first when the buds burst, then after fruits form, and finally when the fruits have reached full size, but well before ripening. Completely replace the mulch each year.

Training and pruning
Container-grown fruit trees can be trained to any of the tree forms (see pages 8–9). They are particularly suitable for single cordon training, that is, growing a single stem at a 45 degree angle against a wall or fence. Single cordons make the best use of restricted space. Bear in mind that trees that need to be moved into shelter during the winter should be trained in a self-supporting round form such as bush or pyramid. Apples, pears, cherries, plums and apricots respond well to sensitive training designed to achieve the dwarf pyramid form.

Apart from training the fruit tree, during its formative years it should be prevented from fruiting too heavily by removing some of the blossoms. Three-year-old apple, pear and peach trees in 10–12 in pots can carry about 6–9 fruits. Plums should be limited to 20 on a three-year-old tree. More fruits can be obtained if the trees are in larger pots or tubs. When mature, all pot-grown fruits should be discouraged from producing too much fruit by thinning at intervals. Provided they are well fed and watered, the final spacing of fruit can be a little closer than that recommended for outdoor trees. The final thinning of stone fruits should not take place until after the stone has formed.

Varieties
The number of varieties suitable for pot growing is legion. The main criterion is that they should not be triploids, because these are too vigorous and they are poor pollinators. Self-incompatible trees need a partner or may require hand pollination. (For details, see page 43). Follow the advice of specialist fruit tree suppliers.

Re-potting

4 When the plant begins to grow, feed with a liquid fertilizer high in potassium once a fortnight. When it is in full leaf, feed every 7–10 days. Stop the feed when the fruits begin to ripen.

5 During the formative years, remove some of the blossom to prevent heavy fruiting. Thin the fruits to leave about 6–9 on three-year-old apple, pear or peach trees; leave about 20 on a plum tree.

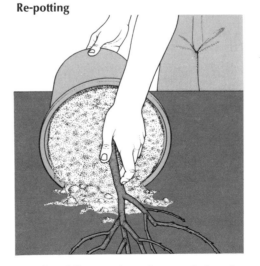

6 In late fall, or early spring, gently knock the plant out of its pot. Trim the roots by about one-tenth. Tease out perimeter roots Remove a little old soil. Re-plant with new soil.

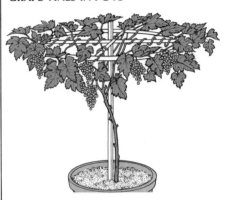

GRAPE VINES IN POTS

Grape vines can be successfully grown in pots in a small greenhouse or on a patio where a large greenhouse is not available. (For full details of growing grapes see pages 38–40).

A vine can be bought as a one-year-old rooted cutting. In the first season, grow the vine in a 7 in pot. When it is in its second season, transfer it to a 12–15 in pot in early spring.

Allow the vine to produce one good cane during this second summer, which should be stopped at about 6 ft. Support the cane with a stake.

In the second winter, prune off the unripe wood. Insert three or four canes into the soil around the pot rim, or insert the kind of wood or metal frame used for supporting weeping standard roses. Tie in the vine cane to this to form a circle. When the circle is complete, stop the vine. Remove the lower side-shoots to create a clear stem up to the ring.

Allow the vine to produce a token crop of two bunches during the second season. In later years, allow the vine to produce progressively larger crops, but no more than one bunch per spur at 12 in apart, making a total of 5–8 bunches.

Prune the vine by the Double Guyot method (see pages 38–40).

Water and feed as described for other pot-grown fruits (opposite). Re-pot or pot on each winter using fresh compost.

Fruit storage

In the past fruit could be stored in the home in two basic ways. Apples, pears and quinces were stored in the traditional root cellar for three to eight months, which is still a popular method; other fruit could be stored only by canning, in jams or jellies, or by drying, all of which affect the basic taste and texture. With the advent of the home freezer, almost all fruits can now be eaten at any time of the year virtually in prime condition.

Traditional storage
The procedure for storing hard fruit such as apples, pears and quinces varies little. Store them separately because the strong aroma of quinces, in particular, can affect other fruit.

Wrapping the fruit

1 Place each fruit in the center of a square of paper. Oiled or waxed wraps can prolong storage life.

2 Fold the bottom point to the middle. Then fold in the two side points to form a firm parcel.

3 Fold down the fourth point and gently place the apple "parcel," folded side down, in the box.

STORAGE BOXES AND TRAYS

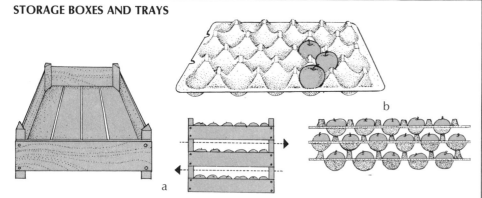

Orchard boxes (a) have slatted sides and corner posts to allow air to circulate and the slats have rounded edges to protect the fruit. Do not wrap fruit packed in polystyrene or fiber trays (b) because the compartments separate the fruit.

Early apples and pears are best eaten from the tree and will keep for only a few weeks. Mid-season varieties generally keep for one or two months, but do not store them with late varieties because the gases given off will hasten the maturity of the later ones. Store late varieties, that mature from late September onwards, for three to eight months.

Picking for storage Pick apples and pears when they are fully sized and when they leave the spur easily with the stalk intact. Very late apples are picked when still unripe; ripeness for eating develops in storage.

Handle the fruit carefully. Bruising can allow fungus spores to enter and rot the damaged fruit. Do not pick the fruit when it is raining because dampness encourages mold. It is best to pick by hand and put the fruit gently into a lined basket or soft bag. Use a fruit picker for the highest fruit (see pages 12–13).

The storeroom If there is a regular and sizeable harvest it may be worth building a special root cellar. However, a basement, cool attic or perhaps a shed is also suitable.

Ideally, the storage area should be kept at an even temperature from 3°–4°C/37°–40°F, but this often requires refrigeration equipment. Most gardeners have to be satisfied with maintaining the storage area at a temperature of about 4°–7°C/40°–45°F during the winter months. Air must circulate freely. To achieve this, fit ventilators at each end covered with wire mesh to keep out birds. The atmosphere must not be too dry or the fruit will shrivel. Damp down the floor occasionally if it is soil, stone or concrete. Keep the storage area clean and remove containers of paint and creosote which could taint the fruit.

A soil floor is ideal because it can be kept moist, but fine mesh wire netting should be laid below soil level to keep out rats and mice. The floor should be firmed down and cleaned each year.

Storage boxes and trays Apples and pears can be stored on slatted shelves inside the storeroom, although wooden orchard boxes and trays and fiber or polystyrene trays are more convenient because they stack on top of one another. They must have corner posts for air to circulate. A thin sheet of polyethylene laid loosely over the fruit helps to delay shrivelling. After use, clean the containers with soapy water and disinfectant.

Preparing the fruit for storage Using only undamaged fruit, store pears unwrapped in single layers on trays. Wrap and pack apples in layers in boxes or in trays. Using special oiled wraps extends the storage life but 8 in squares of newspaper are an alternative for cooking apples. Some gardeners let apples sweat for one to two weeks before storing them, to prevent later condensation and thus possible rotting while in store.

Polyethylene bags Clear polyethylene bags have been tried recently for storing apples and pears and they are particularly successful with varieties that tend to shrivel. Store no more than 4–5 lb of fruit to a bag.

After picking, leave the fruit to cool completely before packing to avoid condensation in the bag. When the bag is packed, fold the top over and place it so that the fold is underneath. Do not exclude all the air from the bag. Make two small holes for every 1 lb of fruit. Alternatively, cut off the bottom two corners of each bag.

Store the bags in the same way as boxes at the coolest temperature possible but not below 3°C/37°F.

Storage problems Generally, problems are the result of storing damaged or contaminated fruit, lack of ventilation, or of fluctuations in temperature in the storeroom. Check all fruit regularly and remove any showing signs of disease or rotting. The most common diseases are brown rot fungus, scald and bitter pit (see pages 14–16).

Freezing
Almost all fruits freeze well, except most types of dessert pears. Berry fruits (currants and gooseberries) are particularly suitable. Freeze as soon after picking as possible.

Drying
Drying is a successful method for storing apples, pears, plums and grapes to be used later for cooking.

Peel and quarter apples and pears, or cut apples into rings $\frac{1}{4}$ in thick. Plums may be left whole or halved and pitted. Leave grapes whole. Arrange the fruit on clean muslin or mesh trays or wooden frames so that it is not touching. Hang apple rings on sticks or bamboo canes across the oven. It is essential to dry fruit slowly or it hardens and whole plums burst their skins. An airing cupboard or an oven that can be heated to low temperatures is ideal. Dry for one hour at 49°C/120°F and then increase the temperature to 60°C/140°F. Leave the fruit at this heat for three to six hours depending on the size. When the fruit is dry, it should be soft and pliable with no excess moisture.

Spread out the fruit on clean paper to cool. Cover with paper or muslin and leave at room temperature for 12 hours. Store in a dry place in boxes lined with waxed paper.

Passion fruit

Passion fruit (outdoors)

The passion fruit (*Passiflora edulis*), a native of southern Brazil, is most commonly grown in Hawaii, but will do well anywhere in zone 10 if protected from cold during the first winter. It is well distributed throughout the Tropics. A vigorous, evergreen climber, the passion fruit plant has deep glossy green leaves and white fragrant flowers. The flowers blossom intermittently throughout the winter.

The fruits (technically berries) are $1\frac{1}{2}$–$2\frac{1}{2}$ in long and oval in shape. Although basically a sweetish fruit, when eaten fresh it has a pleasant, somewhat aromatic tartness. Two forms are recognized: *P. edulis edulis* with deep purple fruits; and *P. edulis flavicarpa* with deep yellow fruits.

Soil The passion fruit plant will grow in almost any soil provided the soil is quite well drained, contains a large amount of humus, and is not extremely acid. Soil infested with nematodes should be fumigated before the plants are set out.

Planting and training Select a location that is protected from strong winds. Support is essential so provide a system of wires as described for grapes (see pages 38–40) or follow the instructions as given in the paragraph below.

The support system should preferably be erected against a wall but may be free-standing.

The illustrations and captions on this page indicate ways to prepare the soil and to plant the passion fruit vine, to hand pollinate the flower, and to train the vine to facilitate natural development.

Grow the plants on a trellis made with three 9-gauge wires. The top wire should be no less than 6 ft above ground and probably at least 7 ft; the middle wire is 18 in lower; and the bottom wire another 18 in below that. Since the vines are extremely heavy, the wires should be run through the posts, not just stapled to them. Space the posts 10 ft apart.

Plant one vine at the base of each post and help it to grow upwards (which usually happens very quickly) by hanging a secured string down the post to which the vine can attach itself and climb.

Feeding and watering Before planting, apply a balanced fertilizer at 3 oz per square yard, and make a similar application about eight weeks after planting. One-year-old and older plants are fed at a slightly higher rate four times a year, that is: before the beginning of active growth; prior to the summer and winter crop; and midway between each growth period.

In Hawaii, a 10-5-20 fertilizer is recommended. Elsewhere use a fertilizer with a lower nitrogen content. Keep the plants watered during dry spells when they are in active growth.

Pruning Pruning should be done sparingly after the winter crop is gathered. Just remove trailing stems and cut out excess growth as necessary to keep the plants from becoming too large and heavy.

Pollination

Passion fruit that is raised from seed may be self-incompatible. If possible obtain clones of the purple-fruited form that are known to be self-compatible. If only seed-raised plants are available, plant two seedlings about 2 ft apart, and allow the shoots to intermingle after initial training. Hand pollinated flowers usually do produce larger fruits than naturally pollinated ones so, where practical, hand pollination is worth while (see page 43). The flowers are short-lived and should be pollinated soon after they open.

Harvesting and storing

For really juicy and good flavored fruits, do not pick passion fruit until it is fully ripe. When mature the fruit attains a strong color, and the skin hardens and begins to shrivel. Once gathered, the fruit should be used as soon as possible but it can be stored a few weeks if kept cool.

Pests and diseases

To control fruit flies, spray with malathion as the flies appear. This treatment may also eliminate mites, the other most serious pest; if not, use a sulfur spray. Always spray when the flowers are closed so that too many insect pollinators are not killed. Flowers of the purple passion fruit open in the early morning and close before noon while flowers of the yellow passion fruit open after noon and close at night.

Second and subsequent years

1 Before planting, apply a balanced fertilizer at 3 oz per square yard. Make a similar application about eight weeks after planting.

2 In spring or early summer, plant two or more seedlings 2 ft apart in the prepared soil. Pinch out the growing tips.

3 During flowering, pollinate with a small brush. Liquid feed every 14 days until the fruits ripen. For further details, see hand pollination, page 43.

4 In spring, train in the new growths onto the 3-wire trellis support system by initially guiding them into position and then allowing them to develop naturally.

Citrus fruits 1

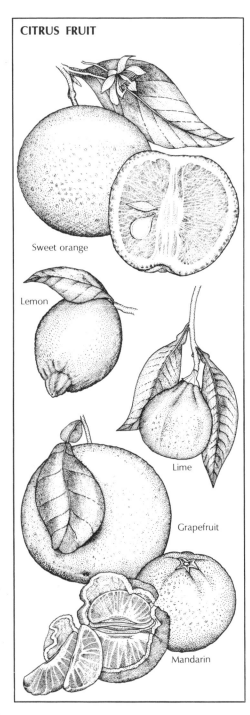

CITRUS FRUIT

Sweet orange

Lemon

Lime

Grapefruit

Mandarin

Citrus fruits can only be grown in the warmest of American climates. Fruits such as the orange, grapefruit, lemon, lime, kumquat, mandarin (including tangerine and satsuma), shaddock, tangelo, and calamondin thrive only in certain zones. For example, the lemon and the lime are restricted to zone 10, while some varieties of other citrus fruits can be cultivated in the southern sections of zone 9. The kumquat, the hardiest species of citrus fruit along with the calamondin and mandarin, can even be grown in zone 8 if the location is well sheltered and sunny.

All citrus trees make attractive evergreen garden specimens as well as being producers of large quantities of enjoyable fruit. With a few exceptions, citrus trees are self-fruitful, making it unnecessary to plant more than one tree of any kind.

Tree selection
The chosen citrus plant should preferably be selected from trees developed by the nursery and grafted on reliable rootstock. Those grown from fresh seeds are inclined to be overly large and may be unsuited to the area in which they are to be grown.

Selection of the right rootstock is difficult for the amateur gardener who has to choose from a wide range of rootstocks, each with characteristics peculiar to the given stock. The nurseryman, preferably a grower who knows local requirements, should be consulted before a choice is made. As a general guide, the gardener should buy either a one-year-old plant having a trunk of $\frac{1}{2}$–$\frac{3}{4}$ in in diameter, or a two-year-old plant measuring $\frac{3}{4}$–$1\frac{1}{4}$ in. The trunk of the plant should be measured one inch above the graft. If possible, the plant should be state-registered as free of serious viral disease.

Cultivation
Citrus trees are not very particular about soil, but do best in loam or sandy loam. Drainage must be excellent and the pH between 6.0–6.5. If the water table is very high or the topsoil is underlain by clay, construct a mound of earth at least 18 in high, 8 ft across at the top, and 12 ft across at the bottom.

Before planting, turn over the soil thoroughly and remove weeds. Mix in a good supply of humus and about 6 oz of balanced fertilizer per square yard.

Locate the trees where they will receive sunlight all day long. Avoid low areas where frost may collect. In regions with occasional freezes, place the trees on the south side of a building, wall or hedge, or near a pond. Oranges and grapefruits require a space of 25–30 ft diameter, calamondins, kumquats, lemons and limes need 15 ft, while other species of citrus fruit benefit from 20 ft of space.

Planting Plant the trees in late winter or early spring after the frost danger is past. Spread the roots out well in the holes. The top roots should be at about ground level and the trunk just a little higher than it was in its nursery container.

After the hole is filled in and the soil firmed, ridge up the soil in a 2 ft diameter circle around the trunk to form a watering basin, and fill this with water. Then, to protect the tree from sunburn, wrap the trunk from the ground up to the lowest branches with loose-fitting newspapers or wrapping paper. Tie the papers in place and leave them on for the next year.

Watering and feeding Citrus trees need considerable moisture, a minimum of 36 in per

1 In late winter or early spring, plant the young, grafted nursery tree in thoroughly turned soil mixed with humus and balanced fertilizer. Spread the roots out well.

2 After the hole is filled in and the soil is firmed, ridge up the soil in a 2 ft diameter circle around the trunk to form a basin. Fill with water.

3 To protect the tree from sunburn, wrap the trunk with paper from the ground to the lowest branches. Use loose-fitting newspapers or wrapping paper.

Citrus fruits 2

year at all times, but especially in the first three years. In dry climates, such as California, build a shallow watering basin that extends about a foot beyond the branch tips of each tree. Also build a ridge of earth close around the tree trunk to keep it dry. Fill the basin with water as necessary. In California first-year trees should be watered every 7–10 days during dry weather, second-year trees every 2 weeks, and older trees every 2–6 weeks.

After they have been planted and have put out leaves, citrus trees should be fertilized on a regular basis to produce good crops. Always just scatter the fertilizer on the ground and water it in. Do not dig fertilizer in, or apply it in holes, because it may burn the roots.

The type of fertilizer and the amount used as well as the schedule by which it is applied varies considerably between citrus regions. In Florida, for instance, a 6-6-6 balanced fertilizer containing magnesium, manganese and copper is recommended, while in Louisiana a 6-12-6 or 8-8-8 fertilizer is used. But, in Arizona, California and Texas, ammonium sulfate is usually satisfactory alone. Established trees should be fed four times a year.

The best way to determine how to care for citrus trees is to send a soil sample to the state agricultural extension service for analysis. On the basis of the analysis, the service can suggest a precise feeding regimen.

Mulching Citrus trees are frequently grown in bare ground, but an organic mulch should be maintained under the tree canopy. This is of benefit to both the tree and the gardener. The mulch should be kept 6 in away from the trunk of the tree to protect it from moisture, fungi and other pests. Mulch not only helps to hold in moisture and keeps down weeds, it also contributes to soil fertility.

Frost protection

Until a citrus tree has developed a low-hanging canopy, the trunk should be banked with soil in late November if the area is subject to occasional freezes. After November, the gardener can take several precautions if frost is predicted. For example, the trees can be covered with large sheets of fabric, fans can be set up to keep air circulating around the trees, or tree heaters can be placed near and under the trees. Tree heaters are not permitted in some areas.

Trees damaged by frost should not be pruned until growth starts again and the damage has been assessed. If the damage is severe, delay pruning for six months. This gives the trees a chance to recover from the shock of freezing.

Harvesting

The first fruits of young trees up to about four years old are of poor quality and should be either pulled from the tree when immature or thrown away at harvest time.

When harvesting fruits in later years, cut the stems close. Do not pull the fruits. Take care not to bruise or cut the rinds if the fruits are destined for storing.

Allow the fruits to ripen on the tree before picking. Citrus fruits, unlike other fruits, do not have to be picked as soon as ripe because they do not deteriorate immediately, indeed they may be safely left for a long time. Fruits picked soon after they ripen can be stored for a considerable period in open boxes at 16°C/60°F. The longer the ripe fruits are left on the tree, the shorter the storage period. Juice from citrus fruits can be canned, and peel from oranges and grapefruit candied.

Pests and diseases

Citrus fruit trees are susceptible to many diseases, as well as attacks from insect and animal enemies. The best method of warding off most disease is to begin with healthy, virus-free plants on recommended rootstocks, and to prevent wet soil from remaining in contact with the trunks for long periods. Eternal vigilance seems the only remedy against deer, armadillos, gophers, land turtles and other animals that damage trees.

To control insects, follow a regular spray schedule as recommended by the state agricultural extension service.

Serious burning of tree trunks, caused by long exposure to the sun, can be prevented by whitewashing until the branch canopy is large and dense enough to shade the trunks.

There is no reliable preventative measure to stop the splitting of fruit because the precise cause is not known, although this may be the result of an extremely uneven water supply or lack of minor nutrients in the soil. Or it may be a combination of these detrimental factors. Take advice from state agricultural extension services about local pest and disease problems.

4 After the trees have been planted and have put out leaves, scatter fertilizer on a regular basis. Always water the fertilizer in.

5 Maintain an organic mulch under the tree canopy. The mulch should be kept 6 in away from the trunk of the tree to hold in moisture and keep down weeds.

6 In late November, bank the tree with soil as a frost protection precaution. The tree will eventually develop a low-hanging canopy that will help ward off frost.

7 After November, two frost protection methods are to cover the trees with large sheets of fabric and/or to set up fans to keep the air circulating.

Coconuts

The coconut palm tree (*Cocos nucifera*) is a common feature of natural beauty on the ocean fronts of tropical regions. In the United States, it grows best in Hawaii and less well in zone 10 of Florida. The tree's slender trunk can raise the crowns of feathery fronds and substantial clusters of large nuts with yellow-brown husks some 100 ft high. The nuts of the self-fruitful coconut palm tree ripen one by one in all seasons of the year.

A disease that has been named lethal yellowing has, to a large extent, destroyed the coconut palm tree in parts of Africa, the Caribbean islands and Florida. Nearly 100 percent of the stands of *Cocos nucifera typica* in Miami's Dade County have been removed because of lethal yellowing disease and have been replaced by two resistant varieties. These are the 'Dwarf Golden Malay' or the Malayan dwarf palm, and the 'Maytan', a hybrid coconut palm tree. The resistant varieties ultimately reach the same height as the standard palm. The hybrid is especially vigorous. Malayan dwarfs need somewhat better soil and more water and fertilizer.

The Malayan dwarf palm takes about three years to produce nuts and will eventually bear 100 or more each year in contrast to the common coconut palm's 30–40 fruits.

Cultivation

Coconut palm trees can be propagated with ease, but it is important in specific regions to keep in mind a few precautions before proceeding with planting. In Florida, for example, it is preferable to buy trees from a horticultural supplier to be certain of obtaining a yellowing-resistant variety. This is because all coconut palms cross-pollinate freely, and nuts picked from the tree, off the ground, or even purchased from a grower, may produce a tree that is not yellowing-resistant. The state agricultural extension service should be consulted.

Hawaii, however, is free of the disease. The home gardener in that region can simply allow a nut to mature on any vigorous, productive tree and then cut it down when the husk turns brown and begins to dry.

Planting The nut, with husk, should be planted in a partially shaded seedbed. In planting, the nut should be placed in a horizontal position, with the eye end slightly higher in elevation, and the longest side of the husk on top. Mount soil mixed with humus up to the top third of the husk and keep moist.

The nut will send up a single sprout in about three months. When this is 6–12 in high, move the entire plant, including the husk, into its place in the garden or to a container, such as a 5 gal can, for further development.

Coconut palms grow best in sandy loam combined with plenty of humus. Dig an extra-large hole and set in the tree so the husk is covered with a very thin layer of soil. In the garden, coconut palm trees are often planted in groups of three which are spaced 8–10 ft apart. Give single specimens a space of about 20 ft in diameter. Do not plant the trees near buildings, terraces, driveways, and so on, where falling nuts and fronds can be dangerous to life and limb, or can damage property.

Watering and feeding The trees should be regularly watered while young to encourage rapid growth and, thereafter, should be adequately watered during dry spells. Although coconuts are highly drought-resistant, they should have about 1 in of water per week at all times of the year.

Several months after planting a tree, apply 4 oz of a balanced fertilizer, such as 10-10-10, followed by three similar applications at three-month intervals. In the second year, apply 8 oz of balanced fertilizer every three months. Double the size of the applications in the third year, again in the fourth year, and once more in the fifth year. This rate of fertilizer application can be continued thereafter, but the total annual dosage can be applied two or three times in the year instead of four times, if preferred.

During the first four or five years, reduce competition with other vegetation by cultivating the soil around the tree or mulching with 3–4 in of pebbles. Older trees can also be cultivated or mulched. Alternatively, the grass can be allowed to grow right up to the trunk, provided it is mown.

Coconut palm trees do not require pruning.

Harvesting

Nuts that are to be consumed should be harvested only when the husks turn brown and begin to dry out. If selecting coconuts for their 'milk', picking should begin when the full-size husks are still green. The use of long-handled pruners to cut the coconuts free for gathering from the ground is the least arduous manner of harvesting.

Pests and diseases

Pests, apart from scale insects, are rarely much of a problem. Scale insects can be controlled by spraying the trees with malathion.

Propagation

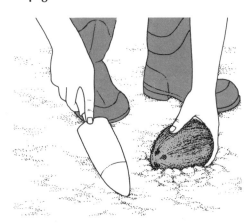

1 At any time of year, plant the nut horizontally in a seedbed with the eye end highest. Cover two-thirds of the nut with soil. Keep moist.

2 In about three months, when growth is 6–12 in high, move the plant into the garden or a container for further development. Do not place containers in the shade.

3 When the tree is ready for planting, dig a large hole and set the nut in so the husk is completely covered. Groups of three or more trees should be 8–10 ft apart.

4 During the first four or five years, reduce competition with other vegetation by cultivating the soil around the tree or mulching with 3–4 in of gravel.

Avocados and mangoes

Avocados

The avocado (*Persea americana*) is a small, tropical, more or less evergreen tree with round to pear-shaped fruits that vary considerably in size. The skin is generally green, but may be black, purple or reddish.

Generally speaking, the trees grow in zone 10 and the warmest parts of zone 9, but differ considerably in their resistance to cold, depending on whether they are West Indian, Guatemalan or Mexican strains. The West Indian strain, usually grown in Florida, is the least hardy and does best at low elevations. Guatemalan or Mexican strains come from the highlands and are hardier and more resistant to drought. They are generally grown in California and Hawaii, although the Guatemalan trees also grow in Florida.

The fruits of each strain are harvested in different seasons of the year. West Indian avocado trees are harvested in summer and fall, Guatemalan trees in winter and spring, and Mexican trees in summer.

Cultivation

Given protection from strong winds and planted in a well-drained soil, avocados will grow almost anywhere within their region. Addition of humus to the soil is always desirable but not essential. When the holes are dug, mix a modest amount of fertilizer into the soil. In California, calcium nitrate, ammonium sulfate or ammonium nitrate is used; Florida and Hawaii use a balanced fertilizer.

Planting Avocados can be grown from seed, but the trees take a long time to bear fruit and do not come true. So it is best to start with grafted plants from a nursery. Varieties are classified into A and B types according to their flowering schedules. To ensure fruiting, plant both A and B varieties.

Space the trees 25 ft apart. Firm the soil around the roots and water well to settle the tree.

Watering and feeding Avocados require deep watering about once a week in dry weather. If the water available contains a high concentration of salts, the trees must be flooded periodically to leach out the salts from around the roots.

Feeding requirements vary between the three states in which the trees are grown. In all cases, the trees should be fed several times a year, but the total annual feeding is not particularly large. Follow the recommendations of the state agricultural extension service.

Pruning Little, if any, pruning is required. But it may be desirable in the first two years to remove a few branches to improve the shape of the tree. Therefore, simply cut out wood that is damaged. As the tree increases in size, the tops may be cut back to simplify harvesting, reduce spraying and lessen storm damage. All pruning should be done soon after harvest. Except for reducing fruit production in the following year, very hard pruning does not hurt the trees.

Harvesting

Green-skinned varieties should not be picked until the skin becomes smoother and develops a yellowish tinge. Dark-skinned varieties are picked when the skin begins to turn from green to a dark complexion. Do not pull off the fruits. Cut the stem close above the fruits. The fruits do not ripen until picked, and ripening takes three to eight days, if the proper stage of maturity has been reached.

Pests and diseases

Diseases and pests rarely cause serious problems to avocados, but it is advisable to apply a copper fungicide every month for three months before the fruits mature to prevent disease.

If scab is a nuisance in the local growing area, grow varieties that are resistant to it.

Mangoes

The mango (*Mangifera indica*) is one of the most highly esteemed of tropical fruits because it is not only delicious to eat fresh but can be made into highly palatable jam, jelly, pies and other delicacies.

The mango tree is also an outstandingly attractive specimen for the garden. The dense evergreen tree can reach 60–90 ft in height in the wild, but is generally much smaller when cultivated in the garden. Large panicles of pinkish flowers festoon the tree in winter. The fruit is yellow to reddish in color, fleshy and sweet, and can average up to 5 in in length. It grows in zone 10 and in the very warmest parts of zone 9 in sheltered locations.

Cultivation

The trees grow in sun or partial shade, but are more productive in full sun. Protection against wind is essential. Almost any soil will do, but it must be well drained and should not contain too much sand or clay.

Purchase grafted plants in containers. One tree is all that is needed as the mango is self-fruitful. The planting hole should be three or four times as wide as the container and at least twice as deep. Mix humus and about 4 oz of balanced fertilizer, such as 10-10-10, into the soil. Set the plants at the same depth as they are planted in the cans. Firm the soil and water well.

Watering and feeding Nature usually takes care of the mango's moisture needs. During the dry months of the year, when the tree starts to bloom, little additional water is required. Thereafter the tree should be watered thoroughly, but only in dry spells.

Three months after the tree has been planted, apply another 4 oz of balanced fertilizer to the soil. The fertilizer application should be increased to 6 oz at the end of the sixth and ninth months, and to 8 oz at the end of the first year. Feedings from those times on are made three times a year during growth periods as follows: 8 oz of fertilizer per feeding in the second year; 16 oz in the third year; 32 oz in the fourth year; and 48 oz thereafter. Bearing trees should be given a little muriate of potash when flowering starts.

Pruning Pruning is unnecessary except to remove dead and damaged wood. The gardener may also want to cut out top growth to keep the tree small enough to care for easily. All pruning is done after harvest.

Harvesting

Mangoes frequently bear well in only two years out of four, and even though the flower clusters seem to indicate an extremely heavy crop, the actual number produced may be rather small. Let the fruits ripen on the tree before harvesting.

Pests and diseases

Anthracnose may be a serious problem, but can be controlled by spraying with captan or a copper fungicide every week from the time the flowers open until the fruits are developed. Spraying with malathion takes care of most insects, which are only rarely troublesome. Consult state agricultural extension services for details of local pest and disease problems.

Planting

Select grafted avocado plants from the nursery. To ensure fruiting, plant both A and B varieties. Space the trees 25 ft apart in a good sunny position. Firm the soil around the roots and water well so that the moisture sinks in.

For mangoes, the planting hole should be four times larger and twice as deep as the container holding the plant. Set the plant at the same depth as it was in the container in soil mixed with humus and balanced fertilizer.

Persimmons

'Fuyu' An Oriental persimmon with deep red, tomato-shaped fruits of medium size. The flesh is light orange and not astringent. Generally self-fruitful...
'Garretson' Native American variety. Small, orange-yellow fruits of excellent flavor. Considered one of the best native persimmons.
'Great Wall' Oriental variety of greater hardiness than most. Fruits are small, slightly square in shape, and very astringent until fully ripe.
'Hachiya' A highly flavored Oriental variety with large, oblong fruits. Orange-yellow skin and yellow flesh. Seedless. In California, the tree is self-fruitful. Plant male and female specimens elsewhere.

'John Rich' Native American. Top quality, small fruits with a heavy red blush.
'New Hampshire No 1' A hardier-than-average native American variety with fruits that are larger than average.
'Peiping' Oriental variety. Fruits of medium size. Hardy and normally self-fruitful.

'Tamopan' Oriental variety. Large, seedless, oddly shaped, red-orange fruits with light orange flesh. Usually self-fruitful.
'Tanenashi' Oriental variety. Fruits of medium size, conical in shape, and light red in color. Seedless. Self-fruitful.

The deciduous persimmon tree (*Diospyros*) forms yellow to orange or blushed red fruit that is prized by some gardeners for its unique taste, although others find the flavor too astringent. In fact, depending on the variety and stage of ripening, the persimmon fruit can be astringent, non-astringent, or very sweet.

A combination of handsome shape, broad leaves that turn pink, orange, red, scarlet or yellow in the fall, and the attractive oblong or oval fruit, makes all varieties of the persimmon tree an enhancement to the visual beauty of any well-planned garden.

Two species grown in the United States are the Oriental or Japanese persimmon and the American persimmon. Generally, both species grow between 20–30 ft in height and produce fruit up to 2 in across, although one variety of Oriental or Japanese persimmon has fruit up to 4 in long and 2½–3 in broad. The American persimmon tree has been known to reach 50 ft in height, but most are moderate-growing small trees.

The persimmon native to the United States can be cultivated in zones 5–9, but in zones 5 and 6 the fruits may not ripen before the first hard fall freeze. The Oriental persimmon, which is more commonly known as the Japanese persimmon although it did not originate in Japan, is a considerably smaller tree than the American species, but has larger, more delicious fruits. It can be grown in zones 8–10 and may also succeed in the warmest parts of zone 7.

American persimmon trees bear fruit only if male and female trees are planted together. Some varieties of Oriental persimmon must be planted in the same way while others are self-fruitful.

Cultivation

The persimmon tree requires little attention, making it an ideal specimen for the busy gardener to cultivate.
Planting Buy one-year-old trees from a reputable grower and plant them in the early spring while they are still dormant. Oriental or Japanese varieties of persimmon tree should be spaced 20 ft apart while American persimmon trees need 25 ft allowance. The soil must be well drained and rich in humus. Dig large, deep holes because the trees put down extremely deep roots.
Support Newly-planted persimmon trees should be well-supported throughout the first three or four years of growth. One method of support is to dig or pound in two strong stakes on either side of the tree. Anchor the tree with jute string or other heavy-duty cord. This is necessary because, in good soil, the persimmon tree grows rapidly and, without support, can be knocked down and ruined by strong winds.
Watering and feeding Mulch the soil around the trees to hold in moisture. Watering is required only when the soil dries out; but water should be applied carefully to be certain that it soaks in well.

In early spring, apply 2–3 oz of nitrate of soda to each new tree. Increase this dosage of nitrate of soda annually until a total of 30 oz is being applied in the sixth year. Thus the rates are: year one, 3 oz; year two, 6 oz; year three, 12 oz; year four, 18 oz; year five, 26 oz; and year six, 30 oz. The amount of annual fertilizer increase will vary, depending on a number of factors. It is not necessary to increase the amount of fertilizer beyond 30 oz per year.
Pruning In late winter, prune the persimmon tree carefully to encourage the development of a scaffold system of four or five strong branches in the second and third years. Thereafter, prune just enough to keep the tops of the trees open. Cutting back some of the side branches forces out the new growth on which fruits are borne.

Harvesting

Persimmon fruit should be allowed to ripen on the tree before harvesting. Each fruit should be carefully cut off so that a portion of stem remains with the fruit. Persimmon fruits can be stored in the refrigerator.

Hard-ripe persimmon fruit is dried by peeling and hanging from a string. Place strings of fruit in a sunny place and leave until dried.

Pests and diseases

The persimmon fruit tree is practically free of pests and diseases. See pages 14–16 for general precautions.

1 In early spring, plant the nursery tree in a hole large enough to take the deep roots. Space Oriental or Japanese persimmon trees 20 ft apart; American trees need 25 ft.

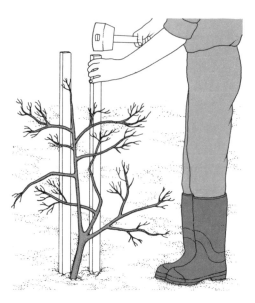

2 To provide a secure support system for the newly-planted tree, drive two sturdy stakes into the ground on either side. Anchor it to the stakes with strong cord.

3 In early spring, apply 2–3 oz of nitrate of soda to each new tree. The dosage should be increased over six years and stopped at a 30 oz application each year.

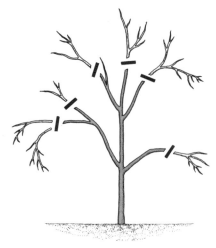

4 In late winter each year, prune the persimmon tree until a scaffold system of four or five strong branches has developed in the second or third year.

'Eleuthera', or **'Penambuco'** Sweet, juicy fruits up to 4 lb with a slightly yellowish-white flesh.
'Natal Queen' Excellent yellow-fleshed fruits to about 3 lb.

'Smooth Cayenne' Large (up to 6 lb) fruits with yellow flesh. Probably the best variety, but generally not as well suited to the home garden as the above. The leaves are spineless.

Pineapples

The pineapple is one of a family of American plants (*Bromeliaceae*) with stiff, densely-packed rosettes of spiny leaves resembling swords. The leaves group around a central stem that bears a single, large, yellowish fruit. The plant, which grows in zone 10 and also responds to cultivation indoors, can reach a height of about 3 ft.

Cultivation

Pineapples prefer a sandy, somewhat acid soil with a great deal of humus. Good moisture retention as well as good drainage are essential. If nematodes are present, fumigate the soil. Set the plants 18 in apart in rows 24 in apart. A black polyethylene mulch surrounding the plants will reduce the need for frequent weeding.

Water regularly. The plants need a considerable supply of moisture, but excess surface water should be drained off as this may damage the plants.

About four months after planting, apply $\frac{1}{2}$ oz of a balanced fertilizer with a low phosphorous content such as 7-2-7 or 8-3-8. Repeat the fertilizer applications thereafter every four months. The alternative for the second and all succeeding feedings is to use a foliar spray composed of $\frac{3}{4}$ lb of urea in 1 gal of water. It is advisable to apply an iron spray at the same time.

Pineapples can also be cultivated quite successfully in containers such as cans of 3–5 gal size. But the roots must be kept at 70°F or above. Feed monthly with a foliar spray of 20-20-20 fertilizer containing iron and magnesium.

Pineapples grown indoors may not fruit, but make attractive house plants. They can be moved outdoors in summer.

Propagation

Most home gardeners in the United States propagate their own pineapple plants by one of the four following methods. Propagation by suckers produces fruit more rapidly than propagation by crowns.

The first method is to remove the crown of leaves from the top of a fruit with a sharp knife, trim off the flesh at the base, then cut the bottom until root buds are exposed. Remove three or four of the basal leaves and let the crown harden upside down in a shady, dry place for about a week. When the cut begins to form a callus, plant the crown right side up in soil mounded to support the fruit in an upright position. Do not let soil get among the leaves.

The second method is to cut off the suckers sprouting from the stem below the fruit and then to carry out the propagation procedure outlined in the first method. If there is a knob at the base of a sucker, cut it off before drying.

The third method is to plant the large suckers that arise from the leaf axils near the bottom of the plant stem. These can be prepared as outlined in the first method.

The fourth and most direct method is to cut off the ratoons or underground suckers sprouting up through the ground surrounding the plant and to plant them immediately.

Whatever propagation method is used, the new plants should be dipped in a mixture of 2 tsp malathion and 1 gal of water before actual planting. If this is not done, mealybugs are likely to become a rampant problem.

Harvesting

The fruit matures in summer within 15–24 months depending on the method of propagation. When the fruit is consistently yellow, cut it off just below the base.

After harvesting, one of the ratoons or underground suckers will start to develop, producing a new fruit. If pineapples are allowed to reproduce in this manner, the fruits will diminish in size until they are of little value. It is therefore advisable to remove the original plants once they have fruited and to replace them with new ones.

Pests and diseases

Mealybugs are the worst pineapple pests. If, despite initial treatment of new plants, mealybugs are a problem, drench the plants frequently with malathion spray until a week before harvest. Mealybugs can also be controlled by the destruction of ant hills.

The most serious disease is heart-rot, a fungus disease that blackens and loosens the center leaves. Plants with such rot can sometimes be saved if captan is poured into them. But the preferred course is to destroy the plants and start anew.

Propagation

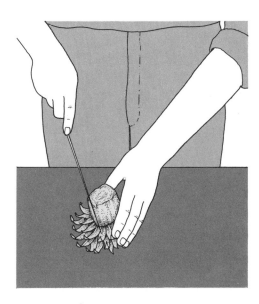

1 **Remove the crown** of leaves from the top of the pineapple with a keen knife. Trim off the flesh at the base, cutting the bottom until the root buds show.

2 **Remove three or four** of the pineapple's basal leaves and let the crown harden upside down in a shady, dry place for about a week. Plant it right side up.

Alternatively, cut off the suckers sprouting from the stem below the pineapple fruit. If there is a knob at the base of a sucker, cut it off before drying. Prepare and plant.

Alternatively, carefully remove the large suckers that arise from the leaf axils near the bottom of the stem.

Pecans

The pecan tree is a hickory species (*Carya illinoiensis*) that can attain a height of 150 ft in the wild, but is usually trained to grow to a much lower height in the orchard or garden. It is a handsome, if craggy, specimen in the large garden. To ensure a harvest of pecan nuts, it is necessary to plant two trees of different varieties, that is, a variety that sheds pollen early and a variety that pollinates later. Even if this precaution has been taken, a crop is not a certainty unless the fruit has had five to seven months of warm weather to mature without unfavorable conditions such as drouth. Good management is essential.

Pecans are probably the most popular nuts in the United States and among the most widely grown next to peanuts, which are not true nuts. They do best in zone 8, but are also productive in zones 7 and 9. Small crops of pecans may even be harvested in zone 6 and the southern part of zone 5 with careful cultivation.

Cultivation

Although the pecan tree will tower above other trees within a number of years and so obtain the necessary sunlight to thrive, it should not be planted in semi-shaded areas. Nursery pecan trees that are one year old and 4–6 ft in height should be given plenty of space to develop rapidly and more than average care if they are to survive the first summer. Choose nursery trees that have been freshly dug from the field.

Soil of enough depth to accomodate the long tap root ($2\frac{1}{2}$–4 ft) and large lateral root system of the pecan tree should be chosen. A well-drained, humus loam is preferable. If the soil contains much sand, mix in large amounts of organic matter; if there is too much clay, mix in gravel as well as organic matter. Soils infested with nematodes should be fumigated before planting.

Planting Make the planting holes at least 6 in deeper than the roots of the young tree and at least 30 in across. This can be done, for example, by using a 12 or 14 in power auger or post hole digger. Trim the roots only if they are damaged. Set the tree and fill the hole with loose soil. Thoroughly water the basin formed around the tree until it is full to settle the soil, then add more soil to raise a mound.

Watering and feeding Irrigate deeply throughout the first growing season. Mulching with organic matter to a depth of 6 in is advisable. After the trees have developed leaves, work in 4 oz of 10-10-10 fertilizer, and make a second similar feeding about six weeks later, but not after the beginning of August.

Maintenance of a good moisture supply at all times during the growing season is essential. During dry weather, soak the ground thoroughly so the water penetrates to the root ends.

Fertilize the trees in early spring with ammonium sulfate or another nitrogen product, applying about 10 oz per year of tree age. If the ground under the trees is cultivated or mulched, scatter the fertilizer over the entire root area, scratch it in lightly and water well. In a lawn, where the nitrogen would probably kill the grass, drop the fertilizer into holes made with a crowbar at 2 ft intervals throughout the root area.

Such care will help to counteract the tendency of some trees to bear in alternate years. It also helps to assure that the kernels fill out properly.

Pruning and training When the young trees are planted, cut the top back, leaving a 36 in trunk. Wrap the trunk with burlap or paper to within 6 in of the top to prevent sunscald, retard drying, and to discourage pests. Maintain the wrapping for two years, replacing and renewing it as necessary.

Train one of the upper branches as an extension of the trunk by tying it to a stake when the tree starts putting out growth. From this will arise the main (scaffold) branches. There should be four or five of these, spaced about 18 in apart, up and down the trunk and growing out in different directions. Do not remove the branches below the scaffolds, which start at 5 or 6 ft above ground, for three or four years.

Once the basic structure of the tree is well developed, little pruning is necessary. Just cut out dead and damaged branches as well as upper branches that prevent sunlight from penetrating the base shape formed by the scaffolds. Remove also branches which cross over others and which cut off light from the main branches.

Harvesting

Pecan trees do not start to bear heavily until they are about ten years old, but nuts can be gathered in small quantities after the fifth year. The nuts are ready for picking when the husks open at the tips and the color begins to fade. They can be allowed to fall naturally or can be knocked out of the trees with lightweight bamboo poles. Dry pecan nuts thoroughly before bagging. Halved pecans can be added to crocked fruit mixtures.

Pests and diseases

Keeping fallen nuts, leaves and twigs raked up is the best way to protect trees. For safety's sake, however, young trees should be sprayed with dodine or zineb when the first leaves show and the buds burst; repeat when the leaves are half developed. Then use a combination of dodine and malathion or zineb and malathion when the tips of the new nuts begin to turn brown, repeating the treatment at 3–4 week intervals. Dodine is used for varieties susceptible to scab and zineb for those tolerant or resistant to scab.

To prevent rosette, a physiological disorder resulting in the yellowing of the leaves, thickening of leaf veins and a bunching up of small leaves at the ends of short twigs, apply zinc sulfate to the soil at a rate of 16 oz per in of trunk diameter. Spread this over the entire root area and work it in thoroughly using a rake or a garden fork.

Varieties

There are three groups of pecan varieties: Eastern, Western, and Northern. Eastern varieties are fairly resistant to scab and other diseases, and grow best in the southeast. Western varieties, on the other hand, are extremely susceptible to scab and other diseases. They grow in moderately dry climates from central Texas to areas westward of that state. Although Northern varieties are tolerant of disease and mature more rapidly than the other varieties, crops are small or non-existent. They are grown more for ornament than utility.

Planting and training

1 Make the planting hole 6 in deeper than the roots of the tree and 30 in across, using a power auger if necessary. Set the tree and fill the hole with loose soil. Water the basin to settle the soil and then mound in additional soil.

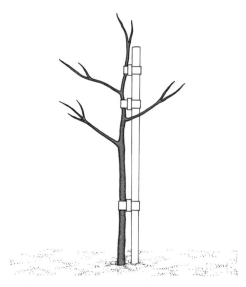

2 Train one of the upper branches as an extension of the trunk by tying it to a stake when the tree starts giving out growth. From this will arise the four or five main scaffold branches protruding from the trunk about 18 in apart.

Papayas

The papaya, or papaw, (*Carica papaya*) looks like a small evergreen tree, but is, in actuality, a perennial. It has huge, deeply lobed leaves and is prized for its big, long, juicy, yellow fruits with orange flesh. The tree, which can grow to about 25 ft in height, is cultivated in zone 10 and the warmest parts of zone 9.

Cultivation

Papayas grow in many different soils. But, for best results, dig large planting holes and mix in a substantial amount of humus and about 8 oz of superphosphate in the zone below the roots of the new plants. Drainage must be excellent, and the location chosen must be sunny and well screened from the prevailing wind.

Planting Although there are self-fruitful bisexual papayas, they are not very productive, and, therefore, both male and female specimens should be planted. But it is impossible to distinguish the sex of a young papaya plant, so it is necessary to plant a number of papayas to ensure both sexes are represented. One male tree is needed to pollinate every 10–15 female trees.

Papaya seeds, extracted from ripe fruits, freed from the gelatinous envelope surrounding them, and dried, grow easily into adult plants. The seeds can be planted at once or stored in air-tight containers for several years before use. Sow the seeds $\frac{1}{4}$ in deep in sterile peat pots. About 2–4 seeds should be sown in each pot, so that, when the seedlings are up, they can be thinned to one plant.

When the seedlings have four leaves, transplant them to the garden where they are to grow. Keep them in their pots and set them a little below ground level. Firm the soil and water well. About a week later, apply a little balanced fertilizer. Keep the plants shaded for two weeks.

Plant 2–3 seedlings 1 ft apart in hills 7–8 ft apart. When flowering starts about four months later, discard from each hill all but one plant of the desired sex. Female trees have flowers with short stems, big petals, and pistils only. On male trees, the flowers are small, appear in hanging clusters on long stems and have ten stamens.

Watering and feeding Up to the time they are thinned, papayas need about an inch of water per week. Thereafter, the supply can be cut almost in half provided that there is ample moisture in the entire root zone at all times. Mulch the plants to reduce evaporation, control weeds, and increase the fertility of the soil.

Regular, heavy feeding is essential. Using a 5-10-10 or 10-10-10 fertilizer, apply 4 oz per tree for a month after setting out in the garden. The fertilizer feeding should be increased to 6 oz in the second month, 8 oz in the third month, 12 oz in the fourth month, and 16 oz a month after that. Continue feeding at this rate at monthly intervals thereafter.

Pruning Trees are not pruned except to remove broken branches. The fruits, however, should be thinned three weeks after they have been set if two or more are growing close together on the trunk.

Harvesting

Papayas start to bear when a year old and continue in good production until they are five years old. Fruits ripen in all seasons except fall. Pick them as soon as they are consistently yellow, using care to prevent bruising. Picking is done either from a stepladder, because an extension ladder cannot be placed against the slender, weak trees, or with a plumber's friend. A plumber's friend is a large rubber suction cup attached to a pole that is used to clear plumbing drains. To use such a device, it is only necessary to place the cup under a fruit and to push upwards, and then to retrieve the fruit.

Pests and diseases

Mites and fruit flies may attack the maturing fruit. Control these pests with malathion. Diseases are relatively rare.

Varieties

Named varieties are grown, but none of them are notably superior.

1 Sow the seeds $\frac{1}{4}$ in deep in sterile peat pots. About 2–4 seeds should be sown in each pot. This is done so that the seedlings can be thinned to one plant after they are ready for transplanting to the garden.

2 When the seedlings have four leaves, transplant them to the garden. Keep the seedlings in their pots and set them a little below the level of the ground. Firm the soil around each seedling and water carefully and well.

3 Plant 2–3 seedlings 1 ft apart in hills 7–8 ft apart. When the flowering of the resultant papaya plants begins approximately four months later, discard from each hill all but one plant of the desired sex for further development.

4 Regular, heavy feeding is essential. Using a 5-10-10 fertilizer, apply 4 oz per tree for a month after setting out in the garden. Slowly and carefully increase the fertilizer feeding to a 16 oz application a month by the fifth month.

Olives

'Ascolano' Top-quality, large fruits early in the season. Tree is resistant to low temperatures.
'Barouni' Large fruits with large pits. Popular for home pickling. A generally consistent bearer.
'Manzanillo' Most popular California variety. Large, fleshy fruits maturing before fall freezes. Tree bears regularly.

'Mission' Small fruits maturing late enough to be occasionally damaged by freezes. Tall tree is likely to bear biennially.
'Sevillano' Biggest fruits with biggest pits. They mature early on easily harvested, spreading tree.

American home gardeners cultivate the olive tree (Olea europaea) because it can be an attractive decorative feature in any garden design as well as being of value for its choice edible fruits. The small, broad-leaved evergreen tree, at maturity up to 25 ft in height, is extremely handsome in appearance. The small fruits, almost black in color when ripened in the fall, are inedible until pickled for the table. Olive oil, of course, is of value for personal or commercial use.

The olive tree (Olea manzanillo) primarily grows in California in zones 9 and 10 and the warmest parts of zone 8. It is most productive in regions with warm, clear summers and fairly cold (down to 15°F) winters. Plant two varieties to ensure fruit production because the trees are not reliably self-fruitful.

Cultivation

An olive tree is more productive if grown in average soil rather than in very good soil. But the chosen soil should be easily and freely drained and a pH test should not show too much above 7.0. Beware of soils infested with the verticillium wilt microbes that chiefly attack tomatoes. Avoid planting in a frost pocket.

Bare-root trees must be planted in December, January or February. Trees in containers such as cans are planted at any time. In both cases, set the plants at the depth that they previously grew. Spread the roots of bare-root trees carefully in the hole. Whitewash the trunks or wrap them in paper to protect the trees against sunburn. Water well and apply a mulch. Bare-root plants must be cut back to a single trunk without branches on planting.

Watering and feeding The olive tree has a high resistance to drought conditions. For improved fruit yield, however, it should be regularly watered. Watering is particularly important in the spring before bloom, especially if the preceding winter has been very dry, as well as in summer after fruit set. If the soil around the roots of the tree has dried out to a depth of 1 ft or more, it is usually an indication that heavy watering is needed. A tensiometer, a device that measures soil moisture content, can be used to test the soil. Established trees can be kept mulched or grown in sod that is regularly mowed.

Apply ammonium nitrate in late December or January. Give first-year trees about 8 oz of ammonium nitrate, adding the same amount every year thereafter until a total of 96 oz has been applied over a 12-year period. Level off at this figure.

Pruning All pruning should be done in summer. In the first year, remove all except the three branches that will be developed into scaffolds to form the framework of the growing tree. These should be evenly spaced around the tree between 12 and 24 in above ground. During the next three years of growth, remove suckers, damaged and crossing branches only.

After trees start to bear, develop a secondary system of three scaffold branches on one of the primary scaffolds. Repeat this procedure on a second primary scaffold the next year.

From then on, prune enough to stimulate the growth of the new shoots on which fruits are carried. Remove branches growing up straight through the center of the tree. Also remove unfruitful and dead shoots.

After a tree is about 18 ft tall, it is wise to cut back upright limbs to facilitate harvesting. If branches spread too far to the sides and tangle with other trees, also cut these back. Shaded branches tend to die.

Thinning There are several ways to encourage annual bearing of trees that tend to alternate-year fruiting. The best method is to thin the fruits between mid-June and mid-July. Wear heavy rubber gloves and strip off all but three to five fruits per foot of twig. The fruits that are left will flesh out more fully.

Harvesting

Olive trees are slow to start bearing, so that a significant fruit yield should not be expected for the first seven or eight years, and full production will not start until the trees are about 20 years old. Once commenced, full production of an olive tree will probably continue for the lifetime of the gardener who planted it.

Pests and diseases

Sap-feeding scale insects are the most troublesome pest affecting the olive tree, but are often held in check by their natural enemies. If scale insects are a problem, however, apply a scalecide from late May to the beginning of July and, if necessary, from mid-July to the beginning of August.

Peacock spot, which occurs in wet seasons, is controlled with zineb sprays. For olive knot there is no cure, but it may be prevented by pruning only in the summer.

1 In late winter, set the bare-root tree at the depth that it previously grew. Spread the roots carefully in the hole. Water well and apply a mulch.

2 After planting a bare-root tree, cut back to a single trunk without branches. Whitewash the trunk or wrap it in paper to protect the tree against sunburn.

3 In summer of the first year, remove all except the three branches that will be developed into scaffolds to form the framework of the growing tree.

4 After the tree starts to bear, develop a secondary system of three scaffold branches on one of the primary scaffolds. Repeat this procedure the next year.

Physalis

The physalis is variously known in different countries and within the United States as Cape gooseberry, golden berry, ground-cherry, husk tomato and, in Hawaii, as poka. Botanically, it is *Physalis pruinosa* syn. *P. Peruviana* or *P. edulis*. It comes from Peru, although it is now cultivated in many areas of the world, and is related to the ornamental Chinese lantern plant (*P. alkekengi*), which also has edible but indifferent-tasting fruit.

The distinctive feature of this fruit is its lantern-like calyx or husk which conceals the golden, cherry-sized fruit. The husk protects the berry from birds and insects, aids the storage of the fruit, and is attractive, as are the small yellow-white blossoms with their purple-black markings. The leaves are large and slightly heart-shaped. The fruit is sweet with a distinctive taste. It can be eaten raw, cooked or preserved. It has a high vitamin C content. Each plant will produce about 1–2 lb of fruit.

Cultivation
The Physalis is a half-hardy perennial usually grown in zones 3–10 as an annual. It can be grown in the open in sheltered areas, or under glass or in pots. It responds to much the same treatment as its relative the tomato.

Soil and situation Do not grow the Physalis in ground just used for tomatoes or potatoes, because it is subject to the same pests and diseases, which may still be present in the soil. A sandy, well-drained soil of pH 6.5 is ideal but it will tolerate a wide range of soils, including limey soil if well laced with humus. It should be planted in a sunny sheltered position.

Propagation The Physalis is grown from seed indoors. The seeds should be sown in gentle heat in early spring. Sow the seeds individually, $\frac{1}{4}$ in deep, in seed trays filled with any proprietary starting mixture. The pots should be covered with glass. A temperature of 18°C/65°F is necessary for good germination. When the seeds germinate in 10–14 days remove the glass. When the seedlings are large enough to grip, prick them into 3 in pots filled with potting mixture.

Planting and staking Prepare the site, which should be cultivated to a fine tilth. No extra fertilizer is needed unless the soil is poor, when a 2-gal bucketful of well-rotted manure should be applied per square yard. An alternative to manure is a dressing of fertilizer such as 10-10-10 at 2–3 oz per square yard.

Plant out after all danger of frost has passed, setting the plants 2½ ft apart. For a slightly earlier start, grow under cloches or tunnels until the danger of frosts and cold winds is past. Plants can be stunted by a cold wind as late as early summer so provide shelter in the form of screens when necessary.

The plants should be supported with individual stakes 3 ft high or with a network of posts and wire. If the plants have not produced flowers by the time they are 12 in high, pinch out the growing points to induce branching and thereafter regular pinching is not needed. Watering should be carefully regulated, for if the plants are given too much moisture they produce growth at the expense of fruit. Give a liquid fertilizer sparingly only after the first flowers appear. Tomato fertilizers are suitable.

Growing under glass In areas where the frost-free season is less than about 80 days, or summers are cool, protection is essential. Grow the plants in pots which can spend the early and fruiting stages inside and the summer in the open.

Seed should be sown in the same way as for outdoor plants. Instead of planting out, the plants should be potted on into 10 in pots filled with about equal amounts of loam and humus. Plants should be staked individually. Or if stood outside, the stakes should be secured to a wire stretched between stronger stakes driven into the soil.

Although plants can be retained for the following year and potted on into larger containers, it is recommended that new seeds are sown each year and the plants discarded after fruiting because thereafter they do not crop so heavily.

Harvesting
In cold regions, fruits grown outdoors may not be ripe by the time of the first frosts. Pot-grown plants can be put back under glass to ripen. The fruits are ready to pick when they turn golden-yellow and the husks have a papery texture. Ripe fruits can be left on the plants for several weeks, the peak of flavor being reached 2–3 weeks after ripening. If frost threatens outdoor plants, gather all those berries that have a hint of yellow color.

Pests and diseases
Outdoor plants should be regularly inspected for aphids, which may gather on the tips of shoots. When seen, spray with malathion.

1 In early spring, sow seeds $\frac{1}{4}$ in deep in seed trays filled with a proprietary starting mixture. Cover the seed trays with glass. Maintain a temperature of 18°C/65°F.

2 In 10–14 days, when the seeds germinate remove the glass. When the seedlings are large enough to grip, prick out into 3 in pots.

3 After last frost, plant out the seedlings 2½ ft apart. For an earlier start, protect with cloches. Remove the cloches when the danger of frosts is past.

4 During the growing season, provide support for the plants. When 12 in high, if they have no flowers, pinch out the growing points. When flowers appear, feed sparingly.

Pomegranates

POMEGRANATES

The pomegranate (*Punica granatum*) is a handsome deciduous shrub or small tree fruit that, judging by historical writings, has changed little in appearance and composition from the fruit cultivated by the peoples of ancient civilizations.

The leaves, bright green to yellow-green and brilliant yellow in the fall, are shining and oblong while the flowers are bright orange-red or scarlet, contrasted by a purple calyx. In spring the scarlet flowers make an attractive show. The color of the resulting fruit is red or brownish-red and the inside flesh is many-seeded, juicy and crimson. Pomegranates, eaten fresh or made into juice and grenadine syrup, have a somewhat acid but pleasant flavor.

Although the tree, which grows to a height of 15–20 ft, is deciduous and drops its leaves annually, in warm climates it is never long without its striking foliage.

Pomegranates are grown in zones 8–10 as much for their ornamental value as for their highly-edible fruit. If fruit is desired, the home gardener should be certain to select those varieties that produce fruit. The most com-monly grown variety is 'Wonderful', followed closely by 'Sweet'. Pomegranates are self-fruitful.

Cultivation

The pomegranate does well in most kinds of soil and will thrive even in the alkaline soils that many other plants cannot tolerate. For improved fruit yield, however, it should be planted in a well drained but rather heavy loam with ample humus.

Fruiting pomegranate trees are generally cultivated as single specimens and are usually spaced 15–20 ft apart. They can also be grown as hedges with spacing distances cut by half of that allowed for trees.

Pomegranate plants can be grown from rooted suckers or from seeds. Dig up the suckers developing around pomegranate trees or shrubs and plant them in early spring where they are to grow, or in nursery beds.

Watering and feeding The trees can withstand the effects of long droughts, but will produce improved fruits if regularly watered during the spring and summer growing seasons. Apply a balanced fertilizer, such as 10-10-10, each spring, giving established plants a 30 oz application and young plants proportionally less.

Training and pruning The natural growth of the pomegranate is bushy and healthy if the plant has been allowed to develop without undue interference. Training of the pomegranate tree, however, will make routine care easier, improve fruit production, and should lead to a good harvest. The aim is to develop a balanced system of scaffold branches, and once this has been achieved, pruning is relatively simple. Pruning then merely consists of removing excess wood and the numerous suckers springing from the roots, and should be done in late winter.

Harvesting

Pomegranate fruits should be picked when dry and before fully ripe. If left on the tree, they are likely to split open. Let them ripen in a cool, shady spot.

Pests and Diseases

No specific pests or diseases trouble the pomegranate tree.

1 Collect suckers from around the base of a mature tree and plant them 15–20 ft apart in nursery beds or in a chosen spot in the garden.

2 Dig a hole to a size that will adequately accommodate the root system of the tree or shrub. Fill the hole, ridge up the soil in a circle, thereby creating a watering basin.

3 Apply a balanced fertilizer, such as 10-10-10, each spring, giving established plants a 30 oz application and young plants proportionally less.

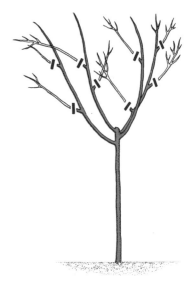

4 Develop a balanced system of scaffold branches. Once this has been achieved, pruning of excess wood from the tree and suckers from the roots is relatively simple.

Index 1

Index 2/Acknowledgements

The Royal Horticultural Society and the Publishers can accept no liability either for failure to control pests, diseases or weeds by any crop protection methods or for any consequences of their use. We specifically draw our readers' attention to the necessity of carefully reading and accurately following the manufacturer's instructions on any product.

Acknowledgements
Most of the artwork in this book has been based on photographs specially commissioned from the Harry Smith Horticultural Photographic Collection.

Artists: Arka Cartographics Ltd, Janet Blakeley, Lindsay Blow, Linda Broad, Charles Chambers, Pamela Dowson, Chris Forsey, Tony Graham, Eric Howley, Alan Male, Ed Roberts, Colin Salmon, Mike Saunders, Stonecastle Graphics, Lorna Turpin, West One Arts.